Comparing Policy Networks

Public Policy and Management

Series Editor: Professor R.A.W. Rhodes, Department of Politics, University of Newcastle.

The effectiveness of public policies is a matter of public concern and the efficiency with which policies are put into practice is a continuing problem for governments of all political persuasions. This series contributes to these debates by publishing informed, in-depth and contemporary analyses of public administration, public policy and public management.

The intention is to go beyond the usual textbook approach to the analysis of public policy and management and to encourage authors to move debate about their issue forward. In this sense, each book both describes current thinking and research, and explores future policy directions. Accessibility is a key feature and, as a result, the series will appeal to academics and their students as well as to the informed practitioner.

Current titles include:

Christine Bellamy and John A. Taylor: *Governing in the Information Age*
Tony Butcher: *Delivering Welfare*
John Ernst: *Whose Utility? The Social Impact of Public Utility Privatization and Regulation in Britain*
Christopher D. Foster and Francis J. Plowden: *The State Under Stress: Can the Hollow State be Good Government?*
Lucy Gaster: *Quality in Public Services: Managers' Choices*
Patricia Greer: *Transforming Central Government: The Next Steps Initiative*
Steve Leach, Howard Davis and Associates: *Enabling or Disabling Local Government: Choices for the Future*
David Marsh (ed.): *Comparing Policy Networks*
O. Morrissey, B. Smith and E. Horesh: *British Aid and International Trade*
R.A.W. Rhodes: *Understanding Governance: Policy Networks, Governance, Reflexivity and Accountability*
Chris Skelcher: *The Appointed State: Quasi-Government Organizations and Democracy*
Gerald Wistow, Martin Knapp, Brian Hardy and Caroline Allen: *Social Care in a Mixed Economy*
Gerald Wistow, Martin Knapp, Brian Hardy, Julien Forder, Jeremy Kendall and Rob Manning: *Social Care Markets: Progress and Prospects*
Spencer Zifcak: *New Managerialism: Administrative Reform in Whitehall and Canberra*

Comparing Policy Networks

Edited by
David Marsh

Open University Press
Buckingham · Philadelphia

Open University Press
Celtic Court
22 Ballmoor
Buckingham
MK18 1XW

email: enquiries@openup.co.uk
world wide web: http://www.openup.co.uk

and
325 Chestnut Street
Philadelphia, PA 19106, USA

First Published 1998

A catalogue record of this book is available from the British Library

ISBN   0 335 19646 2 (pb)   0 335 19647 0 (hb)

Library of Congress Cataloging-in-Publication Data
Comparing policy networks / [edited by] David Marsh.
        p.   cm. – (Public policy and management)
    Includes bibliographical references and index.
    ISBN 0-335-19647-0 (hb). – ISBN 0-335-19646-2 (pb)
    1. Policy sciences. 2. Social sciences–Network analysis.
I. Marsh, David, 1946– . II. Series.
H96.C66 1998
321'.6–dc21   97-43964
                                                               CIP

Typeset by Dorwyn Ltd, Rowlands Castle, Hants
Printed in Great Britain by Biddles Ltd, Guildford and King's Lynn

Contents

vi Contents

Notes on contributors

John Benington is Professor of Public Service Management and director of the Local Government Centre at the University of Warwick Business School. He has authored and edited a number of books. His current research interests include the strategic management of change in local government, the impact of Europeanization on local economies and local democracy and transnational local authority networks and networking.

Elizabeth Bomberg is a lecturer in the Department of Policies at Stirling University. She is author of *Green Parties and Politics in the European Union* (Routledge, 1998). Her primary research interests are European union policy making and environmental policy and politics.

Michael Cavanagh is completing his PhD in the Government Department of the University of Strathclyde. His research deals with health and safety policy in relation to the north sea oil industry in Norway and the United Kingdom.

Alistair Cole is Reader in European Politics at the University of Bradford. He is editor of *French Political Parties in Transition* (Dartmouth, 1990) and author of *Francois Mitterand: A Study in Political Leadership* (Routledge, 1994) and *French Politics and Society* (Prentice Hall, forthcoming).

Carsten Daugbjerg is lecturer in politics at the University of Aarhus, Denmark. He is author of *Policy Networks Under Pressure: Pollution Control, Policy Reform and the Power of the Farmers* (Ashgate Publishing, 1998). He has published articles in Danish and international journals. His current research is concerned with the politics of green taxes in Europe.

Janet Harvey is Senior Research fellow at the Centre for Corporate Change at the University of Warwick Business School. She has published a number of articles in the fields of medical technology, employment relations, work organization and race and gender.

Colin Hay is a lecturer in the Department of Political Science and International Studies at the University of Birmingham. He is also currently a visiting fellow in the Department of Political Science at the Massachusetts Institute of Technology and an affiliate of the Centre for European Studies at Harvard University. He has written widely on theories of the state, the political sociology of post-war Britain and the political economy of environmental crisis. He is the author of *Re-Stating Social and Political Change* (Open University Press, 1996), which was awarded the British Sociological Association's Philip Abrams Memorial Prize.

Peter John is lecturer in politics at the University of Southampton. He is author of articles on population mobility, centre-local relations, regionalism, urban regimes, the EU local dimension and comparative urban politics. His book *Analysing Public Policy* (Cassell) is due in 1998.

Elizabeth McLeay is Senior Lecturer in Politics at Victoria University, Wellington, New Zealand. She has recently published *The Cabinet and Political Power in New Zealand* (Oxford University Press, 1995). Her many publications include articles on political representation, government formation, housing policy, policing, women and politics and comparative public policy.

David Marsh is Head of Department, Political Science and International Studies, at the University of Birmingham. He has published a large number of books and articles including: (with W. Grant), *The Confederation of British Industry* (Hodder and Stoughton, 1977); (with J. Chambers), *Abortion Politics* (Junction Books, 1981); (with M. Read), *Private Members Bills* (Cambridge University Press, 1988); *Trade Unions in a Cold Climate: British Trade Unions in the 1980s and 1990s* (Macmillan, 1992). He has edited four collections: *Pressure Politics: Interest Groups in Britain* (Junction Books, 1983); *Capital in Europe* (Cass, 1983); (with R. Rhodes) *Policy Networks in British Politics* (Clarendon Press, 1992); (with R. Rhodes) *Implementing Thatcherite Policies*, (Open University Press, 1992)

Guy Peters is Maurice Falk Professor of Governent at the University of Pittsburgh. He has held visiting positions at the University of Strathclyde, the University of Manchester and the University of Oxford. Among his many publications are: *The Politics of Bureaucracy*; *European Politics Reconsidered*; *The Future of Governing*; and *Lessons from Experience: Learning in Administrative Reform*.

List of abbreviations

ACPO	Association of Chief Police Officers
AIRLINE	Aerospace Industry Regional and Local Authority Network
APME	Association of Plastics Manufacturers in Europe
CAP	Common Agricultural Policy
CBI	Confederation of British Industry
CCC	Coalfields Communities Campaign
CEMR	Council for European Municipalities and Regions
CIMAH	Control of Industrial Major Hazard Regulations
COR	Committee of the Regions
DEn	Department of Energy
DSD	Duales System Deutschland (Germany)
DTI	Department of Trade and Industry
EAPN	European Anti-Poverty Network
EC	European Community
EEA	European Environment Agency
EEB	European Environmental Bureau
EP	European Parliament
ERR	External Reference Group Regulations
ERRA	European Recovery and Recycling Association
EU	European Union
EURACOM	European Action for Mining Communities
EUROPEN	European Organisation for Packaging and the Environment
FINE	Fashion Industry Network
FoE	Friends of the Earth

HASAWA	Health and Safety at Work Act
HMIC	HM Inspectorate of Constabulary
HSC	Health and Safety Commission
HSE	Health and Safety Executive
INCPEN	Industry Council for Packaging and the Environment
LO/Nopef	Landsorganisasjonen i Norge (Norwegian TUC)
MEP	Member of the European Parliament
MILAN	Motor Industry Local Authority Network
MWA	Mineral Workings (Offshore Installations) Act 1977
NACRO	National Association for the Care and Resettlement of Offenders
NCS	Norwegian Continental Shelf
NGO	Non-governmental Organizations
NPD	Norwegian Petroleum Directorate
OECD	Organization for Economic Cooperation and Development
OFS	Oljearbeidernes Fellessammensutning (Norwegian independent offshore trade union)
OIAC	Oil Industry Advisory Committee
OILC	Offshore Industry Liaison Committee
OLF	Oljeindustriens Landsforening (Norwegian Oil Industry Association)
OSD	Offshore Safety Division (of the HSC/HSE)
PCF	Packaging Chain Forum
PED	Petroleum Engineering Division
QMV	Qualified Majority Vote
SRSCR	Safety Representatives and Safety Committees Regulations
SRB	Single Regeneration Budget
SEA	Single European Act
SEU	Subjective Expected Utility theory
SPAN	Sustainable Packaging Action Network
TEC	Training and Enterprise Council
TEU	Treaty on European Union
TUC	Trades Union Congress
UDC	Urban Development Corporation
UKCS	United Kingdom Continental Shelf
UKOOA	United Kingdom Offshore Operators' Association
WEA	Working Environment Act
WEC	Working Environment Committee
WWF	World Wide Fund for Nature

Introduction

1

The development of the policy network approach

David Marsh

Discussions of policy networks are becoming increasingly common in the analysis of public policy in Britain, the US and Europe. However, whilst there is general agreement that policy networks exist, operating as links between actors within a particular policy domain, there is much less agreement as to the explanatory utility of the concept or the broader significance of the growth of networks. In particular, there are significant differences in the way the concept is used in the US, the British and the German-inspired European literature. Of course, there is common ground. All authors see policy networks as a key feature of modern polities. In addition, there are authors within both traditions who treat the concept merely as a heuristic device, while others see it as having explanatory utility. The key difference, however, is that the European approach sees the growth of networks as having much broader significance; as marking a new form of governance, which they distinguish from two other forms, market and hierarchy. This book is located within the British tradition but acknowledges the importance of the German literature. As such, while this introduction concentrates upon the British approach, it also reviews the German literature. In addition, I shall return in the conclusion to this volume to the question of whether policy networks represent a new form of governance.

This introduction is divided into four sections. It begins with a brief review of the American, British and European literatures which suggests that the key question, in the American and British literature at least, is: do policy networks affect policy outcomes? The second section introduces this question, which is a key focus of this volume, through a consideration of two British approaches. My work with Rhodes (1992) stresses the importance of the

structural aspects of networks and thus of structural explanation, while Dowding (1994a) emphasizes that networks reflect patterns of resource exchange
between agents and, thus, he stresses intentional explanation. The third section
considers a number of related problems: how to define policy networks; how
to classify policy networks; and which methodology to adopt to study the
effect of networks. Subsequently, the final section identifies the key questions
focused upon in the later case studies in this volume.

The development of the policy network concept

A brief summary of the development of the British and American literature on
networks will suffice here as the process has been well documented elsewhere
(see Marsh and Rhodes 1992: Chapter 1).

The American literature

Jordan suggests that the idea of 'a policy network', although significantly not
the term itself, emerged in the United States in the 1950s and 1960s (Jordan
1990b: 320). This American usage emphasized regular contacts between individuals within interest groups, bureaucratic agencies and government which
provided the basis of a sub-government. The approach was a critique, sometimes implicit, of the pluralist model of interest group intermediation, that is of
relations between interest groups and government. It had a significant number
of advocates, but it never dominated. Indeed, as Peters argues in Chapter 2,
there is considerable doubt whether the model ever really applied in the United
States.

Ripley and Franklin effectively characterize the sub-government model
which emerged in the 1960s and 1970s:

> Sub-governments are clusters of individuals that effectively make most of
> the routine decisions in a given substantive area of policy . . . A typical
> sub-government is composed of members of the House and/or Senate,
> members of Congressional staffs, a few bureaucrats and representatives of
> private groups and organisations interested in the policy area.
>
> (quoted in Jordan 1990b: 321)

Other authors, such as Cater (1964) and McConnell (1966), added an
important strand to the position, arguing that the private interests involved in
the sub-governments could become dominant. They could control, rather than
respond to, their members and could capture the government agency which
was supposed to regulate their activities – a phenomenon which became
known as 'agency capture'.

The sub-government literature emphasized the role of a limited number
of privileged groups with close relations with governments; the resultant subgovernment excluded other interests and made policy. Some authors developed more rigid metaphors to characterize this relationship. Theodore Lowi

(1969) stressed the *triangular* nature of the relationships involved, with the central government agency, the congressional committee and the interest group enjoying an almost symbiotic interaction. This insight gave rise to the best known label within the sub-government literature: the 'iron triangle'.

Peters (1986: 24) characterizes an iron triangle as an exchange relationship:

> Each actor in the iron triangle needs the other two to succeed, and the style that develops is symbiotic. The pressure group needs the agency to delivery services to its members and to provide a friendly point of access to government, while the agency needs the pressure group to mobilise political support for its programs among the affected clientele . . . All those involved in the triangle have similar interests . . . Much of the domestic policy of the United States can be explained by the existence of these functionally specific policy subsystems and by the absence of effective central co-ordination.

Faced with such a critique, it is not surprising that the pluralists hit back in the late 1970s. Heclo's (1978) defence of pluralism from attack by the proponents of the sub-government model plays down the restricted nature of access to policy making, emphasizing the importance of issue networks, defined by McFarland (1987: 146) as:

> . . . a communications network of those interested in policy in some area, including government authorities, legislators, businessmen, lobbyists, and even academics and journalists. Obviously an issue network is not the same as an 'iron triangle'. A lively issue network constantly communicates criticisms of policy and generates ideas for new policy initiatives.

Heclo admits that iron triangles sometimes exist but asserts that, in general terms, fairly open issue networks have replaced 'the closed circles of control'.

Pluralist authors have generally not emphasized the significance of sub-governments and have pointed to a dramatic growth in the number of interest groups lobbying national government in the 1970s and emphasized the autonomy of the American executive institutions (see McFarland 1987: 135–6). McFarland's conceptualization contains a renewed emphasis upon two basic tenets of pluralism: the potential independence of government from the pressures of particular interests; and the existence of actual, or potential, countervailing power alliances which prevent the dominance of economic interests. He christened his rediscovery of pluralism a 'theory of triadic power'. Thus, sub-governments may exist but they are rarely exclusive. Characteristically, sub-governments will be based upon a triad involving a government agency, a producer or professional interest group and an *opposing* public interest group, either a consumer group or a social movement. It is noteworthy that this conceptualization keeps the idea that access to policy making is restricted. Indeed, it retains the triangle as an image, but emphasizes that economic groups no longer dominate. Their interests are opposed by powerful countervailing forces and an increasingly autonomous state.

Overall, the American literature has emphasized the micro-level, dealing with personal relations between key actors rather than structural relations between institutions. It initially focused upon the existence of sub-governments and often saw them as constraints upon the democratic orientation of the political system. More recently, however, a wide variety of authors criticized the sub-government thesis. They still recognize the existence of close relationships and accept that these networks can affect policy, but they deny that such arrangements pose a threat to democracy.

Two other points need emphasis, given that most of the case studies in this book deal with countries like Britain in which the legislature plays a minor role in policy making. First, neither the iron triangle model specifically, nor the sub-governments model generally, is directly applicable in such systems. So, in Britain it makes much more sense to talk of a relationship between the Department, the regulatory agency and the interest group(s), leaving out the legislative committee. Second, and this probably follows, the term 'policy network' was developed not in America, where, as we have seen, some variant on the term sub-government is adopted, but in Britain.

The British literature

Rhodes emphasizes (1990) that the British literature on networks owes a great deal to non-American sources. His own work in particular draws upon the literature on interorganizational theory, much of which is German (see, for example, Hanf and Scharpf 1978; Martin and Mayntz 1991a; Jordan and Schubert 1992). However, there is no doubt that both Richardson and Jordan (1979) and Wilkes and Wright (1987) were strongly influenced by the work of Heclo and Wildavsky (1974) on British public expenditure decision making within the Treasury, which emphasized that Whitehall operated like a village or a policy community.

Richardson and Jordan adopt Heclo and Wildavsky's idea of a policy community and suggest that such arrangements are the key to understanding most policy making in stable liberal democracies. They see policy making in Britain as taking place within sub-systems in which government agencies and pressure groups negotiate:

> The policy-making map is in reality a series of vertical compartments or segments – each segment inhabited by a different set of organised groups and generally impenetrable by 'unrecognised groups' or by the general public.
>
> (Richardson and Jordan 1979: 74)

Richardson and Jordan emphasize disaggregation; there are many divisions within government. Society is highly fragmented; a fact which is reflected in the growing number of interest groups. Policy making takes place within a variety of policy networks characterized by close relations between particular interests and different sections of government. Moreover, Richardson and Jordan stress the interpersonal rather than the structural nature of these relationships within policy communities.

Rhodes (1981) takes a different approach, drawing on the European literature on interorganizational relations, rather than on the American literature on sub-governments. For this reason, he emphasizes the structural relationship between political institutions as the crucial element in a policy network rather than the interpersonal relations between individuals within those institutions. In addition, he concentrates on the existence of networks at sectoral rather than sub-sectoral levels.

Rhodes rightly claims that the British literature on networks is distinct, although that literature is disparate, with a variety of authors taking different perspectives. His work became the starting point of the majority of the British literature on networks. It was built on by Wilkes and Wright (1987), although their approach was different; they emphasized the interpersonal dynamics of networks and stressed that networks were located at the sub-sectoral, rather than the sectoral level. However, it is the work of Marsh and Rhodes (1992) which has probably been the most significant development of the Rhodes model and which provides the starting point for this volume. As we shall see in the next section, they emphasized the structural aspect of networks, suggested that networks existed at the sectoral as well as the sub-sectoral level and argued that networks affected outcomes. In addition, they developed a typology of networks which has been influential and is used in this book. The typology is discussed below in the third section of this chapter.

The European literature

The European approach to policy networks is most associated with the work of a number of German scholars concerned with public policy, notably Mayntz, Scharpf and Schneider, who all have associations with the Max Planck Institute. However, recently there has also been a growth of related Dutch literature in the area (see Kickert et al. 1997). Both 'schools' share significant similarities with the British approach. Modern society is seen as characterized by functional differentiation, with private organizations, which control key resources, having an increasingly important role in the formulation and implementation of policy. As such, most authors adopting either approach see policy networks as having a significant influence on policy outcomes, although they are seldom explicit about the causal mechanisms involved. In addition, many of the issues within the network literature, for example questions concerning the relative importance of the structural and the interpersonal dimension of networks, cut across the two approaches. For example, the authors in the Kickert et al. reader (1997) emphasize the importance of institutional structures in much the same way as do Marsh and Rhodes. So Klijn (1997: 33) argues:

the policy network approach draws attention to the importance of the institutional context for the issue of governance. If policy processes take place within a certain institutionalised context (i.e. a stable relation pattern between organisations), it becomes important to understand that context.

However, the European and British literatures do have one fundamental difference. The German and Dutch scholars see policy networks as being of much broader significance. To British authors like Marsh and Rhodes (1992) or Smith (1993), policy networks are a model of interest group representation which is superior to, and indeed can subsume, pluralism and corporatism. In contrast, the Max Planck school and Kickert *et al.* view policy networks as a new form of governance. As Mayntz (1994: 5) puts it: 'The notion of policy networks does not so much represent a new analytical perspective but rather signals a real change in the structure of the polity.'

In this view, a key feature of the modern polity is the growth in the role of private sector organizations and the resultant decline in the capacity of the state; here the ideas have much in common with the British literature on the 'hollowing out' of the state (see Rhodes 1997). So, to quote Mayntz (1994: 5) again: 'Instead of emanating from a central authority, be this the government or the legislature, policy today is in fact made in a process involving a plurality of both public and private organisations.' Similarly, Klijn (1997: 33) argues: '(The policy network approach) leads to a different view of governance. Government organisations are no longer the central steering actor in policy activities.'

In the German literature, networks as a mode of governance are contrasted with hierarchy and markets. Hierarchy is a mode of governance characterized by a very close structural coupling between the public and private level, with central coordination, and thus control, being exercised by government. In contrast, markets as a form of governance involve no structural coupling and outcomes result from the market-driven interplay between a plurality of autonomous agents drawn from the public and the private spheres; there is no central coordination. In contrast, policy networks involve a loose structural coupling; interaction within networks between autonomous actors produces a negotiated consensus which provides the basis for coordination. Some authors see networks as representing an alternative to both hierarchies and networks (see Kenis and Schneider 1991). More authors see networks as a hybrid of the two (Mayntz 1994). Finally, some authors view networks as linked to hierarchy but not to markets (Benz 1995).

The German school argues that policy networks are the emerging form of governance because neither hierarchy nor markets are appropriate forms of governance in a world characterized by increasing interdependence between the state and the private sector; to put it another way, they suggest that the distinction between the state and civil society has been dissolved and this change necessitates a new form of governance. In this view, hierarchies fail as a mode of governance because they produce 'losers' – actors who have to bear the costs of political decisions because hierarchy is based upon systematic exploitation, and who will, consequently, attempt to destabilize the system. Markets fail as a mode of governance because the absence of coordination makes it impossible to prevent, or overcome, market failure. In contrast, because networks involve a horizontal, negotiated self-coordination they can avoid the problems associated with the other modes of governance. The negotiation can produce a positive-sum outcome in which all benefit; it is argued that networks, because of the frequent interactions involved and the consequent development of shared values and trust, develop a problem-solving capacity in which actors do not narrowly forward their self-interests. At the same time, the network provides in effect a shadow hierarchy which can coordinate responses to market failure.

Borzel sums up the argument very well:

> in an increasingly complex and dynamic environment, where hierarchical coordination is rendered difficult if not impossible and the potential for deregulation is limited due to the problems of market failure, governance becomes more and more only feasible within policy networks, in which public and private corporate actors, mutually dependent on their resources, are linked in a non-hierarchical way to exchange resources and to coordinate their interests and actions.
>
> (1997:15)

The Dutch literature, in contrast, distinguishes between the policy network model and the rational central rule model as forms of governance. In the view of Kickert et al. (1997: 7–9) the dominant rational central rule model focuses on the role of the government which is seen as the point of departure for analysis and evaluation. The government is the key actor and the role of other actors in the policy-making process is neglected; there is a top-down view of decision making. Given that there are often a variety of actors involved in implementation, then this model implies effective coordination operated by government. Indeed, to Kickert et al. this is a major weakness because the model implies an almost omnipotent government, with perfect information, attention and control of other actors. It also denies the inevitably political and thus negotiated nature of policy making.

In contrast, the policy network model offers a more realistic, and indeed democratic, alternative (Kickert et al. 1997: 9–10). The government is no longer seen as in a superior, directive, role, but as one actor among a number with roughly equal power. Public policy making in networks is about cooperation and consensus building; it involves an exchange of resources between the actors. Policy failure may result from the absence of key actors, the lack of commitment to shared goals by one or more actors or insufficient information or attention. Thus, the key to effective governance is the effective management of the network.

This book's major focus is not on these wider questions; it is clearly located within the British approach. Nevertheless, as we shall see, some of the contributions here do touch on these issues and, in particular, Benington and Harvey discuss changes in broader patterns of governance in their chapter on transnational networking between local authorities. In addition, because it is an important issue I shall return to it in the conclusion in the light of the case studies examined here. However, two other observations are worth emphasizing before I move on.

First, as Borzel, among others notes, when the German school comes to explain the development of policy networks as a new form of governance, and particularly how they shape policy outcomes, it draws on actor-centred institutionalism which combines elements of institutional theory with rational choice. The argument is that the instututions, in this case the networks, are regulatory structures which constrain and facilitate actors who are striving to maximize their preferences. As we shall see, this approach shares a great deal in common with recent developments in the British literature. In particular, it throws up the same key questions about the relationship between networks as structures and as patterns of exchange between agents which are at the core of the better British literature.

Second, the Dutch literature is similar to the German literature in some ways but different in others. As we saw, both emphasize the importance of institutional structures, but there is probably less stress on the rational choice approach in the Dutch than in the German literature. Certainly, the Kickert *et al.* edited collection places significant emphasis on strategy, which implies calculating subjects acting in structured settings. This approach shares common ground with some of the authors in this volume, especially Hay. The major difference between the Dutch and the German literature results from this emphasis in the former on strategy. The contributions in the Kickert *et al.* collection concentrate mainly on questions to do with the management of the network.

Policy networks and policy outcomes

All the authors discussed to date imply, at the very least, that policy networks affect policy outcomes. Richardson and Jordan (1979) represent a partial exception; they are ambivalent on the issue. In contrast, Dowding (1994a) asserts that the concept of policy networks, as used by most of its proponents, has no theoretical basis and, thus, no explanatory power. In his view, the concept has been used merely as an heuristic device, a metaphor. Network structures *per se* have no influence on policy outcomes. Rather, networks reflect patterns of interaction and resource exchange between agents and it is those resource exchanges which determine outcomes: 'the explanation lies in the characteristics of the actors' (Dowding 1995: 142).

In essence the argument is about the relative importance of structures and agents in affecting policy outcomes. Some authors, for example Marsh and Rhodes, stress the structural aspect of networks while others, like Dowding, emphasize intentional explanation. It is important to analyse both of these positions in some detail as the key question posed in this book is: to what extent, and in what ways, do policy networks affect policy outcomes?

Networks as structures versus networks as patterns of resource exchange

The Marsh and Rhodes approach

There are three key features of the Marsh and Rhodes approach which are relevant here. First, it is essentially structural; they downplay the importance of agents. Marsh and Rhodes see networks as structures of resource dependency and the contributions to their edited collections (1992) emphasize the structural links between the interests involved in the network. Read's conclusion (1992) is typical. He emphasizes that the basis of the British policy network dealing with the smoking issue is the shared economic interest between the Treasury, the tobacco industry and, to a lesser extent, the advertising industry. A more liberal policy on health warnings on cigarette packets or cigarette advertising is in the interest of all actors in the network; the companies will have larger sales, the Treasury greater revenue and the advertising industry more income.

Second, they argue that the structure of networks affects policy outcomes. For example, they suggest that the existence of a tight policy network constrains the policy agenda and tends to result in policy continuity. The best example in Britain is the way in which the very close relations between the Ministry of Agriculture, Fisheries and Food and the National Farmers' Union underpinned a policy of high production and high subsidies for over 50 years from the 1930s (see Smith 1992). While agriculture may represent the archetypal case, continuity, resulting to a significant extent from the existence and activities of a policy network, was also the hallmark of other policy areas considered in the Marsh and Rhodes book, notably smoking, nuclear power, diet and health, health services and sea defence (see Marsh and Rhodes 1992).

Third, while Marsh and Rhodes are less forthcoming on the way in which networks affect policy change, the basic outline of their view is clear. It is suggested that factors exogenous to the network lead to change in both the policy network and the policy outcome. So, policy continuity is the most likely outcome of tight networks, discontinuity is more likely in weaker networks, while policy change would be associated with network change. As such, the implication is that, to understand and explain policy change, we need to understand and explain network change. Marsh and Rhodes discuss network change at some length, although they don't directly relate it to the question of policy change. They argue (1992: 257) that:

> most (network) change is explained in terms of factors exogenous to the network, although the extent and speed of the change is clearly influenced by the network's capacity to minimise the effect of such change.

In their view then, the driving force for change in the network and the outcomes lies in broader economic and political change and changes in knowledge.

Overall, Marsh and Rhodes argue that a large number of the questions raised in the network literature are empirical questions which cannot be resolved by theoretical fiat and the tentative answers they give to these questions rest upon the results of the case studies in their book. However, their case studies do lack empirical detail on the actual exchange relationships involved. In Hay's terms (see below, p. 50) they are more about the network than about networking.

The structural approach has two distinct, if related, problems. First, while it does acknowledge the role of the structure and the agents, there is no doubt it privileges structure. It fails to recognize that the relationship between the two is dialectical; instead, it sees the effect as additive; structures shape outcomes but agents can ameliorate the consequences of this structural relationship. Second, in explaining change it privileges exogenous factors; indeed its explanation is based on a problematic distinction between factors exogenous and endogenous to the network. Clearly, the context within which a network is located affects the shape of the network and the behaviour of the agents in the network. However, it is the agents who have to interpret that context and their behaviour is not determined by that context. In addition, the behaviour of the actors affects both the structure of the network and the broader context within which the network operates.

The Dowding approach

Dowding argues (1994: 69) that network approaches:

> fail because the driving force of the explanation, the independent variables, are not the network characteristics *per se* but rather characteristics of components within the networks. These components explain both the nature of the network *and* the nature of the policy process.

So, to Dowding, policy networks reflect patterns of interaction and resource exchange between agents. In his view, too much of the literature on policy networks deals in broad generalities, failing to establish any direct link between the bargaining which takes place within the policy network and policy outcomes. As such, he criticizes the case studies in Marsh and Rhodes's edited volume for failing to collect sufficient detail about the interactions within the networks analysed in order to allow for any formal, let alone numerical, treatment of the exchange relationships involved. In Dowding's view, such a method is essential because it is the bargaining between the actors which goes on within policy networks, which affects outcomes. While Marsh and Rhodes suggest that change in policy outcomes results from change which is exogenous to the network, although mediated via change in the network structure, Dowding argues it must be explained in terms of endogenous change in the pattern of resource dependencies within the network.

Unfortunately, Dowding is far from clear about his agenda for policy networks research. He certainly emphasizes the need to analyse and quantify the characteristics and preferences of network participants and the bargaining processes within the network. In his initial article (1994b) there was a considerable, but under-developed, emphasis on the utility of rational choice theory. Subsequently, he emphasizes (1995) that to use the network as a key explanatory variable we need to integrate a bargaining model and game theory.

The key problem here is that the rational choice approach privileges agents over structure and assumes preferences. Yet, networks involve structures as well as patterns of interaction between agents. Dowding focuses on the actions of agents and pays no attention to how the structure of relations between agents, that is the structure of the policy network, may affect the process of bargaining, who bargains and what is bargained over. This is a point which is developed in Chapter 4. However, it is important to emphasize here that explanations which exclusively stress either the structural aspects of networks or the interpersonal exchanges of resources within the networks when trying to explain policy outcomes are partial. In my view, the way forward is to acknowledge the dialectical relationships involved. More specifically, I shall suggest in the conclusion to this volume that there are three separate but related dialectical relationships: those between network structure and the pattern of resource exchange between agents; between network and context; and between network and outcome.

Key problems in policy network analysis

Any approach to networks which accords them a key role in explaining outcomes has clear conceptual and methodological implications. In particular, it necessitates: a schema for classifying networks; the integration of network analysis, which is a meso-level analysis, with macro-level and micro-level analysis; and the use of comparative analysis. If a dialectical approach is adopted there are additional implications. We need: a broader definition of networks; to focus on the origins and the development of the network; and the use of qualitative, rather than just quantitative, methods.

Classifying networks

We need to classify different types of networks, because, if policy networks are to be used as a key independent variable to explain change in policy outcomes (the dependent variable) then we must establish and characterize the variation between them; to put it another way independent variables must vary if they are to explain differences in outcomes.

There are a number of different ways of classifying networks. Indeed certain authors have adopted classificatory schema. Here, I adopt that developed by Marsh and Rhodes because the utility of the schema has been established in a series of case studies. Marsh and Rhodes treat policy networks as a generic term and posit a continuum which distinguishes between policy communities and issue networks (see Table 1.1). Policy communities are tight networks with few participants who share basic values and exchange resources. They exhibit considerable continuity in membership, values and outcomes. In contrast, issue networks are loose networks with a large number of members with fluctuating access and significant dispute over values. There is little continuity in membership, values or outcomes.

Various authors have highlighted different characteristics of policy networks and policy communities. Grant *et al.* identify three characteristics of policy communities: differentiation, specialization and interaction (1988: 55). In a similar vein, Rhodes (1988: 77–8) identifies four dimensions along which networks vary – interests, membership, interdependence (vertical and horizontal) and resources. In addition, networks may also be characterized according to the interest(s) which dominate them. It is clearly important not to conflate these dimensions. Nevertheless, the key point must be that the degree to which any one or set of characteristics is present is primarily a matter for empirical investigation, not definition.

Marsh and Rhodes's typology builds upon these points, treating policy communities, policy networks and issue networks as types of relationships between interest groups and government. The typology treats policy network as a generic term. Networks can vary along a continuum according to the closeness of the relationships within them. Policy communities are at one end of the continuum and involve close relationships; issue networks are at the other end and involve loose relationships (see Table 1.1).

A policy community has the following characteristics: it has a limited number of participants *with some groups consciously excluded*; there is frequent and high quality interaction between all members of the community on all matters related to the policy issues; its membership, values and policy outcomes persist over time; there is consensus, with the ideology, values and broad policy preferences shared by all participants; all members of the policy community have resources so the relationships between them are exchange relationships; the basic interaction thus is one involving bargaining between members with resources; there is a balance of power, not necessarily one in which all members equally benefit but one in which all members see themselves as involved in a positive-sum game; the structure of the participating groups is hierarchical so leaders can guarantee the compliance of their members. This model is an ideal type. The actual relationship between government and interests in any policy area can be compared to it, but no policy area is likely to conform exactly to it.

One can only fully understand the characteristics of a policy community if it is compared with an issue network. The issue network involves only policy consultation, characterized by: the involvement of a large number of participants; fluctuating interaction and access for the various members; the absence of consensus and the presence of conflict; interaction based on consultation rather than negotiation of bargaining; an unequal power relationship in which many participants may have few resources, little access and no alternative. Obviously the implication of using a continuum is that any network can be located at some point along it.

Levels of analysis

In my view, policy networks are a meso-level, as distinct from a macro-level or micro-level concept. However, it has little utility as an explanatory concept unless it is integrated with macro-level and micro-level analysis. These rela tionships are the main focus of Chapter 4.

The macro-level of analysis deals with two broad sets of questions concerning the broader structures and processes of government within which any network operates, and the relationship between the state and civil society – that is with state theory. Policy networks occur at the sectoral or sub-sectoral level; so, for example, there may be a sectoral network in industrial policy and/or sub-sectoral networks which are concerned with policy in particular industrial sub-sectors, perhaps chemicals or oil. However, these networks operate within the context of the broader political system which has particular features. For example, a given political system may be characterized by a strong or a weak state tradition; executive dominance or a strong parliamentary tradition; secrecy or openness. All of these factors are likely to shape the policy networks and the way they operate and affect policy. At the same time, state theory offers an explanation of the pattern of inclusion and exclusion in the network and a hypothesis about whose interests are served by the outputs of a network.

The meso-level deals with the pattern of interest group intermediation, that is with policy networks; it concentrates on questions concerning the structure of networks and the patterns of interaction within them. The micro-level of analysis deals with the individual actions and decisions of actors within the networks and must be underpinned by a theory of human behaviour, whether it be rational choice theory or some other.

The need for comparative analysis

In my view, comparative analysis is essential in order to establish both the effect of networks and, more specifically, the relative effect of networks and context, on outcomes. In fact, two different research designs are appropriate, although they may of course be combined. First, we could compare policy formation and outcomes across the same policy area in two or more countries. If the countries shared similar political and economic contexts, but had different types and structures of policy networks, and the policy outcomes were different, then this would suggest that, in this case at least, networks have a considerable effect on outcomes. Second, we could compare policy-making processes and outcomes in different policy areas in a single country over the same period. Using this research design we can hold at least some elements of

Table 1.1   Types of policy networks: characteristics of policy communities and issues networks

Dimension	Policy community	Issue network
Memberhip:		
No. of Participants	Very limited number, some groups consciously excluded.	Large.
Type of interest	Economic and/or professional interests dominate.	Encompasses range of affected interests.
Integration:		
Frequency of interaction	Frequent, high-quality, interaction of all groups on all matters related to policy issue.	Contacts fluctuate in frequency and intensity.
Continuity	Membership, values and outcomes persistent over time.	Access fluctuates significantly.
Consensus	All participants share basic values and accept the legitimacy of the outcome.	A measure of agreement exists, but conflict is ever present.
Resources:		
Distribution of resources within network	All participants have resources; basic relationship is an exchange relationship.	Some participants may have resources, but they are limited, and basic relationship is consultative.
Distribution of resources within participating organizations	Hierarchical; leaders can deliver members.	Varied and variable distribution and capacity to regulate members.
Power:	There is a balance of power among members. Although one group may dominate, it must be a positive-sum game if community is to persist.	Unequal powers, reflecting unequal resources and unequal access. It is a zero-sum game.

Source: Adapted from Marsh and Rhodes 1992a: 251.

the context constant, so that any evidence of different network structures and different outcomes would suggest that the network is having some effect on the outcome.

The structure and focus of this book

No one book could address all the questions raised in this introduction. However, this book advances policy network analysis in two major ways. First, it raises and answers some of the key theoretical questions. As such, Part One includes three chapters which examine these issues. In Chapter 2 Peters reviews the American literature, concentrating on the question of how the policy network concept can be used as an explanatory tool. He also examines the utility of the concept for examining policy making in the United States. In Chapter 3 Hay develops a dialectical approach as a way of transcending the limitations of most existing network analysis. He places considerable stress on the dynamism of networks and, thus, the necessity of a longitudinal study of their development, which pays particular attention to their formation and termination. Finally in this section, in Chapter 4 Daugbjerg and Marsh examine some of the issues involved in integrating the meso-level analysis of policy networks with macro-level and micro-level analysis in order to explain policy outcomes.

Second, this book attempts to establish the utility of the policy network approach. Part Two presents a series of comparative case studies. In Chapter 5 Daugbjerg examines how the different networks in Swedish and Danish agriculture were able to influence policy outcomes when a new issue, the question of environmental pollution, came onto the policy agenda. Cavanagh, in Chapter 6, analyses the development of offshore health and safety policy in Britain and Norway. He pays particular attention to the origins and development of the policy networks in the two countries and indicates how they were both shaped by exogenous factors and influenced policy outcomes. In Chapter 7, McLeay considers the effect of the policy networks on policing policy in Britain and New Zealand. Her work is particularly interesting on how the broader political structures affect the shape of, and outcomes from, networks. Cole and John's concerns in Chapter 8 are different. They offer an analysis of the policy networks in two major European cities: Leeds and Lille. Their chapter shows the utility of the formal, sociometric-based method developed by Knoke and Laumann (1987). In Part Three, the final two substantive chapters deal with another key question in the literature: is the concept useful at the European Union (EU) level? In Chapter 9, Benington and Harvey examine transnational local authority networking within the EU. Subsequently, in Chapter 10 Bomberg considers the utility of the concept for explaining the development of EU environmental policy. The conclusion then reviews the theoretical and empirical contributions of the book before suggesting ways forward for policy network analysis.

Obviously, to an extent, all these case studies raise different questions, so the authors were not given a blueprint for their chapter. However, each was asked to address, where appropriate, the key questions raised in the literature and in the introduction:

- Is the concept a useful tool with which to understand policy making?
- Do the existence and activities of a policy network affect policy outcomes?
- How do networks change?
- How important are interpersonal as compared with structural links within the network?
- Do certain groups dominate the network?
- What methods are appropriate to study policy networks?

Part one

Theoretical developments

2

Policy networks: myth, metaphor and reality

Guy Peters

The concept of policy networks has gained a large number of adherents and occupied a great deal of space in the academic journals over the past decade. This pattern of thinking about politics has made a substantial contribution to the literature on interest groups (Jordan and Richardson 1987; Jordan 1990a), intergovernmental relations (Rhodes 1988), public policy making (Wilkes and Wright 1987; Richardson *et al.* 1992; Smith 1993) and on implementation (Hjern and Porter 1980; Hanf and Toonen 1985). The idea of networks as a means of conceptualizing the relationship between state and society is now pervasive in the European literature, and becoming more so in the North American literature.

There is now, however, a need to examine just what that contribution is, and whether the network approach has yet to achieve the theoretical utility that its advocates appear to assume. In particular, are 'networks' better understood only as a metaphor (see Dowding 1995) or are they also a more substantive means of explaining the dynamics of political interactions and policy making? Do networks exist in any meaningful sense, or are they mere constructs imposed by researchers for their own intellectual convenience?[1] Further, is the model generally applicable or is its utility confined to western European countries and less useful in other industrialized democracies such as the United States and Japan?[2]

The literature on networks has been developed primarily in Europe, although there certainly have been several important contributions from North America (Heclo 1978; Atkinson and Coleman 1989; Sabatier 1989). Indeed, Marsh and Rhodes (1992: 5–8) argue that the American literature served as a foundation for this body of research. The concept of networks actually grew out of the more restricted concepts of interest group politics in the United States, e.g. the famous or infamous 'iron triangles'. The American literature alerted researchers to the structural elements of relationships between state and society and therefore served as a precursor of attention to concepts such as corporatism, networks and communities.[3]

This chapter will address the issue of whether the network approach to policy and politics is as applicable to the somewhat peculiar case of American politics as it is in west European democracies. In particular, it might be argued that the traditions of iron triangles and contested access of interest groups to policy making which have characterized American politics have not been altered sufficiently to make networks descriptive of the reality of American politics. Access may be less contested and restricted than in the past, but interest groups still have less legitimacy in the political process than they enjoy in most European democracies.

In addition to the question of the applicability to the political setting of the United States, there are also several more general questions concerning the approach and its capacity to enhance our explanatory power for public policy. It is clear that in more than a few circumstances there are something like 'networks' existing in a policy area, at least in the existence of a number of groups. The problem is that after those networks are described it is not clear that the knowledge of their existence enhances the ability to predict policy outcomes. Is there sufficient information about the effects of different structures of networks on policy to make adequate predictions? Further, is the conceptualization and knowledge base about how the components of networks interact among themselves adequate to make those predictions? We will argue that, somewhat paradoxically, some of the more important emerging approaches for understanding the effects of networks on policy are derived from the American literature, despite the strength of network analysis in European political science.

The remainder of this chapter will be divided into three sections. The first section will discuss some general theoretical and methodological questions arising in the network literature. The second section will be an appreciation of the network literature from an American perspective, with special attention to the question of whether changes in the politics of the United States can better be described as the creation of networks or as 'hyper-pluralism' (Rauch 1992; see Peters 1994). Both available descriptions assume the involvement of a large number of groups in the policy process, although that involvement would be in significantly different ways. Finally, we will look at several possible ways of addressing the difficult theoretical issues in this literature, and especially those which arise from some of the limited American contributions.

General problems with the network conceptualization

Despite its appeal as a description of some important realities in contemporary political systems, there are also some important questions about using the concept of 'networks'. Several of these questions are definitional, while others are concerned with the capacity of this conceptualization to provide dynamic explanations of policy choices. Most basically, it is not clear if the implicit causal analysis contained within the network approach to policy can be falsified. When there are policy outcomes of whatever sort, they can always be attributed *ex post* to the actions and interactions of the network. While that may well be true, it does not advance the process of explaining and predicting the outcomes unless the nature of the effects can be predicted *ex ante*.

To be effective as an explanation for policy choices the network conceptualization must be able to answer two questions. The first is: how are conflicting policy views resolved within a network? For the 'community' end of the continuum there will be little conflict, almost by definition. For the issue network end of that continuum there is (again by definition) more disagreement and greater conflict and, hence, the need to develop a more common view from the several alternatives within the network. It is not clear that there is an answer to that question coming from the existing literature. The various ideas co-existing loosely within the network must be reduced to a single perspective if the network *qua* network can be said to have an influence.

The second question which must be answered if this conceptualization is to be effective is how issues arising *across* communities, and even across networks, are resolved. There is some tendency in the network literature to focus on a single issue area, or relationships existing with a single government organization (see, for example, the topical chapters in Marsh and Rhodes 1992). The real world of government is generally more complex than that, but even within a single issue area there are often policy conflicts. Therefore, there must be some means of resolving conflicts over policy, often stemming from fundamentally different conceptualizations of the issues involved (Schön and Rein 1994).[4] If, as has been argued, policy coordination and coherence are becoming increasingly significant questions for government, then focusing so heavily on individual policy areas may be counterproductive. In fact, it is particularly counterproductive given that one area in which network analysis should be particularly useful is in the analysis of interorganizational coordination (Chisholm 1989) and perhaps even in the development of mechanisms for enhanced coordination.

In fairness, some of the same critiques could be made with respect to several other models of the relationship between state and society, perhaps especially the pluralist conception (Truman 1971) which has been dominant in the United States for so long. The pluralist conception actually uses some of the same basic ideas as does the network vision of the relationships between state and society. In particular, pluralism as well as network models assumes a number of groups all attempting to influence government in a relatively unstructured manner. Further, both pluralism and the network idea assume that there is a competition for influence over policy, with government itself setting the rules of the game. Finally, the presumed openness of both systems of influence means that no group can expect to win on every decision.

Definitional questions

Before proceeding, we must ask the question of how we can identify a network when it appears in our political universe. What factors differentiate a network or community from other aggregations of groups and organizations? This is one manifestation of the general analytic problem which Sartori (1991: 248–9) calls 'degreeism', in which continua are translated into categorical and definitional variables. So, if networks are defined as having properties such as being 'open', in reality they occupy points along the continuum of 'openness', with a consequent need to identify the points at which the aggregations become networks, rather than the more closed communities. Further, can we differentiate networks from even more loose and open structures that may link government and society? There do not appear to be criteria extant to make those choices in an unambiguous manner.

These problems of defining networks can be extended to differentiating them from alternative structures of interest groups. For example, issue networks are supposed to be 'open' while policy communities are argued to be more 'closed'. Again, it is necessary to define at what point along the continuum of openness one should draw the line that separates the one type of structure from the other. It is by no means clear that the existing discussions of these definitional questions provide adequate guidance to a researcher who might want to engage in research that would separate one system of relationships from another. As Atkinson and Coleman (1989: 50) state: 'Determining just what constitutes centralization and differentiation is difficult in the abstract and is rendered only slightly more tractable by comparing nations.' The comparative element mentioned actually may confound the definitional questions given that perceived centralization in one system may be perceived as being decentralized in others.

There is no shortage of attempts to classify networks and their characteristics. For example van Waarden (1992) classifies networks along seven dimensions. Jordan and Schubert (1992) provide an enumeration of a large variety of types of networks, and Marsh and Rhodes (1992) also detail a number of alternative conceptions of these structures. These are important efforts at cladistics (McKelvey 1982), or as Dowding calls them the 'lepidopterist' approach to networks, but they do not appear to address adequately some of the fundamental theoretical questions already raised. These classifications are all useful descriptively but have not been related systematically to the behaviour of the networks, or of the networks to which they are connected.

These are more than merely definitional questions. If this corpus of social theory is to be able to make meaningful statements about the differential impacts of different types of interest group structures then researchers need to be able to separate one from another. The assumption is that the many differences noted between communities and issue networks in the formal descriptions of the concepts should have significant impacts on policy choices. If, however, the criteria by which these concepts are to be differentiated are not inter-subjectively transmissible then the body of theory may not be able to advance.

Some of the sociological examinations of networks have made strides in providing those more usable criteria for differentiation. For example, there is a substantial literature (Galaskiewicz and Wasserman 1993; Wasserman and Faust 1994) attempting to measure concepts such as openness, centrality and the patterns of interaction among groups in networks. Unfortunately, this set of measurement techniques has only rarely been included in most of the political science discussion of networks and therefore we have yet to be able to specify adequately patterns of influence and their probable effects on policy choices within the networks that can be identified so readily.

Dynamics and explanations

Another fundamental problem in the network literature is the question of the dynamic that motivates the actors and moves the system. The primary motivation of actors (largely groups) within the network appears to be self-interest, with bargaining strategies determined by the interests of the individual member organizations. These multiple and conflicting strategies may determine the interaction of the organizations, but it is not clear that their interactions provide sufficient information to predict outcomes (Marin 1990). For example, there are several possible contents central to the interactions and exchanges in governmental networks – political power, money, ideas, etc. – and different actors may be dominant in terms of one but not all.[5] Therefore, it may matter what is being traded, just as much as it matters who is doing the trading, and perhaps even more.

The point here is that, if *networks* are to explain policy outcomes, or intergovernmental relations, or whatever, then the characteristics of the networks themselves rather than the behaviour of individual organizations should be the primary explanatory element. If network is useful as a concept then there should be some collective explanatory feature, not just a derivative of the individual components. As it is, in few if any of the available network conceptualizations do the networks have sufficient articulation and elaboration to be used as explanatory factors. Indeed, there is a tendency in the literature for networks to be the dependent variable for other systemic changes, rather than an important explanatory factor. Again, as Dowding (1995: 136–7) points out, networks at present appear more useful at the metaphorical level than at the level of models capable of explaining outcomes in a systematic manner. The only hypothesis available is the fundamental one – networks matter – but that alone is almost certainly insufficient as the starting point for a serious theoretical investigation.

Associated with the problem of the dynamics of the system is the absence of more explicit linkage between network models and models of the policy process. With some exceptions the network literature appears to assume that such a connection exists, whether at the stage of formulation or at the stage of policy implementation, or perhaps throughout the process.[6] Unfortunately, a more specific statement of that linkage may be necessary for the more dynamic relationships between networks and policy that we argue are crucial for greater utility for this approach. For example, there should be a very clear linkage between networks and agenda setting (Baumgartner and Jones 1993; Kingdon 1994). The nature of networks should have a great deal to say about the opening and closing of policy 'windows' as well as about how issues are constructed in order to make them more suitable for institutional agendas. Unfortunately, that linkage is rarely made explicitly by network theorists.

A similar set of relationships between networks and the formal institutions of government should exist for policy formulation. This stage of the conventional process model tends to be less clearly explicated than several of the other stages, but one way to think about this stage is through the growing literature on policy instruments (Linder and Peters 1989; Schneider and Ingram 1993). Just as networks may reflect collective preferences about the definitions of policy problems that can influence the final outcome of the process, so too may they manifest those actor preferences in attempts to influence the choices made about the instruments used to address the problems. For example, a network dominated by economic professionals may be more receptive to tax-based instruments than are networks dominated by legal experts.

Summary

The above questions should by no means be taken as a complete rejection of the concept of networks as an approach to political analysis. There can be little doubt that policy-making systems are segmented and that the specialized relationships that exist between the actors within individual segments are important for understanding the decisions made (Jordan 1990b). Indeed, this metaphor has been a useful one in alerting scholars to some very important and rapidly changing characteristics in the socio-economic environment of the public sector. Still, to make the contribution that its advocates would like, theoretical meat must be added to these strong metaphorical bones. That meat must provide a dynamic for change within the policies presumably influenced by the network. Further, it must differentiate among different types of networks in a more useful way than the current distinction between communities and networks. Several of the approaches mentioned below appear to have the potential of meeting those criteria, although none has yet to do so in a satisfying manner.

Networks and American politics

Interest group politics in the United States have traditionally been described using the iron triangle metaphor (Freeman 1965; Ripley and Franklin 1984). This description implied the existence of three powerful actors – congressional committee, administrative agency, and producer-oriented interest group – that could control a policy area and limit access by other actors. American government could thus be seen as a series of 'sub-governments' with the few centralizing forces in the system, e.g. the presidency, attempting to exert control and produce greater policy coherence (Rose 1980; Peters 1996). This highly disaggregated government also could be argued to be capable of producing numerous contradictory and redundant programmes simply because each 'triangle' wanted to control the action in what it considered its own policy domain, or 'turf'.

The strength of the iron triangles actually may have been exaggerated for some time, but it now appears that they have become somewhat rusty. The three powerful actors defining the triangles are no longer able to restrict access to the policy process in the way they once could, and many more groups are now playing the game of political influence. Charles Jones (1979) has argued that the iron triangles were becoming 'big, sloppy hexagons'. Similarly, Hugh Heclo (1978) argued that the triangles were being replaced by more loosely structured 'issue networks', obviously indicating that the network metaphor did appear appropriate to at least one prominent political scientist. The concepts of 'networks' and 'communities' have appeared in other political science writings in the United States, although certainly not with the frequency that the ideas have appeared in Western Europe.

Sociologists in the United States appear to have been somewhat more interested in the network approach than have political scientists, with several of the major works using this approach (Knoke and Laumann 1987) coming from the discipline of sociology. Similarly, much of the conceptual and methodological development of network analysis has been centred in sociology rather than political science. Does this say anything about the perspective of political science in the United States, or is it more of a commentary on the realities of political life, with our sociologist colleagues fundamentally misreading the nature of politics in their desire to employ the tools of their trade in a new domain?

Another way of looking at the proliferation of interest group activity in the United States is to think of it as 'hyper-pluralism'. In this conceptualization there is the expansion of the number of organizations involved in influencing government, but the rules by which they are involved in the policy process are those which have governed pluralism. The network characterization appears to imply that the interest groups have acquired more assured access to the political system. Further, some versions of the network conceptualization imply the involvement of other government organizations, along with interest groups from the private sector, in influencing policy in each issue area. In these ways the network characterization approaches that of 'corporate pluralism' (Rokkan 1966) with the rules of access like corporatism but with a much less restrictive definition of the universe of organizations included in the system of influence.

A hyper-pluralist conception, on the other hand, implies more a set of relationships between groups and the public sector that looks like pluralism writ large, with almost any group which wishes involved. The fundamental question concerns the main direction of bargaining within the panoply of organizations and their involvement with the public sector. One option is a series of bilateral relationships between government departments and the lobbying organizations. This pattern is not dissimilar to the relationships identified within the 'iron triangles' or in pluralistic models of government but differs to the extent that it involves more groups. In particular there are a range of consumer groups and 'public interest groups' that have been created and now are able to exert some influence over policy (McFarland 1984; Rothenberg 1992). These groups will, however, exert this influence sequentially, rather than as a part of a proper network of groups. This pattern of sequential access appears descriptive of several major policy debates in American politics even after the end of the presumed dominance of iron triangles. For example, the tax reform passed in the late 1980s involved a large number of interest groups (Birnbaum and Murray 1987), but they could hardly be said to be working in the structured manner implied by networks. The more recent experience with health care reform also involved a huge number of interest groups (Seelye 1994; Baumgartner and Talbert 1995) with again little or no aggregation of views within the networks. It may be, however, that network conceptualizations are more effective for understanding day-to-day policy making, while the old pattern of restricted group access reasserts itself when major decisions must be made in the United States.

The alternative is a more complex, multilateral, bargaining relationship in which the various interest groups interact among themselves, as well as directly with government. This bargaining relationship may result in issues being processed among the groups prior to any significant interaction with the relevant public sector organization. This bargaining permits taking into account a wide range of opinion while then presenting the relevant organization in government with to some degree a pre-processed decision. This bargaining is all the more effective given that there may be a number of other government organizations involved, so that some of the coordination problems often encountered in the sectorized iron triangle or even corporate model may be minimized (Griffiths 1995; Peters 1995).

The differences between pluralist and network configurations can be seen from the perspective of interest aggregation, to use the term made familiar by Almond and Powell (1965). In the pluralist model of interest group interactions, there is little or no aggregation within the interest group universe. All groups attempt to place their views before government directly and uncompromised and to find some official organization that will be receptive to their demands. On the other hand, groups in a network may be expected to engage in a certain amount of mutual bargaining and aggregation of views.

Even here, however, the definitional questions raised above intrude on the analysis. If we are thinking about the loose network configuration of interest groups then there is little to make us expect any significant 'pre-processing' of issues before the negotiations with government. If, on the other hand, the community conceptualization is more appropriate (or at least more commonly utilized) then there will be more preliminary processing or indeed the processing will have been to some degree performed simply through the selectivity of the membership of the community. There are several significant barriers to the effective use of network conceptualization of political influence in the United States. In the first place, despite academic protestations, iron triangles do appear to survive in American government, and that government is still perhaps more sectorized than many or most European governments (but see Muller 1985). Some analysts have argued that, even if the system of influence appears more open, it is still dominated by a narrow elite surrounding each organization (Heinz and Laumann 1990). This elite dominance may not be the definitive conception of the iron triangle, but neither is it the open participative system of influence envisaged in much of the network literature.

In addition, the continuing absence of legitimacy for interest group influence in politics in the United States makes the development of legitimate network or corporatist patterns of interest intermediation difficult. Although the interest group system may have become broader than in the past, acquiring access still appears to be a principal political task for groups. Furthermore, although more groups may be able to gain access they still may have access one at a time, rather than as part of a collective structure that presses a more unified perspective on government.

Beyond metaphor: saving the model?

As mentioned at the outset of this chapter, we believe that there are some available means of providing greater dynamism and predictive capacity to the network approach to policy making. While there may be others, we will focus on three ideas that emerge from the American literature. This is not out of chauvinism or simply to meet the requests of the editor. Rather, these approaches do appear to address some of the deficiencies in this body of theory that have already been outlined. These three ideas are those of Sabatier (1988) and Jenkins-Smith and Sabatier (1993) about policy learning; the epistemic community approach to policy making (Haas 1990; Adler and Haas 1992); and some components of the agenda-setting literature. The epistemic community research has been developed in the field of international relations but also appears to be readily applicable, if not more applicable, to domestic policy making.

Sabatier argued that in many or most policy areas there would be multiple and conflicting views of the issues and their solutions and that politics would arise between the advocates of these different conceptions. This view is not necessarily different from the general perspectives of the network literature. What does differentiate it is the specification of the manner in which the conflicts would be resolved. The groups involved in the conflict are conceived as having core ideas about the policy and to have more specific ideas derived from those basic ideas. These derivative ideas are more negotiable than are the core values, and groups can also learn from each other as a means of resolving real or potential conflicts.

The fundamental virtue of the Sabatier approach is that it is concerned explicitly with policy change and, therefore, unlike much of network analysis, is also directly concerned with understanding a dynamic process. What matters in the 'advocacy coalition' model is how the different contending policy communities interact with one another to produce a change in the existing policy regimen. It is clear that the several contending groups will bargain and that they will utilize their ideas and knowledge as the basis for those negotiations. That collection of ideas and scientific knowledge will serve as the basis of policy advocacy, which in turn is the *primum mobile* of the entire model.

What is less clear, however, is how the conflicts will be resolved; the assumption is in part through synthesis (the learning aspect of the model) and in part through the triumph of better policy ideas over inferior ideas. These methods are different from the simple application of political power to produce winners which might be expected in a pluralist conception. Likewise, conflicts might be resolved through bargaining and market-like mechanisms. If all these models are possible then we might expect different types of conclusions to the scenario depending upon which method of resolution is dominant so that outcomes here are less predictable than is desirable.

The other obvious weakness of the Sabatier approach as a means of meeting the objections already raised to the network literature is that there is little differentiation of types of networks or communities. In the Sabatier analysis, as well as for most other models, all networks appear to be effectively the same. Thus, there is no real capacity to predict that learning will be more likely to occur in one type of network structure or another.[7] Again, if the discipline is to develop any usable theory about how networks influence policy, we will need to be able to say how and what factors affect the relative capacity of the structures to exert influence.

The concept of epistemic communities as propounded by Haas (1990), Adler and Haas (1992) and others has some of the same virtues as the Sabatier conception of networks and their role in generating policy change. First, the epistemic community approach assumes the existence of multiple and competing communities all attempting to affect policy through their ideas. This assumption is not very different from the Sabatier model, but emphasizes even more the importance of the *content* of the community's thinking as the means of defining the community. While the emphasis on content and especially scientific content is useful for defining the participants, it also highlights difficulties in resolving differences among competing communities in this approach. This difficulty is enhanced by the role of professionals in these networks and their 'trained incapacity' to see problems other than through the lens provided by their training.

Second, by inference this model is arguing that there are different types of networks, with the epistemic community being a particular structural form depending upon knowledge. It thus addresses one of the important weaknesses of the network approach. Even then, however, the answer provided is far from satisfying. While it is clear that epistemic communities are a distinctive form of network, their structural conditions are more adequately defined than their behavioural features. While Sabatier assumes that policy learning will serve as the means of reconciling differences among groups, there is no such mechanism clearly articulated in the epistemic community model. This weakness may be, at least in part, a function of its intellectual roots in international relations. Conflict is much more a matter of course in that body of literature while in domestic policy making there is a perceived need to reconcile competing positions so that governance can be provided to the society.

Third, some of the emerging body of literature on agenda setting offers an opportunity to provide a dynamic element to the study of networks and their linkage to public policy. As noted above, little of the network literature makes the linkage to agenda setting or formulation. On the other hand, the agenda-setting literature does not make that linkage directly either, although it is concerned with how groups and government organizations interact in making policy. Just as agenda setting may be implicit in the network approach, the existence of networks (or something of the sort) appears implicit in the agenda literature.

The potential for this linkage can be seen most clearly in the Baumgartner and Jones (1993) ideas of 'punctuated equilibria' and their ideas about how groups attempt to alter the pattern of influence in the process. The fundamental idea is that agendas in a policy area are relatively stable unless there is some event or political change that upsets the equilibrium. When such an upset of an equilibrium does occur there is the opportunity for a significant realignment of policy priorities. The actors in the process are not, however, necessarily inert and may attempt to generate the crucial changes in the environment of policy rather than simply waiting for them to occur naturally.

Finally, the existing sociological literature on networks offers some promise in how to address the influence of different types of networks on policy. One of the clearest efforts in this direction is the Laumann and Knoke (1987) study of networks in policy making in the United States. This analysis examines the role of networks in three different policy areas and looks at the characteristics of networks in each. This study comes as close as any available in applying the methodology coming from sociological studies of networks to the public sector (see also Knoke 1990). As discussed above, these methodologies permit the identification of crucial variables in networks which in turn will affect their role in making policy.

Summary

It is difficult to deny the strength of the network approach to political science and policy. A number of scholars have demonstrated the existence of these structures and detailed their interactions with state organizations. The existence of these collections of interest groups is undeniable, but what remains less certain is how to understand them and their interactions with the state. Further, it is not clear how best to understand the relationships among the organizations that comprise the structures. It can be argued, in fact, that the component organizations remain at least as important in understanding the outcomes of the deliberations as are the collections of organizations, despite their interactions.

American politics remains more unstructured than that found in most European countries. There are a multitude of groups all seeking individual dominance in the policy area, rather than working cooperatively within network structures. The iron triangles of the past may now be more open to external actors but public organizations still pick and choose among the various groups seeking to influence policy and to some extent can impose their own values on groups, rather than *vice versa*. The fact that the network metaphor does not work particularly well in the United States does not negate its utility elsewhere. But, just as theories based on the American experience should not be taken as general, neither should those which do not fit the American experience well.

Notes

1 A subsidiary question is whether networks have been in existence for some years awaiting the development of the concepts to describe them or whether they are a more recent phenomenon.
2 If true this may be only just, given that so much theory developed in the United States is not applicable outside that one system but is thought by many American scholars to be generic.
3 The dominance of pluralist thinking in American political science may have served as an incentive to find other approaches more suitable to European politics and society.
4 This is the basic logic of the Sabatier contribution to this literature to be discussed below.
5 This is in some ways similar to the assumption in pluralism that no one group will be able to win in all settings.
6 The 'stages' model (Jones 1982), despite its well-documented weaknesses (Sabatier 1991) remains a useful heuristic for examining the process through which policy is made.
7 This is true despite the existence of a large body of literature on organizational learning that should have some applicability.

3

The tangled webs we weave: the discourse, strategy and practice of networking

Colin Hay

The 'network paradigm' in all its mysterious guises is reshaping the political, economic and social landscape of the advanced industrial societies. As practical awareness grows of the seemingly ever more interdependent and contingent nature of the processes of social, political and economic change and their implications for institutions and institutional capacities, the benefits of network modes of coordination have increasingly been recognized (see for instance Ouchi 1980; Aldrich and Whetton 1981; Birley 1985; Thorelli 1986; Antonelli 1988; Jarillo 1988; Lundvall 1988; Imai and Baba 1989; Powell 1990; Miles and Snow 1992). Networking, or so it would appear, offers the potential to establish parameters of stability and predictability within an otherwise unstable, disorderly, unpredictable, path-dependent and rapidly changing environment. In an ever more interdependent and chaotic world, networking can provide a means of mobilizing flexible and reflexive interorganizational responses to rapidly changing circumstances. Networking can at least offer the potential of (however temporarily) removing the strategic decisions of other networked organizations from the list of unknown and unpredictable factors that must be taken into consideration in the formulation of strategy.

So what are networks, and how might we understand their formulation, transformation, failure and termination?

The network concept: definitions, descriptions, and contextualizations

What is a network? Perhaps unsurprisingly there is much at stake in our answer to this question – more so because the term 'network' is not merely an academic abstraction but is an important (and *increasingly* important) lay concept. This presents us with a choice as to strategies of definition: do we seek to impose an abstract analytical definition which might tightly demarcate a subject area and inform an account of interorganizational relations (strategy 1)? Or do we attempt to reflect definitionally what is appealed to in lay discourse when a set of practices and/or relationships is referred to as a 'network' (strategy 2)? Though the two strategies may in fact converge on a similar definition, the distinction is nonetheless highly significant. It is instructive to note that although there have been numerous (often highly commendable) attempts to specify tightly an analytical definition of 'network', variously prefixed (see for instance Rhodes 1988; Coleman and Skøgstad 1990; Knoke 1990; Powell 1990; Rhodes 1990; Atkinson and Coleman 1992; Rhodes and Marsh 1992; van Waarden 1992; Smith 1993; Marsh and Smith 1995), virtually no attention has been given to the *discourse* of networking (for a rare, however partial, exception see Cooke and Morgan 1993: 562–3). In what follows my aim is to attempt to begin to rectify this persistent omission and to consider the implications of so doing for the definition and understanding of the network phenomenon.

The dominance of the former definitional strategy within the existing literature has led to the emergence of a series of distinctive approaches to networks, the most prominent being the 'policy network approach' (Rhodes 1988; Coleman and Skøgstad 1990; Rhodes 1990; Atkinson and Coleman 1992; Rhodes and Marsh 1992; Smith 1993; for an important critique of the theoretical status of this perspective see Dowding 1995, and for a significant advance upon earlier work within this paradigm see Marsh and Smith 1995). Despite its many (and well-documented) analytical strengths, this perspective illustrates well the two characteristic weaknesses of the strategy of fixing analytically the network concept as the basis from which to proceed towards a distinctive 'network theory' of the policy-making process:

1 *The tendency to conflate theory and description*: advocates of the policy networks approach have tended to assume that in defining a range of phenomena as policy networks, in mapping the contours of such network forms, and in detailing the internal operation of such network practices, they have established a distinctive perspective, a distinctive theoretical approach to policy making in its own right. Yet in as much as the content of such 'theory' is dependent upon description, it is tempting to conclude that the policy network approach is less a theory or perspective (far less an explanation) so much as a theoretically-neutral attempt to introduce a (once) new and (still) significant analytical concept into the study of the policy-making process (for a recent recognition of this and an attempt to provide theoretical underpinnings for a distinctive dialectical *theory* of policy networking see Marsh and Smith 1995; cf. Smith 1993; Hay 1995).

2 *The reification of network structure*: a second and more significant weakness of the policy networks approach (despite some recent revisions) and much formal network analysis has been a tendency to concentrate upon mapping

the contours of the network structure at the expense of considering the *process* and *practice* of networking (see for instance Laumann and Pappi 1976; Freeman 1979; Blau 1982; Knoke and Kuklinski 1982; Mintz and Schwartz 1985; Laumann and Knoke 1987; Markowsky *et al.* 1988; Knoke 1990; Borgatti and Everett 1992; Knoke *et al.* 1996). The result has been a characteristic contextual parochialism – a concern with the network itself and not with the broader context within which it is (necessarily) embedded and within which the strategic motivations and intentions of the 'networkers' are (necessarily) formulated. This has in turn led to a certain methodologically-imposed tendency to treat the network as a static and invariant *structure* – as a nexus of structural locations and as a configuration of positional connections – to be elucidated, described and mapped (for a similar critique see Mizruchi 1994; for recent attempts to transcend the limitations of such approaches see Smith 1993; Marsh and Smith 1995). The dynamism of the network form is thus effectively removed from the analyst's focus by methodological and definitional fiat, as a static 'snapshot' is substituted for a moving target. Accordingly, little or no consideration is given to: (i) the pre-network stage; (ii) network formation as *process*; (iii) networking as *practice*; (iv) network transformation (though cf. Marsh and Rhodes 1992: 257–61; Smith 1993: 93–7); (v) network failure; and (vi) network termination. The limitations of such an approach are ever more cruelly exposed by the recent proliferation of modes of networking. For this is driven at least in part by the perception that networks, by virtue of their very dynamism, offer the possibility of strategic flexibility and adaptability in a context of contingency, instability and flux.

The above discussion demonstrates that if we are to make full use of the network concept within a political sociology of social, political and economic change, then there is still much theoretical work that must be done. In this chapter my aim is to suggest theoretical strategies for transcending the characteristic limitations of much existing network analysis as outlined above. The argument proceeds in two stages. In the first section I focus upon the largely ignored discourse of networking, suggesting that: (i) we give far greater attention to *what is being appealed to* by lay actors when they refer to a form of coordination or organization as a network (as distinct, say, from the characteristics we might attribute to such a form of interaction as social scientists); (ii) that we reflect systematically upon the relationship between network discourse on the one hand and the practices of the 'actually existing networks' that are the referent of this discourse on the other; (iii) that we consider what is conferred upon such a form of organization or coordination by lay actors when they refer to it as a network; and (iv) that we consider the discourse of networking as integral to the networking process.

In the second section I propose a *dialectical* or *strategic–relational* approach to networks; an approach which is also developed in the Conclusion to this volume. This perspective does not so much offer a theory of (policy) networks, as apply a theory of (collective) strategic action to the social practice of networking. Such an approach seeks to locate networks within a broader account of the embeddedness of strategic social actors within contexts which: (i) favour certain strategies over others as means to realize strategic intentions; and (ii) are accessed through particular (and always partial) *understandings* of such strategic contexts. By viewing networking as merely one expression of collective strategic action, such a framework counters the tendency towards the reification of networks as structures and as mere configurations of structural locations. Accordingly it places a far greater emphasis upon the essential dynamism of network structures and the practices which recursively reconstitute them. This allows for a consideration of: (i) the processes of strategic calculation and/or intuitive/habitual action through which actors and organizations recognize that their strategic resources can (or cannot) be enhanced by network participation; (ii) the process of network formation through the recognition of common or mutually-reinforcing strategic agendas and the recruitment of network participants; (iii) the practice of networking, specifically the ways in which the changing strategic motivations and the evolving strategic contexts within which network participants find themselves are reflected in the internal dynamics of the network (such as changes in its scope, degree of closure, mode of internal governance, and so forth); (iv) the processes through which network failures are recognized and the degree of flexibility, adaptation and collective strategic learning through which network practices and structures are transformed in response to perceived failure; (v) the processes of network depletion (the shedding or expulsion of networkers) and network termination (whether the intended consequence of collective strategic calculation, or the unintended consequence of network depletion or the exhaustion/full realization of a common strategic agenda). At each stage of the analysis it is crucial to consider: the strategic resources at the disposal of the actors and organizations involved; the nature of the 'strategically-selective' (Jessop 1990) context inhabited by such individuals and the organizations they 'represent'; their understandings of that context and the extent to which they are shared; the time-horizon over which their strategies are couched; the strategies they formulate; and their outcomes (both intended and unintended).

The yarns we spin: the discourse and practice of networking

Having pointed to the limitations of much existing work within the (policy) network paradigm, we are now in a position to return to our initial question of defining the network concept. In so doing it is important, as noted above, that we first consider what it is that is being appealed to by lay actors when they refer to the conduct of their own action (or to that of others) as *networking*, or to forms of organization and coordination as *networks*. Having done so, it is equally crucial that we do not simply conflate the rhetoric and reality of networking, particularly at a time when the 'network paradigm' (cf. Cooke and Morgan 1993) seems to be on the ascendancy and at a time when the discourse of networking is seemingly ever more pervasive. We must, therefore, retain a clear distinction between *network discourse* on the one hand, and the practices and procedures that characterize what might be termed *actually-existing networks* (i.e. those forms of organization and modes of governance referred to as 'networks') on the other.

This has important implications for how we define the network concept. For if we insist definitionally upon a certain combination of tightly-specified criteria as a condition of conferring 'network' status upon an organizational form, then we are very likely to exclude many practices (and the structures through which they are effected) that are routinely referred to by their participants as 'networks'. Similarly, if we extrapolate from network discourse to formulate a definition based, say, on the self-understanding of self-professed network participants, then we are also likely to exclude from the resulting set of networks many of the organizational forms referred to (in part constitutively) by these very same participants as networks. Indeed, should we pursue either strategy, we are likely to be left with a set of networks which is a very small subset *of* (or possibly an entirely independent set *to*) those organizational forms referred to as networks.

Furthermore, if we are to impose tight definitional strictures of the kind outlined above, then we might well find our contemporary interest in networks waning somewhat. For it is unlikely that, by any rigid definition of networks, forms of interstate environmental diplomacy, intra-community relations, or even local growth consortia will satisfy our definitional judge and jury. Moreover, if our interest in such interpersonal and interorganizational relations is animated at least in part by a concern with the (lack of) correspondence between actually existing networks (by which I here refer to the referents of network discourse), and the popular mythologies which surround them (which direct network participants are often extremely skilled in deconstructing, as they switch with unconscionable ease between proffering a strategically-motivated network discourse on the one hand and unpacking its convenient delusions on the other), then it is not a terribly productive strategy to dismiss all but the most ideal (and uninteresting?) actually existing networks as not networks at all.

Yet, tempting though it might seem, it is ultimately no more useful to dispense with definitions altogether. Were we to follow many actor–network theorists, for instance, in conceiving of almost all social processes as network interactions, we would merely empty the concept of all analytical content and rob ourselves of any theoretical work that such a concept might potentially be made to do (see for instance Murdoch 1995a, 1995b; cf. Latour 1986, 1987; Callon and Law 1989; Callon 1991; Law 1994). Choosing to label all aspects of social, political, cultural and economic life in terms of networks is no more and no less useful than dispensing with the concept altogether. It merely establishes a new starting point from which to interrogate the social world, and one from which the potentially useful concept of network (or, more accurately the potentially useful *distinction* between network and non-network) has effectively been removed.

What this suggests then is a minimal and inclusive definition. Such a definition must first allow us to consider *as networks* most (if not all) modes of coordination and organizational forms routinely referred to by direct participants and those excluded alike as networks (as well as a host of interactional forms not similarly understood). Yet it must also allow us to evaluate, interrogate and deconstruct the somewhat mythical status ascribed to such networks in this naming process. Accordingly, it must depart from a mere catalogue of the properties ascribed to modes of organization by lay actors when they refer to them as networks, thereby facilitating a contrast between network rhetoric and reality. Such a minimalist definition might conceive of networks as *modes of coordination of collective action characterized and constituted through the mutual recognition of common or complementary strategic agendas*. Networks, within such an account, are *strategic alliances forged around a common agenda* (however contested, however dynamic) *of mutual advantage through collective action*.

Having formulated an operational definition of the network concept we should not, however, immediately turn our attention from the discourse of networking. For, we might suggest, the self-understanding of network participants as to the type of organizational conduct in which they are engaged and the type of organizational form which provides the setting for such (inter)-action, is in part constitutive of the process and practice of networking. It is thus instructive to reflect upon the discourse(s) of networking as a clue to the nature of the networking process.

Initially it is important to note that as a term with an ever-growing reach and influence beyond purely academic debate, 'network' is neither a neutral nor an uncontested concept. Indeed, as it is ever more widely deployed within organizational, management, political and popular debate, it is seemingly ever less neutral and ever more contested as a description (more accurately ascription). Thus, although often used by direct participants as something akin to a justification of their actions and hence positively associated, the term is often used in a pejorative sense by those excluded from the network 'clique'. In this latter sense the term conjures up connotations of corruption, secretiveness and financial impropriety more akin to the codes, norms and rituals of the Mafia than to those of efficiency, flexibility and responsiveness appealed to in the former construction. Nonetheless, were one wishing to confer pejorative connotations on, say, the Mafia, it is scarcely likely that the term network would be the first to spring to one's lips.

Network discourse: synonyms, antonyms and connotations

Before turning in more detail to the contested connotations and popular resonances of networking, however, it will first prove telling to consider the synonyms, antonyms and universes (the groups of which the concept forms a subset) of the network concept.

Table 3.1   Synonyms, antonyms and universes

Synonyms	Antonyms	Universe
nexus	hierarchy	collective action
web	market	structure
linkage	dissensus	relationship
association	disorder	coordination
mutuality	atomism	order
coalition	rigidity	governance
community	struggle	organization
consensus	individualism	–

The synonyms and antonyms arrayed above give us a greater insight into the network concept and the narrative(s) in which it figures. Networks emerge as patterned linkages that can be depicted in terms of visual and spatial metaphors such as 'web' and 'nexus'; they imply some form of inter-subjective or inter-party recognition and common understanding (mutuality), providing the basis for some form of collective identity, agreement and action (community, coalition, association). Moreover such patterned linkages characterized by mutuality imply a certain orderliness (or, at worst, *regulated* disorder) and flexibility. Network relations can thus be counterposed to dissensus, disorder, rigidity and atomism (the absence of mutuality).

Markets and hierarchies are particularly significant antonyms of network (see especially Thompson *et al.* 1991; cf. Ouchi 1980; Thorelli 1986; Powell 1990). Each might be seen as a mode of coordination. Moreover, it might be pointed out (and with some degree of justification), that modes of coordination do not exist in isolation, but are necessarily articulated. Thus, in advanced capitalist social formations, we should not expect to see hierarchies which are not, at least in some way, articulated with markets; nor for that matter networks which do not display hierarchical and/or market traits. This would seem to imply that hierarchies and markets are not in fact antonymic to networks at all, but are in fact mutually-reinforcing – perhaps even *entailed* by networks. Yet this would be to conflate network discourse and network reality. For clearly if we turn to the practices of any contemporary 'actually-existing network' we are indeed likely to observe both hierarchical and market characteristics. Nonetheless, it is also clear that when lay actors refer to particular (and actually-existing) modes of organization, association and coordination as networks, they are not appealing to their market or hierarchical traits. The analytical distinction between market, hierarchy and network thus makes obvious sense, though it is important to reiterate that such forms of coordination do not exist independently of one another. Similarly, though both struggle and individualism will find themselves expressed (albeit in a variety of different forms) in all actually existing networks, these are not properties ascribed to organizational forms when they are referred to as 'networks'.

Though it might not at first appear so, the column of conceptual universes for the term network in Table 3.1 is perhaps the most revealing. For its entries (like the literature upon which it is implicitly based) span the entire range from agency to structure. Thus the network concept, it would appear, can belong to universes of agency (collective action), process (coordination, governance and organization), *and* structure or outcome of agency (relationship, order, structure). This in turn suggests that agency-centred analyses which focus upon interpersonal and/or group interactions within networks (for emblematic examples see Freeman 1955; Heclo and Wildavsky 1974; Heclo 1978; Richardson and Jordan 1979; Ripley and Franklin 1980; Jordan and Richardson 1987; McPherson and Raab 1988; Jordan *et al.* 1994; Hill 1995) and structure-centred analyses concentrating upon network form (for emblematic examples see Bales 1950; Blau 1982; Burt 1982; Laumann and Knoke 1987; Wellman 1988; Knoke 1990; Borgatti and Everett 1992) must necessarily fail to capture the specificity of network modes of coordination (for more extended critiques of the limitations of such approaches see Hay 1995; Marsh and Smith 1995). Only an account of networks capable of acknowledging the dialectical interplay between structure and agency in the practices and processes of networking would seem adequate to the task. It is to the bases for such a dialectical or strategic–relational approach that we turn in the final section of this chapter (see also Marsh and Smith 1995; cf. Smith 1993).

Before doing so, however, it is important to consider the contested connotations of network discourse. The above list of synonyms and antonyms might be seen as conferring various *positive* attributes upon networks, which are seemingly: (i) non-hierarchical yet constitutive of order; (ii) communal; and (iii) consensual (rhetorically if not in practice). Yet such attributes are not themselves uncontentiously positive, as is starkly revealed by Bernard Ingham's

Table 3.2   Network connotations: harmonious alliance or Cosa Nostra?

Positive connotations	Pejorative connotations
consensual/harmonious	closed/secretive
efficient open-ended decision making	self-serving and self-interested
negotiation/conciliation	clique/cartel
non-bureaucratic	facilitating corruption
organic: network greater than the sum of its components	undemocratic and disenfranchising/de-democratizing
constructive	exclusionary
responsive/flexible	bastion of prejudice
spontaneous as opposed to imposed organizational form	power without mandate; power without accountability
collective/communal	illicit/subterranean
non-competitive yet innovative	serving vested interest by bypassing formal channels
strategic	Machiavellian
non-hierarchically structured organizational form	a reflection of external hierarchy, status and privilege

characteristically brusque comment, 'consensus is something you reach when you can't agree' (1991: 384). Though something of a simplification then, networks can be enlisted within two somewhat different discursive codes: one broadly positive, the other broadly pejorative.

This table gives us a further insight into the network phenomenon. Paradoxically, it is the similarities between these two narratives that is most telling. For it is immediately striking that both discursive constructions share a series of common assumptions about networks. Indeed, in many respects these counterposed and conflicting narratives merely emphasize different *consequences* of the same network traits and properties – these, if nothing else, appear uncontested. Thus the *advocates' discourse* emphasizes (albeit in a somewhat idealized fashion) the consensual and harmonious *internal* relations within the network community, whilst the *detractors' discourse* concentrates upon the processes of *exclusion* and *closure* to those outside, which are the very condition of the network's existence as a bounded community. Similarly, whilst the advocates' discourse focuses upon the efficiency of this open-ended mode of decision making, its non-bureaucratic character and hence its spontaneous, dynamic, responsive and flexible nature, the detractors' discourse reminds us that this is achieved (to the extent that it is achieved) by way of bypassing formal channels and official/legal procedures. Network efficiency, influence and power can thus only be the product (at least within this narrative) of an erosion of democratic accountability and a cumulative process of de-democratization and an effective disenfranchisement of those excluded from the hallowed corridors of 'the web' (virtual or otherwise). The rest follows. If our vantage point is that of one thereby excluded, then networks are self-serving mutual protection societies, cliques and cartels characterized by the illicit, often illegal, and always subterranean pursuit of vested interest through informal channels (cf. Arlacchi 1986; Weston 1988; Gambetta 1993, 1994). If, on the other hand, it is our interests that are being served in this way, and our 'contacts' that serve to spin the web – if, in short, this is the web *we* weave – then networks can only be viewed as *organic* entities in which the strategic resources of all participants are enhanced in and through the very process of recognizing a collective interest or agenda.

The webs we weave: a strategic approach to networking

[T]he recruit is taken to a secluded location (which may also be a private home), in the presence of three or more men of honour of the family, and then the oldest informs him that the goal of 'this Thing' is to protect the weak and eradicate abuses; afterward one of the candidate's fingers is pricked and the blood is spilled onto a sacred image. Then the image is placed in the hand of the novice and set on fire. At this point the novice, who must endure the burning by passing the sacred image from one hand to the other until it is completely extinguished, swears to be loyal to the principles of 'Cosa Nostra', solemnly stating, 'May my flesh be burned like this sacred image if I do not keep faith with my oath.'

(Tommaso Buscetta in 1984, cited in Gambetta 1993: 266)

Not all network initiation ordeals are so ritualistic, nor so onerous upon their subjects. Yet this should not lead us to overlook the fact that all decisions to participate in networks are, in some sense, strategic – as indeed is the very process of networking itself. In what follows it is my central contention that if aspiring networkers, network initiates and hardened network participants alike adopt a *strategic approach to networking* then in seeking to understand the network phenomenon we too should adopt a *strategic approach*. This might seem obvious enough. Yet despite the proliferation of network talk amongst sociologists, political scientists and the like, virtually no attention has been given to networking *as strategic action* – except, that is, for a fairly limited and practitioner-oriented management literature (see for instance Porter and Fuller 1986; Jarillo 1988; Ohmae 1989).

Yet if networks are to be understood as *strategic* alliances forged around common agendas of mutual advantage through collective (again *strategic*) action, then it is clearly important that we rectify this omission and give due consideration to the generation, realization, adaptation, transformation and evolution of strategic agendas, interests and actions within shifting strategic contexts. Once again a strategic approach to the network phenomenon would appear to be called for.

The case for a strategic approach to networking can also be made on rather different and more theoretical grounds. As noted in the previous section, were we to attempt to compile a list of potential conceptual universes for the network concept, we would find it difficult to exclude categories of agency, process and structure from the range of candidates. Accordingly, to develop a structuralist or intentionalist account of networks would be to privilege one moment in what is an essentially dynamic and dialectical process. Networks may well be said to exist as structural forms which may be elucidated and mapped. Yet to dispense with an analysis of the dynamic and recursive process of networking in favour of a structural account of the thereby reified network form is to lose sight of the specificity of networks as distinctive modes of coordination produced and reproduced in and through action.

A strategic–relational or critical–dialectical approach, as I have argued elsewhere (Hay 1995, 1997; cf. Jessop 1990), certainly offers the potential to transcend the artificial and polarizing dualism between structure and agency that finds itself reproduced in the network literature as elsewhere (for a powerful demonstration and critique of its chilling embrace see Marsh and Smith 1995). It does so by suggesting that rather than consign ourselves to references to structure and agency which are, after all, merely theoretical abstractions, we concentrate instead upon the dialectical interplay of structure and agency in real contexts of social interaction. Thus, ultimately more useful than the abstract and arbitrary analytical distinction between structure and agency is that between *strategic action* on the one hand and the *strategically-selective context* within

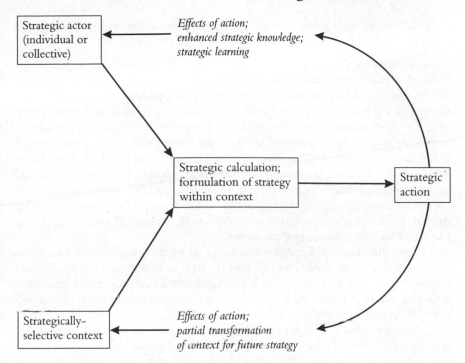

Figure 3.1   Strategic learning within a strategically-selective context
Source: Adapted from Hay 1995: 202

which it is formulated, and upon which it impacts, on the other. Within such a perspective, networking is understood as a practice – an accomplishment on the part of strategic actors (and the organizations they nominally 'represent') – which takes place within a strategic (and strategically-selective) context that is itself constantly evolving through the consequences (both intended and unintended) of strategic action. This is depicted schematically in Figure 3.1.

Within this account, strategies, once formulated, are operationalized in action. Such action yields effects, both intended and unintended. Since individuals (and groups of individuals) are knowledgeable and reflexive, they routinely monitor the consequences of their action (assessing the impact of previous strategies, and their success or failure in securing prior objectives). Strategic action thus yields:

1 *direct effects* upon the structured contexts within which it takes place and within which future action occurs – producing a partial (however minimal) transformation of the structured context (though not necessarily as anticipated); and
2 *strategic learning* on the part of the actor(s) involved, enhancing awareness of structures and the constraints/opportunities they impose, providing the basis

from which subsequent strategy might be formulated and perhaps prove more successful (cf. Bovaird 1994).

Strategic actors (potential and actual networkers for our purposes) are situated within a strategic context with (perceived) strategic interests that might conceivably be advanced through network participation (although whether these actors would continue to think of such perceived desires as representative of their 'true' interests were they in fact realized can only ever be an empirical question. In this sense 'interests' are to some extent necessarily a question of perception (see Hay 1997)). Yet in formulating strategy to advance these interests, such actors can rely only upon: (i) incomplete (often wholly inadequate and demonstrably false) information in assessing current configurations of constraint and opportunity; and (ii) more or less informed *projections* regarding the strategic motivations, intentions and likely actions of other significant players. This raises two important points.

First, the strategically selective context, as noted above, is also *discursively selective* in that it is accessed through perceptions, misperceptions and representations of the existing context. Such perceptions may or may not enhance the ability of actors to realize their intentions, and in certain contexts may militate severely against their realization.

Second, strategic action must be informed not only by representations whose accuracy can at best be an empirical question, but also by anticipated future scenarios. Strategic actors simply cannot assume some unchanging and immutable context within which cumulative strategic learning can occur. Thus to some extent networking (as strategic action informed by strategic learning) resembles playing golf in an earthquake – being able to map the contours of the fairway at one moment in time is not likely to prove a very useful guide to subsequent strategy.

This type of analysis with its focus upon strategic action, strategic learning, and – above all – on the *process of change* can inform an account of networks and networking that is capable of transcending the characteristic tendency to reify network form and structure. Networks are here conceived of as strategic alliances recursively reconstituted through the process and practice of networking. Accordingly, they are viewed as essentially dynamic and ongoing accomplishments on the part of networkers. This allows us to develop an account of the strategic and discursive selectivity of the network regime inhabited by particular network partners and its broader social and political embeddedness.

From the perspective of a potential networker, the structure of the network regime is strategically selective. It comprises all contextual factors relevant to the ability to pursue desired strategies and realize strategic intentions through networking. Such factors might include: the nature of other potential network 'partners' and their perceptions of the organization in question; the internal structure of the organization and the degree of flexibility that this allows to those who 'network' on its behalf; political, economic and juridical constraints (such as the legality and illegality of specific forms of networking);

and the social composition of the network (its degree of closure, rigidity and exclusiveness, its internal codes of conduct, and so forth).

From the perspective of an organization seeking to decide upon potential network partners, the strategically selective context is broader still, presenting: (i) the choice 'to network, or not to network'; (ii) a choice between potential network partners; (iii) a choice of 'what to network about'; and (iv) a choice of how much organizational 'sovereignty' to risk pooling in the network; as well as (v) similar strategic factors to those outlined above.

This strategic–relational approach suggests a dynamic conception of network evolution. Such a perspective can immediately be put to use in informing an account of the transformation of network forms, structures, practices and procedures, guiding our reflections on four moments of network evolution: the pre-network stage; network formation; networking as practice; and network termination. It is to this task that we now turn.

Network formation, network recruitment

Network formation must be regarded as one of the most sadly overlooked, least discussed, and yet obviously crucial aspects of networking (for a very rare though rather specific exception see Benington and Harvey 1994). The assumption seems to pervade the existing literature (be it broadly structuralist or intentionalist) that networks are always already present, always already preconstituted. The question of their formation is thus persistently deferred. This is unfortunate. For if distinctive aspects of network formation and structure are to be *explained* (as opposed to merely elucidated, detailed and described), an understanding of the legacy and hence the very process of network formation is essential. Though networks are dynamic and adaptive strategic alliances, this evolution is nonetheless *path-dependent*. Accordingly, network formation is highly significant in establishing network traits, characteristics and properties which may prove hard to shed, and may decisively influence subsequent evolutionary trajectories.

This process of network formation is schematically depicted in Figure 3.2. For network formation to occur, a number of strategic and contextual factors must be present:

1 The recognition of the potential for mutual advantage through collective (as opposed to individual) action.
2 The recognition of the potential for enhancing the strategic capacities of participant organizations through the pooling of strategic resources (itself often dependent upon pre-established contexts of mutual exchange and communication, or on the activities of a 'lead' organization or network 'hegemon').
3 The recognition and/or establishment of the conditions of network feasibility – it is one thing to recognize a collective interest or common agenda, but another thing altogether for this to prove substantively feasible.

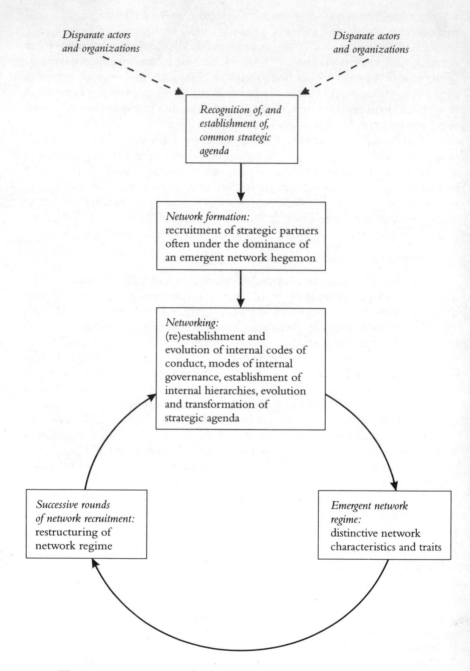

Figure 3.2   Network formation: forging a strategic alliance

Feasibility might here be considered further dependent upon: (i) a degree of geographical or communicative proximity between potential network partners; (ii) a degree of shared cultural norms and values; as well as (iii) the availability and/or willingness of organizations to devote resources of time, money and personnel, and to devolve sovereignty, to networking.

If such criteria are satisfied, a network core can be said to have been established. Network formation, however, is not necessarily thereby complete. Often under the dominance of, or at least at the behest of, a lead organization – an emergent network hegemon – the recruitment of a range of further strategic partners (chosen by virtue of the strategic resources they can muster) is sought. Here we might think of the recruitment of strategic partners to Single Regeneration Budget (SRB) bids under the dominance of a lead organization – generally a local authority (on the composition of SRB bids, both successful and unsuccessful, see Mawson *et al.* 1995; see also Government Offices for the Regions 1994; Hogwood 1995). As SRB passes through successive rounds, such lead organizations (and indeed future lead organizations) will no doubt engage in a process of strategic learning, establishing for themselves an understanding of the array of strategic partners most likely to constitute a successful bid to procure governmental resources. With the early rounds of the bidding process only recently completed (at the time of writing), they still currently have little to go on.

Network recruitment, however, is not merely a process associated with network formation but, within dynamic networks, is a near constant mechanism through which the network is reconstituted, reinvigorated and its strategic resources enhanced in response to changing circumstances.

After an initial phase of recruitment, the network can be regarded as constituted, becoming in turn a site for the practices and processes of strategic networking (and hence *re*-constitution). Emergent network traits and characteristics thus emerge and evolve as internal codes of conduct, modes of network governance, internal hierarchies, and cores and peripheries are all established and *re*-established in and through successive phases of (more or less intensive) network activity. Networks can be characterized in terms of their internal modes of *governance*, and their modes of coping with a range of problems integral to the network process. Chief amongst these is the question of *coordination* – the problem of how an array of often very different organizations and individuals with clearly divergent strategic intentions and motivations, criteria of success and failure, time-horizons, and strategic resources at their disposal can be cemented and drawn together around *either:* (i) a long-term common strategic agenda (in a network); *or* (ii) a short-term, goal-oriented strategic initiative (in a partnership). Here it is likely that other (non-network) modes of coordination will be drawn upon. These might include: (i) hierarchical dominance within the network; (ii) conciliation and compromise (itself somewhat closer to the network 'ideal'); (iii) hegemonic struggles to impose a dominant conception of the 'network-popular' interest (cf. Gramsci 1971: 131); and/or (iv) various forms of strategic bartering such as threats of exclusion to participants, and enticements to non-participants on inclusion.

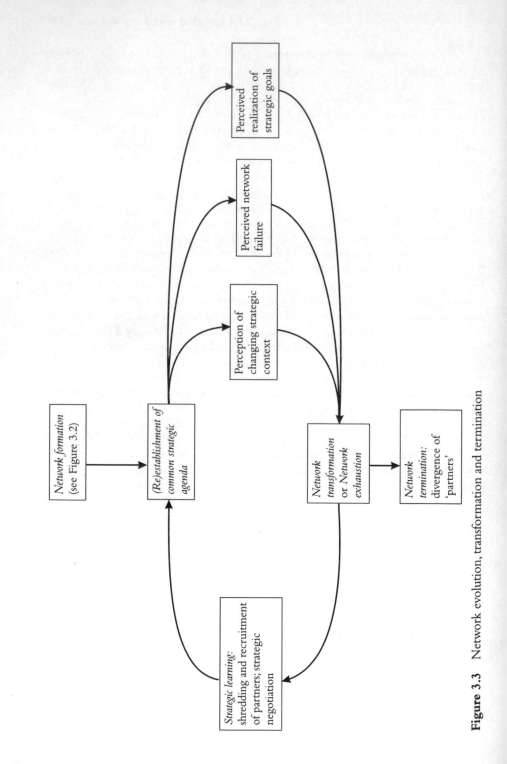

Figure 3.3 Network evolution, transformation and termination

Internal network dynamics

This type of analysis can be extended to inform an account of the evolution, transformation and ultimately termination of specific network forms. Once established, networks evolve through the renegotiation of the strategic agenda cementing the various partners in this constitutive strategic alliance. As the broader social, political, cultural and economic context within which networking occurs changes, the perceived strategic interests of individual network partners and the balance of strategic resources between them also changes. If the network is not to become obsolete, precipitating a premature disintegration and potential termination, then it must prove capable of adaptation to changing external conditions. This is dependent in turn upon the ability to find new foundations for, and bases of, collective strategic action. Networks are transformed, then, in response to: *perceptions* of the changing external context; *perceptions* of network failure; or, indeed, the perceived realization of strategic goals (see Figure 3.3).

In each of these scenarios the basis for continued networking may be exhausted as a mutual recognition of the obsolescence of this strategic alliance is achieved. Of course, such a diagnosis may well be contested, resulting perhaps in a slow disintegration of the network regime, or in a shedding of network partners to leave a smaller derivative progeny network. If network exhaustion and ultimately termination is merely one possibility arising out of perceived success, failure or external change, then a more likely one is network transformation.

This may take various forms, from *tinkering* – the minor reconfiguration of the network and the rethinking of the strategies likely to advance the long-term (collective) strategic goals of its members – to the shedding of partners, the development of a new strategic agenda, and the wholesale modification of existing network hierarchies, practices and modes of conduct: in short, the establishment of the parameters of a new *network regime*. Precisely where along this continuum any specific transformation will lie will depend upon the particular *construction* of the changed and changing strategic context that comes to predominate within the network and, indeed, the extent to which any agreed diagnosis can be reached.

This observation perhaps suggests that the concept of *network failure* (again almost wholly absent from the existing literature, though see Miles and Snow 1992) deserves closer scrutiny and further attention. For, as pointed out above, the identification of network failure is not some uncontentious, uncontested and unanimous process of objectively assessing network performance from a neutral vantage point. All network participants have a strategic stake in network success, and *in a particular understanding of what network success entails*. These different perspectives and vantage points may, and often do, sow the seeds of subsequent failure within network regimes. The immediate problem then of identifying network failure can be captured in the question, 'failure for whom?' Failure for one organization, interest or actor within the network may well constitute and represent success for, and the success of, another. Indeed, (perceived) network success for one organization is not unrelated to its ability to seize and hegemonize the 'common' strategic agenda of the network, thereby subverting the collective interest for the particular interest. This, almost by definition, implies network failure from the vantage point of other network 'partners', other particular interests.

This suggests that network failure is almost entirely a matter of perception. Yet we can take the analysis at least one stage further by identifying and distinguishing (at least analytically) between: (i) *network failure*: a situation in which the collective strategic agenda (constitutive of the network) is subverted in pursuit of a singular interest; and (ii) *network crisis*: a situation in which perceptions of network failure threaten the very continuity of the network (which might in turn be seen as a failure of the internal management of perceptions within the network). Yet this is merely an analytical distinction. Whether such conditions are held to pertain is still, essentially, a matter of perception.

Moreover, even where a common identification of network failure is reached, this, it must be emphasized, is still necessarily a *construction*, a *representation*, a *narrative,* as distinct from any simple reflection of the contradictions of the particular network form (cf. Hay 1995/96, 1996a, 1996b). The evolution – whether through piecemeal adaptation or wholesale transformation – of networks is thus mediated through constructions of failure that emerge and become hegemonic within the network and which may bear little relationship to the 'objective' contradictions of the regime itself. Furthermore, the referent of such constructions of failure and, periodically, crisis may be various. Thus for instance, a perceived crisis of the network regime may be diagnosed (and hence narrated) variously in terms of the following:

1 The subversion of the general interest by the network hegemon or network core. Such a diagnosis may have the effect of precipitating a challenge to the dominance of the lead organization or core, resulting in the emergence of a new hegemon, of a new core, or of a non-hegemonic mode of internal governance.
2 The failure of the existing strategies formulated within the network to pursue collective strategic goals by virtue, for instance, of their obsolescence within a changing context. This diagnosis may result in a modification of strategic thinking – a form of enforced strategic learning.
3 The failure and or outdatedness of the strategic agenda itself and the construction of the common interest upon which it was premised. Such a diagnosis may give rise to the attempted renegotiation of the strategic agenda to reflect the evolving interests of network participants in a changing external context.
4 Failures arising from the inappropriate constitution of the network for the successful prosecution and advancement of its strategic goals and targets. This diagnosis may result in a process of the recruiting and shedding of partners and the adoption of new modes of organization, communication and coordination within the new network regime.
5 Some combination of the above – perhaps the most likely scenario.

However, because of the difficulty of reaching collective agreement amongst network participants on the condition afflicting the network, or even on the existence of network failure in the first place, network transformation tends not to be characterized by frequent decisive interventions of this type. Rather network evolution tends to proceed through piecemeal *adaptation* to changing external circumstances which tilt the balance of power within the network in certain directions, thereby favouring the strategic interests of certain partners over others. The result is the gradual and cumulative rearticulation of network aims, the re- or counter-hegemonization of the network core, and the dropping and gaining of strategic partners.

Unweaving the web: network termination

For similar reasons, network termination – as distinct from partnership termination – tends to be a long-drawn-out process involving the whittling away of strategic partners and the gradual decline in influence of the network. The network form may well continue to linger on long after its strategic significance has been dissipated and the principal strategic attentions of its nominal participants directed elsewhere. By contrast, partnership termination tends to be more decisive and abrupt, as the need for a short-term, goal-oriented strategic alliance is exhausted by the less ambiguous success or failure in the realization of this goal. The (fairly unambiguous) failure, or indeed success, of a city's (or city partnership's) bid to stage the Olympic Games, for instance, may well result in the instantaneous termination of the bid partnership. In contrast, it may also result in efforts to reconstitute the partnership in bidding for other prestige sporting events. Here we might think of Manchester's bid for the Commonwealth Games (see Peck 1995; Peck and Tickell 1995).

Yet we should not rule out the possibility of rapid network termination altogether. Here we might think of the influence of external shocks beyond the control of immediate network participants upon the very continuity of the network. The outlawing of the practices which sustain many networks may well precipitate an abrupt ending, as may the deployment of state resources strictly to enforce laws (say, of insider dealing) that already prohibit network practices. Yet networks can exist behind prison bars too. Moreover, the seeming inability of the Italian state – despite its concerted efforts since 1992 – to uncover, expose, and impose a premature termination upon the Sicilian Mafia should remind us that tangled webs, once woven, are difficult to unravel.

Acknowledgements

The research on which this chapter was based was funded by the ESRC, award number L311253032, and conducted jointly with Bob Jessop, Gordon Macleod and Ufuk Cakmacki. An earlier version was presented at the Political Studies Association's annual conference, University of Glasgow, April 1996. The author would like to thank participants on this occasion as well as Bob Jessop, John L. Campbell and Dave Marsh for stimulating discussion, comments and suggestions.

Explaining policy outcomes: integrating the policy network approach with macro-level and micro-level analysis

Carsten Daugbjerg and David Marsh

As was emphasized in Chapter 1, the key question in policy network analysis is: what is the utility of policy network analysis? In order to address that broader question this chapter is divided into two sections. The first section suggests that the policy network approach is best treated as a meso-level framework, which, if it is to have explanatory utility, needs to be integrated with both micro-level and macro-level analysis. The second, much larger, section then examines how such integration might be achieved.

Levels of analysis and the explanation of policy outcomes

Marsh and Rhodes argued that their typology of policy networks should be seen as a meso-level concept. However, perhaps they are insufficiently clear about what that means. In fact, there have been three interpretations of this claim:

1 A number of authors seem to equate the view that the policy network is a meso-level concept with the idea that networks occur at the sectoral, rather than the sub-sectoral, level (Jordan *et al.* 1994; Dowding 1994b). They argue that Marsh and Rhodes, and authors like Smith (1992, 1993), emphasize that networks exist at the sectoral level and deny that they exist at the sub-sectoral level. Instead, these critics assert the opposite; that networks are largely, if not exclusively, a sub-sectoral phenomenon. In this way, Jordan

et al. (1995) attack Smith for identifying, and concentrating upon
community involving the National Farmers' Union and the 1
Agriculture, Fisheries and Food at the sectoral level in British ;
They argue, contra Smith, that networks in various sub-sectors, f
milk, pigs and poultry, are more important than the putative sect
community in shaping policy outcomes (for a response to this position see
Cavanagh *et al.* 1995).

To be fair, there is some, although not much, evidence to support this
interpretation of Marsh and Rhodes's focus on the meso-level. The case studies
in their edited book did identify networks at the sectoral level. More perti-
nently, in his earlier work Rhodes (1986) did concentrate on the sectoral level.
However, Marsh and Rhodes are clear that networks may occur at either level.
They emphasize that whether networks occur, at what level they occur and the
nature of the relationship between networks at the two levels are all empirical
questions; indeed, these are questions dealt with in a number of the empirical
chapters in this volume.

2 It is clear from the introduction to this book that Marsh and Rhodes's
  analysis emphasizes the structural, rather than the interpersonal, basis of
  policy networks and, as such, pays insufficient attention to the micro-level of
  interpersonal behaviour. Once again, they argue strongly that the extent to
  which interpersonal relations between network participants or structural
  relations between institutions, organizations and companies are more crucial
  within any given network is an empirical question, and this is also a question
  taken up later in this book. Nevertheless, most of the case studies in Marsh
  and Rhodes's edited collection emphasize structural relationships as the crucial element in the policy networks identified. Certainly, they treat policy
  networks as political structures which constrain and facilitate actors within
  the network.
3 Marsh and Rhodes see policy network analysis as providing a model of
  interest group intermediation; that is of relations between interest groups
  and government. They argue strongly (1992: Conclusion) that it is a model
  of interest group intermediation, located at the meso-level, which is superior
  to the pluralist or the corporatist model. Marsh and Rhodes make modest
  claims for the policy network model. They argue that the existence, membership and characteristics of policy networks affect policy outcomes. Networks essentially involve exchange relationships and power dependence is a
  central feature of them. They suggest that the distribution and type of
  resources within a network explain the relative power of its members,
  whether individuals or organizations. In addition, the different patterns of
  resource-dependence explain some of the differences between policy networks (Rhodes 1986: 29). Most significantly, the differences between networks affect policy outcomes. For example, the outcome of a tight policy
  network, in their terms a policy community, is likely to be policy continuity,
  some would say inertia, because participants share a common ideology and,

thus, policy preferences and all participants acknowledge it is a positive-sum game. Similarly, a policy network dominated by professional or business interests is likely to forward policies favouring that interest. It is also interesting here that Scott (1990: especially 135–51) argues that the existence of political structures like policy networks (he still talks of corporatist structures) has broader socio-political consequences. He suggests they are a, if not the, major reason for the rise of new social movements as the middle classes become increasingly alienated from the closed nature of political systems.

We follow this third usage but emphasize that policy outcomes are not just a function of what occurs in the network; they are also strongly influenced by the economic, political and ideological context within which the network operates. In fact, in order to explain the membership of networks, and the outcomes from them, the meso-level policy network model needs to be integrated with both micro-level and macro-level analysis.

There has been a tendency in network analysis to examine the policy process without including the broader state institutions in the study (Atkinson and Coleman 1992: 155, 168). If one's research interest is limited to identifying and describing policy networks, there is no need to integrate these institutions into the analysis. However, by removing the influence of macro-variables from network analysis, one excludes major explanatory variables. So, if the researcher is concerned to explain policy outcomes, particularly variation in outcomes across sectors or countries, s/he can hardly neglect the influence of broader state institutions. Therefore, network analysis must leave: 'some room . . . for the reintegration of macropolitical structures into the analysis of policy outcomes' (p. 163).

Here, the macro-level of analysis deals with the relationships between the state and civil society, that is state theory, and, more specifically, the broader political structures and processes within which the policy network is located. State theory offers an explanation of the pattern of inclusion and exclusion within the network and an hypothesis about whose interests are served by the outputs from the network. The meso-level deals with the pattern of interest group intermediation, that is the policy networks; it concentrates upon questions concerning the structures and patterns of interaction within them. The micro-level of analysis deals with individual actions and the decisions of actors within the networks and must be underpinned by a theory of individual behaviour.

Integrating policy network analysis with a macro-level and a micro-level approach

The aim here is to examine some of the issues involved in integrating policy networks as meso-level concept with macro-level and micro-level analysis. First, we identify how macro-analysis can help explain both the membership of networks and how networks are constrained by the social, economic and political context within which they are located. Subsequently, we consider how micro-level analysis can help network analysis explain outcomes. The approach here is exploratory. The aim is to examine some of the issues involved in integrating the three levels of analysis and provide a framework for further research.

Integrating macro-level and meso-level analysis

Here we shall deal with two separate, if related, ways in which macro-level theory and analysis needs to be integrated with meso-level policy network analysis if the structure of, and outcomes from, networks are to be explained: how network analysis can be integrated with state theory; and the way in which broader political structures and processes impact upon networks. Each of these approaches is important and they are clearly related; here we don't explore that relationship in detail, but it will be a fruitful focus for future analysis.

State theory and policy networks

It is important to integrate state theory with the policy network approach because it is state theory which provides an explanation of the patterns of inclusion and exclusion which characterize networks. Any state theory needs to address four questions. Who rules? Why do they rule? How do they rule? In whose interest do they rule? Policy networks are crucial political structures through which we are governed or ruled. As such, any state theory is likely to utilize the policy network concept as part of its explanatory framework. This is particularly so because, in their modern formulations, all three main traditions of state theory, elitism, pluralism and Marxism, stress the need to disaggregate both the state and the relationships between the state and interests within civil society (Marsh 1995b); network analysis fits very well with this development. At the same time, any attempt to explain how networks affect policy outcomes must deal with the other questions raised by state theory. In particular, it is crucial to explain the membership of the network and whose interests are served by network outcomes; these questions take us into the realm of state theory.

The aim of this section is to examine the possible relationships between policy network analysis and state theory by considering how the modern variants of the three main bodies of state theory can be, and to an extent are, integrated with the policy network model. We emphasize both that policy network analysis needs to be integrated with state theory and that the policy network concept can be, and has been, integrated with different models of state–civil society relations. There is no space here to chart the recent development in each theoretical position (for an exposition of recent developments in state theory and the putative convergence between the three positions see Marsh 1995b). Rather, we will concentrate upon two issues: how the policy network model can be integrated into each position; and what hypotheses about networks would be generated by each position.

Elitism. Two of the variants of modern elitism deserve particular attention: the sub-governments approach; and radical Weberianism. As we saw in the introduction, the work of Lowi (1969) on sub-governments offered a critique of the pluralist model of decision making and power distribution. Lowi argued strongly for the need to disaggregate when looking at the distribution of power and the process of policy making. For Lowi, there was pluralism in certain policy areas in which benefits were non-divisible (for example, government regulations) and where there were a variety of well-organized interest groups. On the other hand, plural elitism occurred in those areas in which benefits were divisible (for example, government grants or tax subsidies). Here, particular interests enjoy privileged access to, and close relations with, government; they control and defend their own turf and trade benefits with other interests in similar positions to preserve the power bases of each.

To Lowi, the latter, distributive, mode of politics had come to dominate the American political system in the 1970s. As such, a wide range of decisions had been turned over to sub-governments, which McFarland defines as:

> a coalition of interest groups, public administrators and members of Congress serving on the relevant committees that control the administration of public policy for the benefit of those within the sub-government. Such policies usually benefit established economic interests.
>
> (McFarland 1987: 135)

Lowi argues then that the interest groups, the executive agency and the congressional committee, make policy within an exclusive, closed and secret policy network. Thus, he stresses the existence of close, closed and continuing relations between interest groups and sections of the government which negotiated policy between them to their own mutual advantage. This model of interest group intermediation clearly implied an elitist power structure. It was particularly starkly captured by the image of the 'iron triangle', but also emphasized the importance of a disaggregated approach to government and to policy making. In addition, this literature focuses on the way in which political structures, like sub-governments or policy networks, can have a crucial effect on political outcomes. However, as McFarland points out, Lowi emphasized the importance of economic interests and played down the possibility of state autonomy.

In the radical Weberian elitist model, the political system is characterized in terms of structured inequality; thus, some interests are consistently favoured over others. There are a number of bases of structured inequality, none of which inevitably, or always, enjoys primacy: (i) economic/property resources – a basis of division obviously most associated with Marxism, but also crucial in the Weberian tradition; (ii) gender – due to the influence of feminist theory, gender inequality has received much more attention; (iii) political resources – including membership of policy networks; (iv) knowledge – a basis of division closely associated with the Weberian position and emphasizing the role of professionals. So, membership of a policy network, and the political resources which are associated with such membership, is an important basis of privilege. However, other bases of structural inequality will be strongly related to policy network membership; so economic interests and professional interests are likely to be vastly over-represented in networks. In addition, in order to explain policy outputs from networks it is essential to locate them within the context of the balance of social forces: the structured inequality reflected in society outside the policy network.

Overall then, utilizing the policy networks model within an elitist position would generate a series of hypotheses:

- Policy networks may occur at the sub-sectoral or the sectoral level, but the outcomes from the policy network at the sectoral level are likely to have considerable influence on the membership, operation and output from the sub-sectoral network(s).
- Many policy networks will be tight; in the terminology adopted here there will be a number of policy communities.
- Networks will be based on structural rather than interpersonal relationships.
- There will be a consistent pattern of inclusion and exclusion across networks; so networks will generally be dominated by a narrow range of interests, particularly economic, professional and state interests; although it is acknowledged that state interests particularly need to be disaggregated.
- Policy networks are a restriction on democracy because the tighter networks reflect a consistent pattern of structured political inequality and are characterized by the exclusion of most interests; outcomes serve the interests of the members of the networks.

Pluralism. Pluralism has changed significantly in the last 30 years and theoretical and empirical work on sub-governments and policy networks has had significant influence on those changes. So, as we saw earlier, the origin of the work on sub-governments in America was as an elitist critique of pluralism. Subsequently, these ideas have been taken up, developed and criticized by pluralists. In Britain the relationship between policy network analysis and pluralism was, initially at least, even closer. Certainly, the work of Richardson and Jordan (1979) on policy networks was explicitly developed from within the pluralist position. These two cases amply illustrate the extent of the convergence which has occurred between the pluralist and the elitist positions – a theme Marsh has developed elsewhere (Marsh 1995).

Lowi's work provoked a wide variety of criticisms of the sub-government thesis from pluralist authors and such criticisms have been crucial in the development of the pluralist position. Authors like Heclo (1978) and McFarland (1987) still recognize the existence of networks involving close relationships, but they: focus on issue networks rather than sub-governments or policy communities; emphasize the autonomy of government; stress the importance of countervailing power; and are critical of the view that such arrangements pose a threat to democracy. Of course, this conceptualization retains the idea that access to policy making is restricted. Indeed, McFarland's triadic theory retains the triangle as an image but emphasizes that economic groups no longer necessarily dominate. Their interests are opposed by powerful countervailing forces and by a potentially autonomous state. As such, government is not identified with any particular interests; and actual and potential countervailing power alliances prevent the dominance of economic interests.

As indicated in Chapter 1, in the British context, Richardson and Jordan (1979) were most concerned to relate the existence of policy networks to questions of power. They see policy making in Britain as taking place within sub-systems in which government agencies and pressure groups negotiate. As such, unlike some of the American pluralists, they accept that, in Britain at least, there are a number of relatively closed policy networks. In their view, the existence of such networks is not inconsistent with pluralism or democracy because there are a variety of policy networks in which *different* interests enjoy privileged access. Jordan in particular has strongly argued (Jordan *et al.* 1994) that networks will usually be located at the sub-sectoral, rather than the sectoral, level. Certainly, in Jordan's view, no one interest dominates broad areas of policy and the government enjoys considerable autonomy; it is often, perhaps even usually, the dominant partner. In this way, Richardson and Jordan are proponents of a model, which we would characterize as the plurality model, in which disaggregation and plurality are seen as synonymous with pluralism. There are many divisions within government, civil society is highly fragmented – a fact reflected in the growing number of interest groups – and policy making takes place within a variety of policy networks characterized by more or less close relations between different interests and different sections of government. In fact, this is the same model of power which is implicit in Vogel's criticism of Lindblom (Vogel 1989) and shares much in common with MacFarland's view.

Overall then, utilizing the policy networks model within a pluralist position would generate a series of hypotheses:

- Policy networks are much more likely to occur at the sub-sectoral than at the sectoral level.
- Most policy networks will be loose rather than tight; in the terminology adopted here issue networks will be much more common than policy communities.
- Networks will be based on interpersonal rather than structural relationships.
- There will be no consistent pattern of inclusion and exclusion across networks; so networks will not be generally dominated by a narrow range of interests.
- Policy networks are not a restriction on democracy because they are numerous, relatively open, being usually issue networks, and not all dominated by the same interests. Plurality equates with, indeed is the essence of, democracy.

Marxism. Marxist state theory has changed fundamentally in the last three decades. While few Marxists have discussed the sub-government or policy network literature directly, the emphasis in modern Marxism on the autonomy of the state, the need for disaggregation and the importance of political structures clearly fits happily with the literature on sub-governments and policy networks (see Marsh 1995a; Taylor 1995).

We shall concentrate here upon Jessop's strategic relational approach (1990), perhaps the most interesting of the modern Marxist treatments of the state. In Jessop's view, all structures – in his terms accumulation regimes, state forms etc. – are the outcome of past strategic struggles; once the accumulation regimes or state forms have become relatively stable they then comprise the strategic terrain on which current strategic struggles occur:

> [S]trategic selectivity refers to the structurally mediated bias which means that particular forms of state privilege some strategies over others, some time horizons over others, some coalition possibilities over others. A given type of state, a given state form, a given form of regime, will be more accessible to some forces than others according to the strategies they adopt to gain state power. And it will be more suited to the pursuit of some types of economic and political strategy than others because of the mode of intervention and resources which characterise that system.
>
> (Jessop, quoted in Hay 1994b)

The state structures, which of course need to be diasaggregated, thus privilege certain social forces and certain hegemonic projects. However, the outcome of current struggles is not determined; it is contingent and there is no guarantee that the current strategic struggles will be contained within, or reproduce, existing state forms, or accumulation regimes.

Jessop thus has a distinctive view on the relationship between the state and civil society. To Jessop, the state is an institutional ensemble shaped by the outcome of past strategic struggles between social forces. Civil society is divided along class lines but there are other crucial social divisions which have political resonance. Class is not privileged in theoretical terms, although in any concrete analysis class-based strategies may prove to be most important in shaping current structures and, thus, future outcomes. It is perhaps worth emphasizing here that, while in his theoretical work Jessop may deny the primacy of economic relations and critize the use of functional explanation, much of his own empirical work treats political change as a response to economic crisis. Hay (1994b) argues that this is because some of Jessop's empirical work neglects the insights of his theoretical analysis but it needs to be recognized that Marxism does retain strong economistic residues. So the state form, and indeed the accumulation regime, are inscribed with biases, but those biases do not determine outcomes; there is crucially space for the development of new strategies which will overcome that bias, establish a successful hegemonic project, and/or restructure the state, and/or restructure the accumulation regime.

It should be clear how the policy network model could fit with Jessop's broader theoretical approach. Policy networks are an important feature of the precise form the state takes and, in particular, of the way it relates to civil society. Their structure and membership, and particularly the pattern of inclusion and exclusion reflected in the membership, reproduce the broader structural inequality in society which is the result of the outcome of past strategic struggles. As such, from Jessop's perspective we would expect policy networks to be common and to be tight with a limited number of interests dominating a variety of networks; inevitably, certain interests would have much greater access to policy making and their strategies, and policy preferences, would be privileged.

Utilizing the policy networks model within a Marxist position would generate a series of hypotheses which are very similar to those generated by elitism:

- Policy networks may occur at the sub-sectoral or the sectoral level, but the outcomes from the policy network at the sectoral level are likely to have considerable influence on the membership, operation and output from the sub-sectoral network(s).
- Many policy networks will be tight; in the terminology adopted here there will be a number of policy communities.
- Networks will be based on structural rather than interpersonal relationships; but the strategic calculations of groups and individuals have a crucial influence on both the membership and the outcomes of networks. So the emphasis is upon strategic rather than structural selectivity and the relationship between structure and agency is viewed as dialectical (Hay 1995).
- There will be a consistent pattern of inclusion and exclusion across networks; so networks will generally be dominated by a narrow range of interests, particularly economic, professional and state interests. However, both gender and racial inequality will also clearly be reflected in the membership and outcomes of policy networks.
- Policy networks are a restriction on democracy because the tighter networks reflect a consistent pattern of structured political inequality and are characterized by the exclusion of most interests.

This section has been concerned to examine how policy network analysis can be integrated with different state theories. What is very noticeable from this discussion is the similarity between the hypotheses which would be generated about policy networks by researchers operating from within the elitist or the Marxist positions. In contrast, operating from within a pluralist position throws up significantly different hypotheses.

Obviously, these hypotheses about policy networks can, and should, be tested empirically; and indeed a number of the empirical chapters in this collection deal with some of those isssues. However, the key point here is that policy network analysis can, and must, be integrated with state theory if it is to offer an explanation of policy outcomes.

The macro-level political system and meso-level networks

One way of integrating macro-level theories with theories developed at the meso-level is to start off from the macro-level, as we saw in the last section. The alternative is to put the meso-level at the centre of the analysis and search for macro-level variables which have a direct impact upon the meso-level. While the approach starting from the macro-level is crucial for explaining broad questions about the whole political system, for example who rules and in whose interest, the meso-level approach is most appropriate in accounting for variation, both cross-sectoral variation within one country and variation between similar sectors in different countries.

Rhodes (1988) utilizes the approach in which the researcher begins from meso-level analysis and attempts to identify the characteristics of the broader macro-context which influence meso-level processes. In his study of sub-central governments in Britain, he applied macro-level analysis as a method of exploring 'those features of the national government environment which directly impact on the sub-central system . . .' (p. 48). By 'national government environment' Rhodes means 'central government institutions and their socio-economic environment as they impact on [sub-central government]' (p. 48). He uses several characteristics to describe the national government environment of Britain. These features are:

> an unstable external support system; the decline of the mixed economy; the growth of the welfare state; the extension of the allied process of functional differentiation and professionalization; the development of a social structure characterized by multiple (non-class) cleavages; and the continuing stability of political tradition characterized by a two party system, a unitary institutional structure and a central élite ideology defending the mixed economy welfare state.
>
> (p. 49)

The strength of Rhodes's work is that it outlines a method for the integration of meso-level and macro-level analysis. Its weakness is that it is under-theorized. Since there is no shortage of macro-variables which influence meso-level processes (Atkinson and Coleman 1992: 166), we need to work towards a theoretical model which can identify the macro-variables which have most influence. In addition, the model must define the variables accurately. More importantly, it must be capable of suggesting how these variables influence sectoral policy making; in particular, it must specify the conditions under which a certain outcome is likely to occur (p. 167). In other words, we need to establish the causal links between the variance in the macro-variables and the variance in the meso-level variables. It is too optimistic at present to expect anyone to develop a theoretical model which specifies how all poss-ible values in the macro-variable are linked to certain meso-level outcomes. As both types of variables can be seen as continuums, the starting point of model building is to account for the outcomes the *extreme* values on the macro-level variable produce at the meso-level; for instance, we could spec-ify how centralized and decentralized states influence the formation of policy networks. At this stage, we should be satisfied with such propositions but, later on, research must lead us towards more precise theoretical models.

In this section, we identify two macro-features of the state which are key characteristics of a nation's political system and, at the same time, have meso-level effects. We shall argue that both the parliamentary support enjoyed by various social groups and the organizational structure of the state influence meso-level policy processes.

Parliaments and policy networks. Relatively few political scientists have studied the relationship between interest groups and parliamentary parties (Grant 1993: 125). Insofar as such studies have been undertaken, some focus on the way in which interest groups can use political parties to gain influence and what the limitations are of using the party channel of influence (e.g. Jordan and Richardson 1987: ch. 10; Wilson 1990: 6; Grant 1994: ch. 7). Others attempt to map the interactions between parties and organized interests and to reveal their importance (e.g. Damgaard 1982, 1986; Norton 1991). In the latter type of studies, there seems to be an implicit assumption that the pattern of interaction reflects the influence of various interest groups. It may be so; however, their influence may not only be reflected in the pattern of inter-action. No doubt the exercise of non-structural power, that is the exercise of power arising not from structure, rules, procedures and beliefs, but from situations in which actors apply their resources and skills (Smith 1990: 35), is an important aspect of interest groups' attempts to influence political parties but the structural power arising from the political parties' sympathy towards various social groups is an even more important factor explaining interest groups' influence in the policy process. Therefore, in revealing how the political parties privilege certain interests, and not others, we can examine their ideologies, general policy positions and electoral appeals. These bias the policy process in a direction which favours some groups over others.

Few studies acknowledge the importance of how the party system influences meso-level processes (Steen 1985 provides an exception). Indeed, there is a strong tendency in network analysis to regard the policy process as non-parliamentary. Jordan and Richardson (1987: 234–8) argue that the party system is a weak determinant in the policy process. However, what goes on in a sectoral or sub-sectoral policy network 'is structurally constrained by the parliamentary system' (Judge 1993: 125). Since representative democracy is the major form of governance in Western societies, it does not make sense simply to argue that parliaments are excluded from influence because we cannot observe their direct effects upon the policy outcome. Parliaments do, however, rarely change policy proposals agreed on in sectoral policy networks, but this does not mean that they are too weak politically to oppose such proposals, rather it suggests that their views are taken into account in advance (see Olsen *et al.* 1982: 65; Olsen 1983: 39). The notion that legislatures have very limited influence is based on conclusions arising from the application of inadequate research methods which focus only on the observable behaviour of parliament; thus they only reveal the exercise of the non-structural power. The power of parliaments also rests on the exercise of structural power. Overlooking the role of parliaments in analyses of public policy making is, therefore, a great mistake (Brand 1992; Judge 1993).

Social groups may either enjoy wide support among the political parties or support only from one or a few parties. A social group facing the latter situation is not necessarily in a weak position because a party which is sympathetic to its interests may possess a strategic position within the party system, enabling it to ensure that the policy decisions which the group favours are delivered. The structure of party loyalties has an impact upon the formation of meso-level policy networks. Political parties tend to favour some groups' interests by giving them access to policy networks and by excluding others. When an interest group has a wide or strategically-positioned sympathy within the party system and its counterparts are not in such a privileged position but have only weak support, it can form a policy community with the state actor which is responsible for the policy area with which the network is to deal. Such a construction gives both of them a central position within the network and enables them to exclude others. Counterparts may perhaps become members of the network but they are likely to be located in its periphery and therefore unable to achieve more than marginal influence. A policy community is not likely to be created if an interest group enjoys limited support among the political parties. Other groups which in various ways are affected by the policy with which a network is to deal will find it relatively easy to become members of the network. When a group's interests are balanced in parliament by another group, then a policy network in which both conflicting groups are represented together with state representatives may be constructed. Issue networks tend to occur when a large number of interest groups with stakes in a policy issue each have some support in parliament. The parliamentary support does not need to be as direct as suggested here. Occasionally, bureaucrats and interest group representatives can form policy networks without the involvement of parliament. This is possible when parliament does not oppose the network construction.

Although one should not overlook the role of parliament in the formation of meso-level policy networks, it is important not to overestimate it. Parliamentary support is a necessary but not a sufficient condition determining their nature. Parliament may give an interest group access to a network but this does not necessarily mean that the interest group obtains a central position because it may not possess the resources which the other network members value. What parliaments can do is to give interest groups access to a policy network but the pattern of resource interdependencies, to a large extent, determines their position within the network.

Support from the political parties is not derived from the electoral power of a social group alone; it often has historical roots. The formative phase in a party's history continues to condition its political behaviour in many ways (Panebianco 1988: xiii, 63). Panebianco (1988: 16) argues that:

[A party's] original official aims are never abandoned, nor do they ever become a mere 'facade' . . . [The party] continually engages in certain activities related to these aims, for it is precisely upon these activities that the party's collective identity and the leadership's legitimacy are based.

The original aims are often linked to the interests of the groups which were the party's electoral basis in its formative phase. The interests of such groups are favoured by the party in the political process because the party, to some extent, acts as their agent. It is, however, important not to conceive of political parties as merely being agents of special interests. Even the most narrowly focused parties must deal with broader issues, particularly if they are in power (see Jordan and Richardson 1987: 243–4). As Wilson (1990: 156) points out: 'No political party can win a majority by being identified with a single interest' (see also Grant 1993: 126). As a result of their claims to democratic legitimacy, political parties generally enjoy some autonomy from interest groups.

Political parties may change because they are vulnerable to changes in social structure. The concomitant of an increase in voters in one social group is a decrease of voters in another. The decline in the number of a party's core voters, due to social changes, presents it with a dilemma. It has to choose whether to stick to the interests of its traditional voters and face declining electoral support or to transform and attract votes from new social groups in order to maintain, or even increase, electoral support. Parties react differently to these changes in the social structure. Some transform whereas others remain loyal to their core voters (Lane and Ersson 1991: 112). Under some circumstances, party change may be an important source of network change. If the network produces outcomes which are acceptable to groups and state actors outside the network, or at least do not bring about opposition, party change may not have any immediate consequences for the network. But once the outcome becomes a source of opposition, party change may have an impact. If the groups favoured by the outcome produced by the network have lost parliamentary support because of party change, pressure for reform can lead to a reorganization of the network so that new interests are included.

State structures. From a structure–agency perspective, there are two ways of viewing the state. While some writers view it as an agent (e.g. Nordlinger 1981), others view it as a structure (e.g. Hall and Ikenberry 1989). Skocpol (1985: 27–8) tries to bridge the gap between the two positions by suggesting that it can be both; however, her contribution does not overcome the confusion. The state-centred approach views the state as an agent. For Nordlinger (1981: 11), who advocates a strong version of the state-centred approach (Thomsen 1994: 39), the state 'refers to those individuals who occupy offices that authorize them, and them alone, to make and apply decisions that are binding upon any and all segments of society'. Attempting to avoid the confusion within the state debate, we distinguish between the state and state actors. The *state* refers to: '[a] set of institutions . . . [which] are at the centre of a geographically-bounded territory . . . [and which] monopolises rule making within [the nation state's] territory' (Hall and Ikenberry 1989: 1–2). Using Nordlinger's definition of the state, we define a *state actor* as an individual, or group of individuals, who occupies an office that authorizes her/him, or it, to make and apply decisions on behalf of the state which are binding upon some or all segments of society.

Studying the state is important because: '(its) organisational configurations . . . encourage some kinds of . . . collective political actions (but not others), and make possible the raising of certain political issues (but not others)' (Skocpol 1985: 21; see also Katzenstein 1978; Skocpol and Finegold 1982; Atkinson and Coleman 1985). An important organizational configuration which influences meso-level policy processes is the internal division of authority within the state. It has an important impact upon the power of state actors versus private interests. Katzenstein (1978: 323) argues that the more centralized a state, the stronger it is *vis-à-vis* organized societal interests; and the stronger the state, the more it can intervene in a nation's industrial sectors. Katzenstein's strong–weak state distinction has been criticized for being oversimplified; reality is often much more complex than the distinction suggests (see Wilkes and Wright 1987: 281–5; Grant et al. 1988; Atkinson and Coleman 1989: 48–9).

In an attempt to overcome the problems with Katzenstein's strong–weak state distinction, Atkinson and Coleman (1989; see also 1985) apply it at the sectorial level, but point out that we should not be tempted to lose sight of macro-level analysis (1989: 49). By focusing on the sectoral level alone, Atkinson and Coleman do, indeed, overlook the fact that the overall structure of the state has important consequences for sectoral state actors dealing with a particular segment of civil society. States in which authority is dispersed are likely to develop competing decision-making centres which, in turn, constrain the power of state actors interacting with interest groups. In such a situation an interest group can play the competing state actors off against each other. It can also take advantage of the situation if a competing state actor allies with it in order to achieve control over the policy process. In both cases the interest group can exercise considerable political influence. The least centralized states tend to be federal states and states with strong parliaments which limit the power of the executive. Such states develop competing decision-making centres. Fragmentation emerges from competition between national and regional (or sub-national) decision-making centres, from competition among state actors at the same administrative level of the state and from checks and balances between the legislature and the political executive. Division of authority occurs as a result of constitutional or informal rules of governance.

State structures influence the formation of meso-level policy networks. State actors who can aggregate authority within the state are powerful and can, thus, construct policy networks including two opposing economic interests (Atkinson and Coleman 1985, 1989: 57). In this way, such state actors increase their autonomy versus the interest groups, a major objective of most political actors. State actors which cannot aggregate authority are weak and, therefore, conflicting government agencies and interest groups enter the network. The relationship between the participants tends to develop into an issue network which has many participants and suffers from frequent and fundamental conflicts (Smith 1993: 63). Policy communities are likely to emerge when state actors are in intermediate positions upon the strong–weak state continuum. On the one hand, state actors cannot introduce a countervailing power into the network, while, on the other hand, they can exclude certain interests. The state does not have a competing decision-making centre which has sufficient power to support the interest groups excluded. If a state actor attempts to introduce a countervailing power into the network, the insider interest group can mobilize resistance to this elsewhere in the state structure, particularly in parliament.

Although there is a tendency that certain state structures are associated with certain types of policy networks, a closer examination of state structures can help to explain why policy networks vary within a political system. The state structure may facilitate the coordination of state action and thus aggregate power within some policy sectors, whereas it may impede coordination in other policy sectors with the effect that power will be dispersed to a number of state actors (see e.g. Skocpol and Finegold 1982). As a result, there will be policy communities or other types of tight and closed networks in some sectors and looser networks or issue networks in others. Although state structures are usually stable for long periods, network change can occur. In states with a relatively low degree of centralization, a government department can be the hegemonic state actor in a policy network for a long period because other departments were too weak to gain access to the network when it was formed or because they have no interest in becoming members. Over time, outside state actors may threaten the dominance of the hegemonic state actor because they become aware of the political and/or economic costs of the policy outcomes produced by the network. Outside state actors and their traditional allies will then try to gain access to the network. Since states with low degrees of centralization have weak coordination mechanisms, there is a possibility that many new actors will enter the network so that it becomes an issue network or another type of loose network. In centralized states where coordination mechanisms are well-developed, network transformation is likely to be more ordered. In order to avoid the network losing its policy-making capacity, only a very limited number of new actors will be allowed to enter.

The two macro-level approaches which we have presented here are not competing; rather they are complementary. The approach using state theory can be used to explain the overall nature and consequences of policy networks within a political system. Bearing in mind that variation in government–interest group relations was an important starting point for, and focus of, network analysis, we need to explore why policy networks in some sectors may differ from the overall pattern predicted by state theory. The macro-level approach focusing on broader political structure can help to account for this variation. Therefore, to explain the nature and consequences of policy networks convincingly, we need to use both approaches. If we, on the one hand, limit the macro-level analysis to include only state theory, one can explain the overall tendency in government–interest group relations, but not the deviations from it. On the other hand, when utilizing only the approach stressing the broader political structures, we can explain why policy networks vary, but we may lose sight of the overall nature and consequences of policy networks. In this section, we have presented two macro-level approaches and we have briefly outlined how they should be combined. Of course, we need to study the link in more detail. This is an important task for future analysis of the relationship between state and organized interests.

Integrating micro-level and meso-level analysis

We also need to integrate meso-level analysis with micro-level analysis if we are to explain the behaviour of the individuals in the policy network. Obviously, this is crucial because it is the behaviour of actors which leads to policy outcomes. However, we must acknowledge that actors behave in structured contexts and that a policy network is a structured context. Our argument here then has two key elements: first, rational choice theory is the obvious micro-level theory to be utilized; however, second, any explanation of behaviour in networks must acknowledge the dialectical relationship between the structure of the networks and the actions of the members of the network.

Using rational choice theory

At the micro-level we need a model of individual/group behaviour which will explain how individuals in networks act given the constraints, both inside and outside the network, with which they are faced. The classic intentional explanation in social science is provided by rational choice theory. As yet no-one has systematically applied it to the study of policy networks. As we saw in Chapter 1, Dowding (1994b, 1995) strongly advocates such a development, but fails to show how it could be done. In our view, two developments are crucial if rational choice theory is to be used. First, we need to use a rational choice model which operates with a conception of bounded rationality and subjective expected utilities. Second, we need to recognize that agents' actions are constrained or facilitated by structures.

Dowding strongly criticizes the case studies in Marsh and Rhodes (1992) for failing to collect sufficient detail about the interactions within the networks analysed in order to allow for any formal, let alone numerical, treatment of the exchange relationships involved. For Dowding, such a method is essential because it is the bargaining between the actors which goes on within policy networks which affects outcomes (1995: 145–6). In his view, too much of the literature on policy networks deals in broad generalities, failing to establish any direct link between the bargaining in the policy network and policy outcomes. Outcomes, and especially change in outcomes, must be explained in terms of endogenous change in the pattern of resource dependencies within the network.

Unfortunately, Dowding is far from clear about his agenda for policy networks research. He certainly emphasizes the need to analyse and quantify the characteristics and preferences of network participants and the bargaining processes within the network. In his initial article (1994) there was a considerable, but under-developed, emphasis on the utility of rational choice theory. Subsequently, he emphasizes that to use the network as a key explanatory variable we need to integrate a bargaining model and game theory (1994). We accept the implication of Dowding's analysis: rational choice theory is a useful tool for analysing the effect of networks on policy outcomes. However, it is only useful if we make realistic assumptions about individual behaviour; in particular we need to consider how individuals make rational decisions.

If one is to utilize a rational choice model it is important to specify the assumptions which are being used. A lot has changed in rational choice theory since the 1970s; in particular, the assumptions of the model have been relaxed. Much of this change results from criticisms of the model by other rational choice theorists; what Ward (1995) calls the internal critique. More specifically, these changes are a response to the two key problems of rational choice theory: its unrealistic assumptions about the knowledge available to, and the attention paid by, actors; and its failure to acknowledge that the calculations of actors involve subjective judgements of costs and benefits.

Bounded rationality. Rational choice theories have increasingly accepted the notion of 'bounded rationality'. Simon's work (1982) has been particularly influential. He argues that, faced with limited information and limited time, and given limited attention and even interest, individuals use standard operating devices as a shorthand guide to rational action. In this view, decision makers are satisfiers rather than the classical rational choice theory maximizers. Their decision-making schemes represent a simplification of 'reality'. Of course, there are likely to be common ways in which different individuals simplify 'reality'. So, civil servants in a particular Department or members of a particular policy network may share the same shorthand guide. A rational choice approach to networks needs to use a model of bounded rationality and concentrate upon the methods used by the individual and the group to make strategic decisions, their shorthand guide and their perceptions of both the decision-making scheme with which they are faced and the costs and benefits attached to various choices.

Introducing subjective judgements. This second point is also crucial. Individuals make strategic judgements in the light of their subjective perceptions of the costs and benefits involved. Opp calls this approach subjective expected utility theory (SEU):

> For each type of behaviour the SEU is defined as the sum of the utilities for each behavioural consequence multiplied by the subjective probability of each consequence.

> (Opp 1986: 89)

Opp also emphasizes that individuals value a series of 'soft incentives', those for which 'the utility is not attached to a material phenomenan' (p. 88). So, individuals in a network may value the status involved in membership, or the feeling of belonging to a potentially influential group, and this may influence their judgements about the costs and benefits attached to various strategies, options or outcomes.

In our view, recognizing that individuals use simplified models of rationality and that their strategic judgements are based on their subjective assessment of the decision-making scheme and the costs and incentives involved is crucial if rational choice theory is to be used to explain policy outcomes from networks. However, any move in that direction has significant methodological implications and is not achieved without some cost.

An attempt to establish the nature of an individual's or a group's shorthand guide for processing information and making strategic decisions involves the use of different methods. Rational choice theorists have tended to concentrate on 'objective', quantitative, data; for example, Dowding (1995) emphasizes the need to collect data on the number of times individuals or groups interact, the resources they bring to the exchange etc. In contrast, an SEU approach would concentrate upon the individual's perception of the decision-making scheme and the costs and benefits of particular policy options. As such, it is likely to involve extensive interviewing; often using qualitative, and probably non-numerical, data.

Such an analysis marks an important advance on classical rational choice theory. Certainly, the assumptions and the methodology are more appropriate. However, this advance is not achieved without cost. We are no longer dealing with the 'hard' numerical data beloved of economists. The incentives are 'soft' but so is the data; it is often recall data and is based on subjective evaluation by participants. It is not merely that economists might deny its utility. In addition, the great appeal of rational choice models has been their rigour and their parsimony. Including a much broader range of incentives certainly reduces parsimony and introduces much greater problems of measurement and validation.

Privileging agents
In our view, the key problem with the rational choice approach is that it privileges agents over structure and assumes preferences. As we saw in Chapter 1, Dowding (1995) focuses on the actions of agents in networks and pays no attention to how networks – the structure of relations between agents – may affect the process of bargaining, who bargains and what is bargained over. Although structures don't exist independent of agents, neither can they be reduced, as Dowding implies, to the preferences and actions of agents. In an earlier piece Dowding recognized that preferences can be shaped by institutions:

> When explaining a particular political process and its resultant outcomes
> by means of individual behaviour one does not need to do so without

taking into account the institutional structures which help to shape that behaviour. Even in individualist analysis the institutions which help to shape behaviour are, in many ways, what carry the explanatory force.

(Dowding 1994a:13)

It is important to acknowledge and extend that point. Structures shape preferences and policy networks are structures which shape the preferences of the actors within them. In addition, both the networks and the preferences of the actors reflect broader patterns of structural and strategic privilege. At the same time, we must recognize that the relationship between structures and agents is dialectical. The actions of agents change structures which, in turn, form the context within which agents act. Structures may constrain or facilitate agents but they are not given; rather, they are capable of interpretation and renegotiation and, thus, subject to change. Of course, it is agents who interpret/use these constraints, who attempt to minimize the constraints/maximize the advantages and who, more broadly, aim to renegotiate/change the decision-making scheme. From this perspective the policy network is a political structure which can constrain and facilitate the actions of agents. At the same time, policy networks are the product of patterns of structured privilege, based on access to a control over resources, and are constructed and reconstructed through the actions of agents. To Dowding (1994b, 1995) this means that everything can be explained in terms of the preferences and actions of agents. It seems to us that Dowding fails to acknowledge the importance of the structure/agency problem, taking refuge in the intentionalism and methodological individualism which underpins rational choice theory. If we are to integrate meso-level and micro-level analysis in this area a dilectical approach is crucial. We need to recognize that, while networks shape preferences, the actions of agents mediate and renegotiate these structural constraints. This issue is returned to in the conclusion.

Conclusion

Our aim here has been to show how a meso-level concept, policy networks, can be integrated with macro-level and micro-level analysis to produce an explanation of policy outcomes. More specifically, we have argued:

- If policy network analysis is to have explanatory power it needs to be integrated with macro-level analysis and micro-level analysis.
- At the macro-level, network analysis needs to be integrated with a state theory, which accounts for the structure of the network and the pattern of inclusion and exclusion within it.
- It is possible to integrate network analysis with any of the three broad state theory traditions, Marxism, elitism and pluralism, although each would lead to the generation of different hypotheses about the structure and operation of the networks.
- Policy networks are articulated with key features of the broader political system, for instance the structure of interest groups' support in parliament

or the state structure. The links between networks and broader political structures help to explain why the structure of networks varies across policy sectors.

- It is useful to utilize rational choice theory as the micro-level of analysis, but it is crucial to operate with a model of bounded rationality and acknowledge that actors make strategic judgements on the basis of their perceptions of the decision-making scheme and the costs and benefits attached to various options.
- Any analysis must recognize the dialectical nature of the relationship between the networks as structure and the actions of the agents who occupy the structural positions involved.

Overall, we need to recognize the utility and the limitations of network analysis. It can't explain policy outcomes simply by reference to the strutures of the network or the behaviour of the agents. We need to know why the networks take the form they do, how they relate to the broader political system and how network structures and actor behaviour affect outcomes and restructure networks.

Part two

Policy networks in comparative perspective

5

Similar problems, different policies: policy networks and environmental policy in Danish and Swedish agriculture

Carsten Daugbjerg

Western states became deeply involved in the business of agriculture in the early 1930s. Food importing countries developed agricultural policies which restricted food imports in order to safeguard farmers against the impact of the world market. Countries exporting food responded to this protectionism by adopting agricultural policies which aimed at ensuring the survival of their agricultural industries and maintaining farmers' income. Ever since these formative phases of agricultural policy making, Western states have continuously intervened in agriculture. Agricultural policy making took place in closed arenas in which the public and most members of parliament had a very limited say. Policy making was, in other words, depoliticized. Agricultural policy networks existed more or less in isolation from the rest of the political system.

Of course, decades of state intervention in agriculture did not pass by without the development of strong regulatory traditions. State actors and farmer representatives developed policy rules which defined the content of agricultural policy. A major rule, and probably the most important one, concerned the role of the state. The state in Western countries has traditionally taken a large responsibility for economic imbalances in agriculture when compared to most other sectors. States have either guaranteed minimum prices for the most important agricultural products or given direct income support in order to ensure a certain income for farmers. Writing about the Common Agricultural Policy (CAP) of the EC in the early 1980s, Harris *et al.* observed:

> Market prices are administered, not competitively determined, and they are set at such levels that even high cost producers can earn a living. Within the CAP prices no longer have the limited role of bringing about an efficient allocation of resources and production; the implications for the incomes of farmers are judged to be unacceptable. (1983: 40).
>
> (Harris *et al.* 1983: 40)

In other words, the EC has taken a large responsibility for the economic well-being of the farmers. The rule on state responsibility for economic imbalances in agriculture has been, and still is, a major advantage for farmers. Without it, farmers would face unstable prices for their products which would, in turn, cause unstable incomes and, perhaps, increase the number of bankruptcies. It would also make production management much more difficult because increased uncertainty in the market would require farmers to pay more attention to market forces when they plan their production. Although Harris *et al.* write about EC agricultural policy, the same could be said about the agricultural policies of other Western states, in particular Sweden which stayed outside the Community until 1995. Swedish national agricultural policy was, until 1991, based upon the same model as the Common Agricultural Policy of the European Community (Kjeldsen-Kragh 1995: 122).

The 1980s brought changes in the agricultural sector. Environmental problems caused by farmers caught the eye of environmental authorities and interest groups. These political actors were outsiders; that is, they did not belong to the agricultural policy network. As a result, the established political order in the agricultural sector was seriously disturbed. Since the late 1960s and early 1970s, environmental policy making has been on the political agenda in Western countries. Thus, environmental authorities had also developed regulatory experiences and traditions. The basic rule in environmental policy making is the Polluter Pays Principle. It was first adopted by the Organization for Economic Cooperation and Development (OECD) member states in 1972 and by the EC in 1973 (OECD 1989: 27; Baldock 1991: 15). The Single European Act strengthened the rule in the EC in 1986 when it became a part of the Treaty of Rome (art. 130A) (Baldock 1991: 17). OECD countries have, however, interpreted the principle in various ways, allowing for different types and levels of state subsidies (OECD 1989: 27–30). Denmark and Sweden have officially recognized that the principle should be applied in environmental policy making (Christiansen 1996: 3; Proposition 1987/88, 85: 42).

Basically, the Polluter Pays Principle is incompatible with the dominant rule in agricultural policy making, the state responsibility rule. Applying the latter rule invalidates the former, because the state pays the costs of pollution control and not the polluters themselves. A political struggle over which rules to apply, therefore, is likely to emerge; one which can easily become very conflictual. Agricultural policy has a positive image for farmers because the rules upon which it is based benefit them. In contrast, the efforts of environmental interests to introduce a new policy issue into the sector, explicitly criticizing the existing policy, are viewed negatively by farmers (see Baumgartner and Jones 1993: 81–9). Consequently, farmers will oppose agri-environmental policies based on the Polluter Pays Principle.

Environmental interests, and environmental authorities in particular, set a new political agenda in Swedish and Danish agriculture in the 1980s. Agricultural policy makers could no longer ignore the issue of pollution and environmental damage; in particular water pollution caused by nitrate run-offs. They had to deal with it. Although Swedish and Danish environmental and agricultural policy makers faced similar types of nitrate pollution problems, they chose different solutions, the result being that Swedish farmers bear a larger share of the perceived costs of environmental regulation than do their Danish colleagues. This difference indicates that Swedish farmers were less successful than the Danes in transferring the main rule of agricultural policy making (the state responsibility rule) to nitrate policy making. Hence, the Danish nitrate policy is, to a large extent, based upon the state responsibility rule whereas the Swedes, by and large, base their nitrate policy upon the Polluter Pays Principle. Since farmers in both countries had been benefiting from agricultural policies based on the state responsibility rule, they had every incentive to attempt to transfer it to the new policy issue. What is more important, it came naturally to them to transfer the policy rule because this would make it possible to cope with the new policy problems by using well-known methods. By applying these methods, agricultural policy makers could reduce uncertainty in the policy process.

A key to understanding the variation in policy outcome is the difference in the agricultural policy networks which have been regulating agriculture since the early 1930s. Certainly, the policy network approach provides the starting point for an exploration of the reasons why policy outcomes are different in the two countries. However, in its current state, the network approach only offers a poor contribution to explaining how well-established policy networks influence the choice of policy when actors outside these networks have forced a new policy issue onto the political agenda.

As we saw in Chapter 1, Dowding does not believe that we can explain policy choices within a network perspective because: ' "policy community" and "issue network" are merely labels attached to an explanation of differences between policy formation in different policy sectors. The labels do not themselves explain the difference. The explanation lies in the characteristics of the actors' (1995: 142). Instead, he offers an agency-centred approach. A similar analytical downgrading of political structures is fairly common in the policy networks literature as we saw in Chapter 4. So, for example, Jordan (1990a: 301) argues: 'Political outcomes are the result of processes and not simply the consequence of structures.'

In contrast, this chapter supports Stones's (1992: 224) counter-argument that an important 'assumption of the policy network approach is that particular types of policy networks will tend to have distinctive effects on the shape of policy decisions' (see also Marsh 1995b). In other words, *network structures make a difference*. To give this argument force, we need to establish the causal link between network type and the type of policy decision. Showing that there is a correlation between the two is not in itself convincing.

The policy network approach has not yet developed a theoretical model for explaining policy outcomes. However, the approach has made some useful observations: a policy community produces policy continuity, while loose networks are associated with unstable and unpredictable policy outcomes (Rhodes and Marsh 1992: 197; Smith 1993: 71, 75; Marsh 1995b). The network approach is even weaker in explaining policy outcomes in situations in which changes in the environments of a policy network lead to political demands for changes in the sector where the network governs. Unless the alterations in the environments are dramatic and threatening for the survival of the network itself, the members of a tight policy community are unlikely to address problems arising outside the network. Therefore, demands for changes which threaten the stability of a network only reach the political agenda if there is an outside political actor who carries the new demands into the policy process. The effects of such demands depend on the type of network which exists in a policy sector: 'Where there is an issue network or looser network the effect of social and political change is likely to be greater than where there is a closed policy community' (Smith 1993: 87). Establishing this correlation does not, however, establish a causal link. We are not told how the members of a policy community can limit the effects of changes in its environment and why members in looser networks cannot do so. Therefore, we need to explore, on the one hand, how a sectoral network influences the opportunities of outsiders to cause change in a policy sector in which they do not traditionally participate. On the other hand, the analysis must establish how networks can become an important resource for insiders who attempt to limit the effects of outsiders' activities. Finally, we need to establish how different network types influence the choice of policy when outsiders have succeeded in setting a new agenda in a policy sector.

The theoretical model which I develop argues that the success of environmental interests depends mainly on the network type existing in the sector in which they attempt to bring about change. If there is a high degree of cohesion among the members of the network, farmers may attract significant support from the other members, in particular agricultural state actors. Consequently, environmental interests have to accept that the rules of agricultural policies will guide agri-environmental policies. Such an outcome is beneficial to farmers. On the other hand, if the degree of cohesion among members of the network is low, environmentalists have a much greater chance of influencing the rules of policy making.

The best way to test whether network structures make a difference in explaining policy outcomes is to apply the comparative case study method. Comparative and cross-national studies of policy networks are the exception rather than the rule. Compared to single case studies, the major advantage of comparative studies is their ability to generate results which can be generalized beyond the immediate case studies undertaken. By choosing cases which are different with regard to both the dependent variable (the policy) and the independent variable (the network), this study sets up the comparative case study design which provides the most favourable conditions for generating theoretical statements. We can, thus, test theoretical models, establishing the conditions under which a particular outcome occurs and the conditions under which it does not occur. The logic underlying this type of multiple case study design is what Yin (1989) calls theoretical replication in which each case is regarded as an experiment. The more case studies, producing the outcome predicted by the theory, the more convincing becomes the theoretical model (Yin 1989: 52–4, 112). To undertake this form of comparative case study, one must first develop the theoretical propositions which the empirical case study is to test.

Old policy networks and new policy issues

Policy networks structure the decision-making process and provide outsiders and insiders with different opportunities for respectively changing or maintaining the existing order in a sector (Smith 1993: 97). Whether reformers will succeed 'depends on the *opportunities* embodied in the network' (Döhler 1991: 239; emphasis in original). Some configurations of policy networks facilitate changes whereas others prevent them (Lembruch 1991: 125). The key to revealing the different opportunities for reform embodied in a network is to analyse the degree of cohesion in the network.

Over time, a policy network develops a certain degree of cohesion among its members, resulting in certain patterns of collective action. Cohesion among a policy network's members emerges when there is a consensus on what should be the contents of public policy, what problems the network should deal with and how they should be solved. For those wanting to maintain the existing order in a policy sector, a sectoral policy network which has a high degree of cohesion among its members is a very powerful political resource. On the other hand, it is a major problem to outsiders demanding that new policy principles should be introduced into an old sector. They may be forced to pay a high price for a compromise or they may even fail completely; however, policy learning can strengthen their position over time (Jenkins-Smith and Sabatier 1993).

Cohesion among members of a policy network is associated with the type of network existing in a sector. While cohesion characterizes policy communities (Stones 1992: 201), issue networks lack it. The development of cohesion is facilitated if the membership of the network is very restricted and if the degree of integration is high. The fewer the members, the fewer the interests which have to be reflected by the policy rules and, thus, the more manageable and predictable the policy process becomes (Daugbjerg 1994a: 462).

Hence, the members can more easily achieve consensus among themselves. 'Frequent [and high-quality] interaction between all members of the community on all matters related to the policy issue' (Rhodes and Marsh 1992: 186) also eases the development of cohesion. Intensive information exchange implies that each member achieves insight into the others' situations, interests and values. This makes it possible to achieve consensus on what rules, procedures and norms should prevail in policy making.

In a policy community, policy rules, norms and procedures are well developed. These institutional factors become more important in public policy making over time than the pattern of resource exchange. Members increasingly handle policy problems by referring to rules, procedures and norms. The policy-making procedures, which are laid down in the formative phase of a network, do, to a large extent, define which resources are important in policy making. Thus, the policy-making procedures outline the pattern of resource dependency. Actors developing resources which are not defined as being relevant to policy making will, therefore, be unable to gain access to the network.

The high degree of cohesion in a policy community influences its members' formation of policy preferences. In particular, the network structure influences the policy preferences of the state actor most centrally positioned in the community. State actors, for example ministries of agriculture, do not have policy preferences which are as obvious as those of interest groups. The formation of their preferences is contextual. Olsen argues that the views of top civil servants 'are formed by the tasks they are responsible for, by the institutions and the professions to which they belong, and by the parts of the environment they interact with' (1983: 145). In sectoral policy making, state actors' 'interests develop from contacts with groups, and often within networks' (Smith 1993: 227). The interests of the state actor may, therefore, develop to be rather similar to those of a particular organized interest. Interest groups' policy preferences are, to a large extent, derived from their position in the economy or from the functions they perform. However, network structures have considerable influence upon how they transform these interests into policy preferences.

When a new policy issue is placed on the political agenda and can no longer be avoided or downgraded, members of a policy community are forced to act. They will, because it comes naturally to them, apply well-known methods to solve the new problems. The experience derived from earlier decision-making processes forms the basis of approaching new problems (March and Olsen 1989: 22, 38, 167–8; see also Hall 1986: 233). Members of a policy community eventually match a situation to the demands of established policy rules (March and Olsen 1989: 23), thus classifying the new problem into well-known problem categories. Then, action can follow certain well-established rules. Members of a policy network, in other words, try to transfer the existing principles, rules, norms and procedures to policy making in the new policy issue. Outsiders' opportunities for forcing new policy rules into an old regulated sector in which a policy community exists are limited. They will meet strong united resistance. The state actor which is a member of the established network allies with the interest group. The cohesion is, in some cases, so strong that the network can be said to act in unity, especially if all members feel they are being threatened by an outsider (Daugbjerg 1994b: 13). Outsiders have few chances of gaining sufficient support to ensure that their policy rules form the basis of the new policy. As a result, the established policy rules of the sector are transformed to the new policy issue.

Members of a policy community may, however, give some concessions to the reformer to avoid an increase in the conflict to a level at which the issue becomes highly politicized and, thus, even more out of their control. If the issue becomes highly politicized, the political decision-making process moves from the political administrative arena to the cabinet and perhaps to the parliament. Policies which are adopted in these two arenas may – due to a high level of public attention – result in outcomes disadvantageous to those who are the targets of regulation (see Schattschneider 1960: 15, 36). However, as public attention decreases, members of an existing network may regain their power. They react to the policy output by entering into the political–administrative process in which they try to turn the implementation process in a direction which limits their perceived costs of the policy. They do so by influencing the administrative rules concerning how the policy instruments are to be applied, by influencing which public agency is to implement policies and, to some extent, by persuading public authorities to downgrade the importance of policy goals. This sort of feedback moves the system back to its *own* equilibrium. External pressures introduced into a system can cause disequilibrium for a period. Baumgartner and Jones (1993: 16–17) call this negative feedback; a process in which external pressures result in a system being changed without returning to its former equilibrium they name positive feedback. Even though an outsider may seem successful in the short term, it may in the medium term be content that at least something is being done, although the policy measures are not what it wanted in the first place. In the long term, policy learning may, however, provide an outsider with strong evidence and argumentation, enhancing the opportunities for successful changes later (Jenkins-Smith and Sabatier 1993).

Members of an issue network react rather differently to new policy issues. Issue networks are characterized by a low degree of institutionalization. There is no dominant coalition which has the power to lay down a set of policy rules, policy-making procedures and norms which can guide policy making. Members of an issue network constantly struggle over rules, procedures and norms. The low degree of institutionalization implies that policy making is, first and foremost, guided by resource exchange from case to case or from sub-issue to sub-issue. The pattern of resource dependency is unstable because actors move in and out of the policy process. They are included in the policy process if they have resources in the particular case whereas they are excluded in cases in which they lack resources. Due to the ever-present struggle over policy rules, norms and procedures, no cohesion among the members will develop. However, to decrease uncertainty they may make a compromise on some rules, but the network is basically unstable because it is not based upon a shared understanding (see Smith 1993: 126–7). When issue network members confront a new policy issue, they continue to struggle over policy rules to apply in policy making. Each member, or group of members, pursues what it perceives as its narrow self-interest, trying to achieve support for policy rules which would benefit them in present and future policy making.

A low degree of cohesion implies that outsiders have better opportunities for successful changes in a sector in which they do not traditionally participate in policy making. Not only can they ensure that the new problems are being dealt with, they also have good opportunities for gaining political support for the policy rules they favour. In policy networks where the degree of cohesion is considerably lower than in a policy community, members can only form a weak alliance of resistance, if any. This provides outsiders with reasonable chances for success, as they may be able to split the alliance, or even form an *ad hoc* coalition with one or more of the members. The interest group whose members are to bear the costs of regulation is, therefore, left without centrally placed political actors, in particular state actors, which can support it in the policy process. State actors within established networks either become mediators between outsiders and the interest group who represent the new policy's target group or they pursue their own bureaucratic interests. Consequently, new policies will be based on policy rules which are significantly different from the established ones.

So far, it has been argued that the established policy network in a sector influences the policy output in situations in which an outsider forces policy makers to deal with a new policy issue which has a negative image for those who are to be regulated. While the network members will attempt to transfer the policy rules of the established, and beneficial, policy to the new policy issue in order to limit costs, outsiders will do everything they can to apply rules which favour their interests. These two sets of policy rules are likely to conflict with each other. Outsiders tend to be successful if the established network has only developed a low degree of cohesion, whereas they will fail if the network is cohesive.

Nitrate policy making in Swedish and Danish agriculture

This chapter focuses on the environmental problem in agriculture which has received most attention from policy makers and the public in both Sweden and Denmark: the nitrate contamination of ground and surface waters (see Andersen and Daugbjerg 1994; Eckerberg 1994). In both countries, environmental interests favoured the Polluter Pays Principle as the main policy rule of the nitrate policy, whereas farmers preferred the state responsibility rule. The choice of policy instruments reflects which one of these two rules is applied in Swedish and Danish nitrate policy. Policy instruments which produce limited perceived costs to farmers indicate that the state responsibility rule has, to a large extent, been transferred to nitrate policy making. In contrast, if the policy employs instruments which farmers perceive as costly, then the Polluter Pays Principle is the prevailing policy rule. Interpreting which rules have been influencing the policy output is a more valid empirical research method than trying to reveal the rules directly. The most important reason for this is that actors do not argue in terms of rules in policy making, at least not in public. Instead, argumentation in policy making is technical; for instance, by referring to the technical feasibility and efficiency of a certain kind of policy output (see e.g. Landbrugsministeriet 1991). But, basically, the decision-making process is political, although argumentation is veiled in technical terms (Daugbjerg 1995). Thus, trying to reveal the rules directly may turn out to be extremely difficult and may even result in invalid conclusions. Certainly, it is important to emphasize that it is *the perceived costs and benefits* that matter in politics, not the 'objective' ones (see Wilson 1980: 366). In consequence, the farmers' perception, not the investigator's, must be the basis on which one assesses policy instrument costs.

This section compares the nitrate policy process in Sweden and Denmark. The first aim is to reveal whether there are any differences in policy contents. The second aim is to examine the policy positions of the political actors involved, in particular those of agricultural authorities. How sympathetic were agricultural authorities to the interests of farmers?

At first sight, the contents of the nitrate policy in Swedish and Danish agriculture seem similar. However, a closer look reveals that there are important differences in the choice of policy instruments. A policy instrument is a political method which aims at obtaining a certain behaviour among individual members of the target group through learning, compulsion or economic incentives (Daugbjerg 1995: 34). First, the Swedes have applied environmental taxes which, so far, has been impossible in Denmark. Second, in Denmark the major policy measure in the nitrate policy is a highly complicated regulatory instrument which takes into account the individual conditions of each farmer's production. Both Danish and Swedish farmers preferred this instrument rather than environmental taxes, but the Swedish farmers did not succeed in achieving this aim. Third, the level of environmental subsidies in Denmark is higher than in Sweden. In other respects the nitrate policies of the two countries do not show significant differences (Daugbjerg 1995: 42–3).

In Sweden, a 5 per cent fertilizer tax was introduced in 1984. The farmers' association heavily opposed it, but could not achieve sufficient support to avoid it. Instead, they wanted improved advice and information on environmental protection. It is not surprising that the Swedish Environmental Protection Agency supported fertilizer taxes, but it certainly is surprising that the Swedish National Agricultural Board remained silent on the issue (SOU 1983, 10: 18–23, 297–305), considering that it had been very sceptical about agri-environmental policies in the 1970s (Interview, SEPA (Swedish Environmental Protection Agency) 1994). Three years later, Swedish farmers again came under pressure. A working group (the Intensity Group) consisting of traditional agricultural policy makers and environmental interests was set up in 1987. The group addressed the surplus production of cereals and agri-environmental problems. It suggested that the fertilizer tax should be raised and, again, farmers opposed the proposal. The agricultural authorities represented in the working group did not oppose the tax increase but accepted it as long as the tax revenue was used for funding agri-environmental measures (Proposition 1987/88, 128: appendix 2: 85–6). Acknowledging that solving the nitrate problems demanded more than improved advice and information, farmers wanted regulatory instruments which took into account the conditions of production of each farmer, or group of farmers (Jordbruksdepartementet 1987: 68–86). In 1988, the *Riksdag* (the Swedish Parliament), against the wishes of the farmers, doubled the tax on fertilizers to 10 per cent (Proposition 1987/88: 128). Although the tax is rather low, its symbolic value is high. It makes the defeat of the farmers very visible. Swedish farmers were in a weak political position during the nitrate policy process because the agricultural state actors did not ally with them. Thus, they had to accept defeat.

In Denmark, there has also been a struggle over environmental taxes in agriculture. In 1984, the Danish Environmental Protection Agency put forward a proposal to diminish nitrate run-offs from agriculture. The proposal included a tax on fertilizers (Miljøstyrelsen 1984: 141–7). The tax was strongly opposed by the Ministry of Agriculture (Miljøstyrelsen 1984: 7–8) and the Danish Farmers' Union (Landboforeningerne 1986: 107–10). The chairman of the Smallholders' Union suggested a small fertilizer tax as a political compromise but had to withdraw the proposal because of opposition within the union (Interview, Sørensen 1993), but presumably also because of heavy opposition from the Farmers' Union (Landboforeningerne 1986: 107). The opposition to the tax was so strong that the *Folketing* (the Danish Parliament) turned down the proposal, but only after long, highly politicized, debates. In 1986 and 1987, the issue of the fertilizer tax again became a subject of political dispute. Once again, farmers, heavily supported by the Ministry of Agriculture, were able to prevent a fertilizer tax being adopted (ATV 1990; Andersen and Hansen 1991; Dubgaard 1991; Andersen and Daugbjerg 1994). The policy process was one of the most chaotic and politicized in recent decades in Danish politics. In 1991, the proposal on a fertilizer tax appeared once more on the political agenda. As in the previous cases, farmers avoided the tax with support from the Ministry of Agriculture, although the tax had considerable support in the *Folketing* (Dubgaard 1991: 39–40; Landbrugsministeriet 1991; Udvalget vedr. en Bæredygtig Landbrugsudvikling 1991; Andersen and Daugbjerg 1993: 12–15). The success of Danish farmers in avoiding the fertilizer tax, to a large extent, depended on the wholehearted support of the Ministry of Agriculture. In other words, farmers were able to ally with a state actor centrally placed in the policy process.

Instead of adopting a tax on fertilizers in 1991 and 1992, Danish politicians adopted a highly complicated regulatory instrument. The policy instrument requires farmers to work out fertilizer and crop rotation plans and fertilizer accounts. These are subject to inspection by the Ministry of Agriculture. The Ministry expects to inspect the plans and accounts of 30,000 farmers which is about half the total number of plans being worked out (Interview, Ministry of Agriculture 1993). Both the Farmers' Union and the Smallholders' Union could accept this alternative, except for its emphasis on inspections. In fact, they had suggested the instrument themselves (Landboforeningerne 1991: 24; Danske Husmandsforeninger 1991: 11). Swedish farmers also preferred this alternative to taxes, but were unable to mobilize sufficient political support for it (Proposition 1987/88, 85: appendix 5.2: 137–8 and appendix 10.3: 443).

Both countries have subsidized the enlargement of the storage facilities for manure, but the levels of support are different. In Sweden, the state covered 20 per cent of the costs of the investments at each entitled farm, the maximum amount being 25,000 Swedish *kronor* (£2275 at 1990 exchange rates). The scheme was in effect from 1989 to 1991 (SFS 1989: 12; SFS 1991: 238). In Denmark, the state covered 40 per cent of small farms' costs, 32.5 per cent for medium sized farms and 25 per cent for the largest ones; the maximum amount being 100,000 Danish *kroner* (£9877). In 1992, the maximum subsidy was increased to 150,000 Danish *kroner* (£13,465) and the regulations were changed so that all farms were entitled to a 35 per cent subsidy. The subsidy scheme was in effect from 1987 to the end of 1994 (Lov no. 16 1987; Lov no. 1172 1992).

Comparing the nitrate policies of the two countries shows that Danish farmers have avoided more of the perceived costs of environmental regulation than their Swedish colleagues. The nitrate policy instruments in Danish agriculture are more acceptable to Danish farmers than the instruments applied in Sweden are to Swedish farmers. Hence, Danish farmers have been most successful in transferring the state responsibility rule from agricultural policy making to environmental policy making. Swedish farmers had to accept that the Polluter Pays Principle was applied more strictly.

The cohesion of Swedish and Danish agricultural networks

According to the theoretical model, the variation in policy in the two countries can be explained by differences in the cohesion of the established agricultural policy networks. If the theoretical model is valid, then an empirical examination must show that the Danish agricultural policy network has a higher degree of cohesion than does the Swedish one. We can establish the cohesion of the networks by examining the extent of consensus on the state responsibility rule in the network. This can only be established through a study over time. Limiting the examination to a certain point in time, or a short period, would yield invalid results (see Sabatier and Jenkins-Smith 1993: 16; Smith 1993). For example, what looks like consensus may, in fact, only be a temporary compromise which one or more of the members may question from time to time.

As in most Western countries, the Swedish and Danish state became deeply involved in the agricultural sector in the early 1930s. In Sweden, the agricultural policy network did not develop the same degree of cohesion as it did in Denmark. In the period from the early 1930s to the 1990s, the official goals of Swedish agricultural policy were unstable, indicating that a consensus on the state responsibility rule never developed. From the 1930s until 1947, social concerns for farmers became more and more important in agricultural policy. In 1947, they became explicit in their policy objectives. The main goal of agricultural policy was to ensure that farmers' average incomes were equal to those of industrial workers. The goals of agricultural policy were questioned in the early 1960s, with the result that the government adopted new goals in 1967. These goals indicated that state responsibility for imbalances in the agricultural sector had diminished. The emphasis on farmers' income decreased and became less precise than earlier. What emerged was an emphasis that agriculture should, to a larger extent, be subject to the market forces which applied to business and industry. In 1977, the pendulum swung back towards more social concerns in agricultural policy, so that the income goal was again given higher priority (SOU 1977: 110–13; SOU 1984: 75–6; Steen 1988: 76–80; Micheletti 1990: 91–3, 101–3). In the mid-1980s, the priority of goals changed again and the income goal was given lower priority (Proposition 1983/84, 76: 6). A major change took place in 1990. The domestic system of price regulations was removed for some products and considerably simplified for others, giving market forces much more influence on price setting (Jordbruksutskottets 1989/90: 25; Daugbjerg 1996). Consequently, the state responsibility rule was no longer the major rule in agricultural policy making.

The instability of the goals of Swedish agricultural policy shows that a long-term consensus did not develop within the agricultural network. From time to time, the state responsibility rule was challenged and its importance changed, implying that the degree of cohesion is low. The instability of policy making is closely associated with the increasing consumer influence in the Swedish agricultural policy network. In 1963, the Consumer Delegation, which consists of representatives from the trade unions, the Cooperative Union and Wholesale Society and wholesale trading companies and business associations not belonging to the farmers' movement, achieved the right to participate in the price negotiations between farmers and the Swedish state. Micheletti (1990: 94–7, 133) and Steen (1988: 214–18) conclude that, since the early 1970s, the Consumer Delegation has been exercising considerable influence on agricultural policy making. However, on the one hand, the presence of consumers in the network did not result in lower levels of agricultural subsidies in Sweden than in the EC. On the other hand, the consumer representation may have prevented the level of subsidies from increasing to the high Norwegian level – one of the highest levels in the world. So, from 1979 until 1986, the average proportion of the agricultural production value (the PSE percentage) which could be put down to direct and indirect agricultural state subsidies was 70 per cent in Norway. It was 44 per cent in Sweden and 37 per cent in the EC. By 1990, the proportion had increased to 75 per cent in Norway, 57 per cent in Sweden and 46 per cent in the EC (OECD 1994: 107–8). Overall, the most important influence of the consumers in Swedish agricultural politics is that they prevented the agricultural network from developing a high degree of cohesion.

In Denmark, the agricultural policy network has been, and still is, much more cohesive. From the early 1930s until the present, the main aim of agricultural policy has been to maintain the international competitiveness of agricultural production in order to uphold a high level of export earnings and a high level of employment in the agricultural sector, especially in the food processing industry. When agriculture has faced economic problems, the Danish state has taken responsibility for solving them. In the 1930s the state provided the legal framework for export regulations which the agricultural organizations needed (Just 1992: chs. 3–4). From the late 1950s until Denmark became a member of the EC in 1973, the state responsibility rule was again in effect. The exclusion from EC markets caused economic problems in agriculture. To cope with these problems, agriculture received considerable subsidies 'through home market schemes, tax reliefs, direct subsidies, support to young farmers etc.' (Just 1994: 44). There was no criticism of this policy within the network.

Agricultural interests have been closely tied to the national interest (Buksti 1980: 288–9), notably after Denmark's entrance into the European Community in 1973, as Denmark has a net benefit from the membership, primarily through EC agricultural subsidies (Tracy 1993: 251–2). EC membership, therefore, has contributed to the maintenance of the consensus within the agricultural network. Entry into the EC meant that the Community took over the responsibility for imbalances in the agricultural sector, implying that the costs of agricultural policy were passed on from the Danish state to the other EC member states. In consequence, no Danish state actor has had any incentive to question the rule on state responsibility.

The Danish agricultural policy network is characterized by consensus on the aims of agricultural policy, unlike Sweden. The stability of the network is closely associated with the membership of the network itself. Since the early 1930s, the core of the network has consisted of the Ministry of Agriculture and the agricultural associations (Just 1992, 1994: 39). Entrance into the EC in 1973 changed the internal organisation of the network as the Ministry of Agriculture strengthened its position in relation to the agricultural organizations (Buksti 1980: 288; Just 1994: 44), but the main policy rule remained the same. Further, the reorganization introduced a countervailing power into the network as the Consumer Council became a member; however, consumers never gained more than marginal influence. As a result, they have not been able seriously to challenge the rule on state responsibility for imbalances in the agricultural sector (Daugbjerg 1996).

The comparison of the agricultural policy networks in the two countries shows that an important reason why Swedish farmers bear more perceived costs than Danish farmers is the presence of a less cohesive network in Sweden. Consensus on the state responsibility rule did not develop in the Swedish network. Consequently, Swedish farmers could not mobilize strong support from agricultural state actors. In Denmark, there is, by contrast, a strong consensus on the rule. In other words, the Danish agricultural policy network comes closer to a policy community on the Marsh and Rhodes continuum (Marsh and Rhodes 1992; Rhodes and Marsh 1992) than the Swedish one. Thus, Danish farmers were able to achieve support from the Ministry of Agriculture and could, thus, transfer the state responsibility rule from agricultural policy making to nitrate policy making to a larger extent than their Swedish colleagues. The alliance with the Ministry of Agriculture was a very important political resource for Danish farmers. The structure of the Danish agricultural policy network favoured the interests of farmers much more than the Swedish network.

It is important to point out that it is not the national economic importance of agriculture, but rather the importance of established political structures which explain why Danish farmers could minimize the perceived costs of environmental regulation, although the national economic importance of Danish agriculture and the benefits of Danish EC membership did strengthen the consensus on the state responsibility rule in agricultural policy making. The economic importance of an industry may have important consequences in the formative phases of policy making and network building. However, if policy networks become institutionalized, changes in economic importance are rarely reflected in the network design and in policy making. A comparison of agri-environmental policies in Norway and Sweden demonstrates that we cannot explain differences in policy by differences in the national economic importance of an industry. Agriculture in these two countries is equally important for their national economies; however, in Norway the level of agri-environmental subsidies is much higher than in Sweden. If the economic importance of agriculture was a crucial independent variable, there should be little difference in policy outcomes (Daugbjerg 1995: 43).

Conclusion: do network structures make a difference?

Environmental policy making is approached in an untraditional way in this chapter. Demands for pollution control are viewed as a disturbance to an old and well-established order in the agricultural sector. This approach is more fruitful for analysing environmental policy making than focusing upon it in isolation from the existing sectoral order – most notably in highly regulated sectors. Viewing environmental policy making from this perspective helps explain why different policies are chosen in similar sectors in various countries.

The comparison of the nitrate policy-making processes in Sweden and Denmark shows that Danish farmers were more successful than their Swedish colleagues in transferring the main rule of agricultural policy making, the state responsibility rule, to environmental policy making. Environmental actors in both countries based their policy proposals on the Polluter Pays Principle. Basing the nitrate policy upon this principle would inflict costs upon farmers. Environmental interests and farmers were, therefore, likely to come into conflict. By transferring the state responsibility rule from agricultural policy making to nitrate policy making, farmers could escape the costs of the Polluter Pays Principle. Differences in the structures of the existing agricultural policy networks explain why the two countries adopted different policies. The Danish agricultural network is much more cohesive than the Swedish one, so Danish farmers could mobilize the support of the Ministry of Agriculture. In Sweden, farmers were not able to form such a strong coalition because the network is less cohesive. Therefore, Swedish farmers had to accept that the Polluter Pays Principle came to play a large role in Swedish nitrate policy.

The main purpose of this chapter has been to establish the causal link between policy network type and policy choice in situations in which an actor outside an established network tries to bring about change. What happens in such situations has hitherto been a weak point in the network approach. The degree of cohesion in different network types is the key variable explaining coalition-building among the political actors involved in the policy process. Cohesion influences the formation of policy preferences; in particular those of state actors, since their interests are rarely straightforward. In this way, network structures affect the strength of coalitions. Thus, the characteristics of the actors themselves do not explain policy. Danish and Swedish nitrate policies are different because the established agricultural policy networks had a different effect on the agricultural authorities' formation of policy preferences. Therefore, we cannot take preferences as given; they need to be explained. In my view, the independent variable is the network structure, not the actors' policy preferences. Policy preferences are intermediate variables affecting the choice of policy. Attempting to explain why policies are different by attributing explanatory force to differences in actors' resources alone is also unsatisfactory. What counts as a valuable resource is influenced by the context in which actors employ their resources. A resource which is highly valued in one setting may only have limited value in another setting.

This chapter also demonstrates the advantages of the comparative case study method in generating theoretical insights as regards the influence of network structures. By choosing cases which vary both in network type and in policy choices, it was possible to test empirically whether the network model establishing the causal links was plausible. Single case studies are less suitable for this purpose because such a research method does not allow us to test models which attempt to establish how variation in the independent variable is linked to variation in the dependent variable. Further, single case studies involve the risk that the researcher reduces network structures to actor preferences and, thus, overlooks the influence of the network itself.

The influence of meso-level organizational arrangements has been emphasized in this study; however, policy networks and political actors are embedded in a broader context. To explain meso-level phenomena, we also need to undertake a macro-level analysis (see Chapter 4). As Atkinson and Coleman (1989: 67) put it: 'Meso-level phenomena cannot be explained in isolation from broader political institutions.' Hence, a fully fledged explanation would also have to include the influence of these institutions.

6

Offshore health and safety policy in the North Sea: policy networks and policy outcomes in Britain and Norway

Michael Cavanagh

The unprecedented loss of 167 lives in the Piper Alpha disaster of 1988 brought home the extreme dangers involved in the offshore oil industry. It also re-established the issue of offshore health and safety on the British political agenda. Piper Alpha was the latest and most devastating loss of lives offshore, but it was certainly not the first.

This chapter will examine the development of offshore health and safety policy in Britain and Norway, paying particular attention to the most recent period. More specifically, I shall compare the role of policy networks in this area across the two countries and across time. This comparative perspective will allow me to address one of the key questions in the network literature: the extent to which the structure and operation of policy networks affect policy outcomes. In addition, because offshore health and safety policy is, in effect, a policy area which, in crucial senses, is a sub-sector of broader policy concerning the oil industry, this case study allows me to discuss another important issue in the policy network literature: the relationship between sectoral and sub-sectoral networks.

This analysis involves a comparison of two similar cases (on the comparative method see Mackie and Marsh 1995). Indeed, this comparison is particularly powerful because both Britain and Norway display many similar characteristics, making it easier to isolate the effects of policy networks on policy outcomes. Oil activities in both countries are carried out in the same waters of the North Sea with only an invisible boundary line separating offshore installations. In addition, the same international oil companies have been involved in the development of both industries, utilizing the same technology within identical climatic conditions. At the same time, both countries became oil- and gas-producing nations in the mid-1960s. What is more, both countries are western European states with similar modern advanced economic systems and strong liberal democratic traditions.

The chapter is divided into two parts. First, I outline the development of oil-related activities in both countries, examining the legislative process and regulatory procedures. This includes an analysis of the relationships between both states and the respective interests involved in forming policy networks and influencing policy outcomes. The second aspect will concern itself with an analysis of factors exogenous to sectoral and sub-sectoral networks; the structural constraints which form the broader context of network activity and influences the membership and viable policy options of policy networks themselves.

The transformation of the offshore health and safety policy networks in Britain and Norway

The present system of safety management and regulatory control, like the types of policy network involved, have undergone major changes since the first contacts between the oil companies and the British and Norwegian Governments in 1962.

Britain

The process leading to the proclamation of sovereign rights over the United Kingdom Continental Shelf (UKCS) began with the Continental Shelf Bill being introduced into the House of Lords in November 1963. By mid-December the frantic pace of the parliamentary process reached comical proportions when the Third Reading of the Bill was scheduled for December 19, just two days after it had reached the Committee Stage. This pace was maintained throughout the first quarter of 1964, as the House of Commons came under constant government pressure to rush the Bill through before the imminent general election (Carson 1982: 141–3). Carson argues that the implications for health and safety were significant as the rush to establish a legislative framework for future exploration resulted in the issue becoming more peripheral.

Certainly concerns over safety issues were raised, but they went largely ignored in the process leading up to the Continental Shelf Act coming into force in 1964. Such pressures as did exist resulted in the extension of the 1934 Petroleum (Production) Act, to include the UKCS. This was achieved through section 1(4) of the 1964 Act and focused upon section 6 of the Petroleum (Production) Act, which required the relevant Secretary of State, then the Minister for Power, to issue 'model clauses' which were to be incorporated into any licence allocated. The aim was to use the model clauses to issue safety regulations. However, soon after the successful passage of the 1964 Act there was a debate about whether the model clauses actually had to refer to health and safety at all (Carson 1982: 144; Barrett *et al.* 1987: 40).

During this early period some observers argued that existing onshore provisions for health and safety could be made applicable offshore. However, successive government decisions indicated that not all UK law applied offshore (Carson 1982: 145–6). More importantly, there was little, if any, regulation of offshore health and safety conditions. The regulations which did exist emerged from the sectoral level, developed within the sectoral policy network. Safety was a peripheral issue dealt with in the policy sector concerned with oil production and licence allocation. The key network members were the oil companies and the Ministry of Power. The Ministry could in theory regulate the industry, either by direct intervention or by threatening to withdraw (or actually withdrawing) the operator's licence. However, the first option was not viable; the regulatory authority lacked the technical and economic resources to intervene. The latter option would have been effective, but there was no political will to take such measures; the prospect of future gas (and subsequently oil) revenues were too important. In the event, neither option was utilized, despite evidence of flagrant abuse of the regulations contained within the model clauses (Carson 1982: 146–8).

In 1965, the capsize of the Sea Gem 'jack-up' rig, which resulted in the death of 13 men, revealed the basic weakness of the model clause system. The subsequent tribunal highlighted the fact that, while the Sea Gem licence did have model clauses attached, they had been ignored. The Sea Gem tribunal was highly critical of the model clause system and called for the creation of 'a statutory code supported by "credible sanctions" '. The Labour Government did not act on the tribunal's recommendations until some four years after the Sea Gem disaster and even then the legislation failed to pass before the 1970 general election (Carson 1982: 150).

In the period from 1964 until the early 1970s there was little concern with health and safety provisions. The existing regulatory controls lacked any authority as the government and its regulatory agency demonstrated a total unwillingness to impose sanctions on operators who violated the requirements of the model clauses. This point is supported by the evidence given to the Robens Committee by the representatives of the Petroleum Production Inspectorate, then under the Department of Trade and Industry (DTI). They argued that '[t]he Petroleum (Production) and Continental Shelf Acts do not provide for the specific enforcement of safety requirements'. In addition, they emphasized that the only powers available to the Petroleum Production Inspectorate were those included in the licence (Cmnd 5034 1972: vol. 2:372). This suggests that there was no policy network at the sub-sectoral level and that a sectoral-level policy community successfully minimized the extent to which health and safety was able to become a policy issue. In effect, there was a highly integrated structural relationship in the policy sector which, for a time, successfully depoliticized the health and safety issue, minimizing its intrusion onto the political agenda.

However, the pressures on government, from sections of parliament and labour organizations, to introduce a proper regulatory system for offshore health and safety resulted in the Mineral Workings (Offshore Installations) Act, 1977 (MWA). The MWA was a belated reaction to the Sea Gem disaster and at least 14 subsequent deaths in the oil-related activities on the UKCS. The legislation was specifically tailored to regulate the offshore industry's activities through 'criminal sanctions imposed in the interests of the health, safety and welfare . . .' (Barrett *et al.* 1987: 40).

The MWA allowed the regulatory agency, then the Petroleum Production Division of the DTI, to formulate and issue regulations relating to offshore health and safety. However, Nicholas Ridley, then Under-Secretary of State for the DTI, stressed the importance of not issuing strict regulations which might impede the technical development of the industry, instead suggesting that 'enabling provisions' should be adopted to allow the dynamic nature of the technical development of offshore oil-related activity to continue (Carson 1982: 151).

Criticism of the MWA focused on both the extensive exemption powers within the Act and the subordination of safety to the production-related demands of the industry (Carson 1982: 151). Such criticism reflected the contradictions involved in creating a regulatory body which was responsible for both health and safety and production. Branch 2 of the Petroleum Production Division was concerned with health and safety; but it was under the control of the same Under-Secretary responsible for maintaining and increasing production. This created a potential conflict of interests which, perhaps inevitably, led to the relative neglect of health and safety (p. 195).

During the parliamentary passage of the MWA, the Robens Committee was involved in an investigation of health and safety (Cmnd 5034 1972). The Robens Report, published in 1972, was intended to bring about the rationalization of health and safety legislation. The report was commissioned in the light of the complex tangle of legislation and regulations which had resulted from the piecemeal development of health and safety provisions and the emergence of a number of regulatory agencies. Therefore, Robens recommended that a single regulatory body should be created to implement broad health and safety regulations and to stimulate greater self-regulation (Cmnd 5034 1972). It criticized the introduction of the legislation and argued that the MWA, along with other legislation, 'should be brought within the unified system . . . unless very sound reasons can be adduced for leaving them outside' (ibid.: 35).

The development of the MWA regulations was slow. The capsize of the Transocean 3 in 1973 stimulated criticism over the time being taken to formulate regulations. The government responded by declaring that six regulations had already been drafted and that a further two were nearing completion. The problem was that none of the regulations mentioned were concerned with offshore safety; they were all administrative in nature (Carson 1982: 155).

The Department of Energy (DEn) was 'hived off' from the DTI in the wake of the oil crisis of 1973. This new Department, established in 1974, had responsibility for the potentially conflicting functions of health and safety and production. In the same year the Health and Safety at Work Act (HASAWA) was introduced, breaking the practice in the post-war period whereby it was the norm for the sponsoring Department to have responsibility for all aspects related to 'their' industry. As Carson (1982: 166) states:

> the point to be underlined is that for some years after 1974, safety continued to be combined with other functions inside a Department which now had rapid development not only as one objective, but as part of its very *raison d'être*

As such, the continued inclusion of responsibility for health and safety in the sponsoring Department was against the trend in onshore industries.

In 1977 there were two important developments related to offshore health and safety. The first was the creation of the Petroleum Engineering Division (PED) within the DEn. This agency was delegated authority over most health and safety matters offshore. The second development was the extension of the HASAWA to include the UKCS.

The HASAWA was based largely upon the recommendations of the Robens Report. The Act aimed to establish a unified health and safety agency which would secure adequate working conditions and allocate responsibilities to employers, employees, contractors and others. In addition, the Act established the agencies necessary to accomplish such tasks. The HSC was to be responsible for defining UK health and safety policy and was to comprise eight members: three each nominated by the Confederation of British Industry (CBI) and the Trades Union Congress (TUC), while the remaining two members were to be nominated by local government. The specialized functions and day-to-day inspection were to be performed by the Health and Safety Executive (HSE) (Wilson 1985: 112).

The introduction of the HASAWA and the HSE into offshore health and safety policy meant that existing relationships were under threat. This intervention suggested that offshore health and safety would be incorporated into existing onshore policy, challenging the 'unique' status that the industry and successive governments had long been asserting. The oil industry was consistently referred to as a 'pioneer' and 'frontier' industry. This status, based on technological expertise, was used as a defence against any suggestion that a unified, or more rigid, form of regulation should be introduced.

The HSC/E did not revolutionize either the existing relationships or the offshore safety system. Their involvement offshore was to be frustrated by the government's imposition of an agency agreement with the DEn, whereby the HSC determined broad policy, but the PED carried out the detailed inspection and the issuing of regulations (Cmnd 7866 1980: 7–8). Therefore, the HSC did not have the power to monitor the industry or to determine the substance of new regulations.

Tony Benn described the relationship between the PED and the offshore operators as 'cosy' (Carson 1982: 175). Certainly, PED officials defended the operators' safety record when it was criticized and the operators returned the favour when the PED came under fire (p. 176). As such, their relationship was mutually supportive.

The 'cosy' relationship developed as a result of the highly integrated and specialized world in which the PED and the operators existed. The consultation process was limited to the PED and the operators, with the operators having a 'duty to consult' the workforce. In addition, the PED was largely staffed by ex-oil company personnel and there is even an example of a senior PED official resigning to take up a position within the United Kingdom Offshore Operators' Association (UKOOA) (Cmnd 7866 1980: 59; Carson 1982: 174). Some argued that this relationship constituted a real danger to the development of offshore health and safety. As Lyons and Millar observe: 'The possibility of shared values and membership of groups amongst offshore management can have a tremendous implication for the independence of inspectors involved' (Cmnd 7866 1980: 59).

Another aspect of the relationship between the PED, successive governments and the operators was reflected in the adoption of regulatory provisions which were designed to allow for the 'need for constant changes to keep pace with technological innovation' (Carson 1982: 178). This would appear sensible given that the oil industry is involved in pioneering technology. However, the problem lay in the fact that safety regulations lagged behind because the focus of the technological development was on production.

Oil companies and the government favoured a high depletion-rate policy which meant that priority was given to the production aspects of offshore activities. Such an attitude inevitably led to an emphasis on production increases at the expense of safety. This atmosphere enabled the oil companies to disregard the detailed, non-statutory Guidance Notes attached to the 'broad brush' regulations. The capacity to ignore such guidelines illustrates the deference to technology and productive capacity which was a characteristic of the PED-operator relationship (Cmnd 7866 1980: 16; Carson 1982: 179).

This relationship continued when the HSC took responsibility for defining general offshore health and safety policy. The role was frustrated by the non-cooperative activities of the PED and the DEn. The DEn failed to keep the HSC informed of inspection findings. In addition, there was a reliance on the MWA, rather than the HASAWA, for the legislative framework for regulations. Similarly, the PED maintained its exclusive relationship with the operators; this was a direct challenge to the HSC and the HASAWA, both of which involved a tripartite system of cooperation and consultation.

The contrasting concerns of the PED and the HSE were to lead to an interdepartmental conflict which was fought out in the Burgoyne Committee. The Committee was established to review the DEn's existing offshore legislative and regulatory provisions, and was convened in response to the Ekofisk 'blow-out' in the Norwegian Continental Shelf (NCS). The evidence to, and outcome of, the Committee's report represented a concerted attack on the HSE's activities.

Burgoyne decided to go beyond its original remit after the weight of response from the oil companies and the PED had focused on the HSE's role offshore. The chronology of events and the extent of the criticism voiced against the HSE is suspicious when one considers that, although the extension of the HASAWA had been established through an Order in Council in 1977, it was over a year before the agency agreement was formally reached. This was actually after the Burgoyne Committee had begun its investigations, but still the HSE were heavily criticized for their approach to safety regulations. Carson (1982: 197) notes that even the limited involvement of the HSE had 'touched on some very raw nerves indeed'.

The Burgoyne Report recommended the transfer of responsibility to a single regulatory agency: the PED under the DEn. Burgoyne noted that a conflict of interests could arise as a result of giving responsibility for safety and health and production to the same Department, but discounted such concerns (Cmnd 7866 1980: 15). Burgoyne also stated that one of the reasons for the transfer to the DEn was that the HSE lacked specialized inspection capacity (Cmnd 7866 1980: 16). This point is less than convincing given that the same report detailed that the PED had no staff trained in occupational health and safety or in the practical application of legal enforcements (Cmnd 7866 1980: 59–60). One of the recommendations of the report concerned the introduction of safety representatives and safety committees. The Safety Representatives and Safety Committees Regulations (SRSCR) had been introduced through the HASAWA in 1977, but had not been extended offshore. The Burgoyne Report regarded safety representatives as desirable, but not to the extent of making them a statutory requirement; instead it favoured a negotiated approach to their introduction. The negotiations were carried out within the Oil Industry Advisory Committee (OIAC), a tripartite legacy of the HSC/E intrusion, but resulted in total failure as the PED hosted negotiations between the unions and UKOOA which dragged on for eight years. UKOOA's intransigence meant that no concessions were made and the farce was eventually resolved by the intervention of Cecil Parkinson, then Minister for Energy, who tried to limit the political damage from the Piper Alpha disaster by forcing an agreement (Foster and Woolfson 1992: 6–7).

The transfer of responsibility involved the revision of the existing agency agreement and essentially downgraded the role of the HSE to that of a support agency; thus, the pre-1977 status quo was re-established. The transfer was completed in 1981, recreating the previous 'cosy' relationship which persisted until the Piper Alpha disaster (Cm 1310 1990: 254).

The change in government was an important factor as far as the timing of the Burgoyne Report was concerned. The development of new oil fields in the North Sea held obvious appeal for the new Conservative Government (Foster and Woolfson 1992: 5). In addition, the Thatcher Government was highly critical of organized labour, which meant that the tripartite foundations of the HSE were regarded with some antipathy. As a result, the government instructed the HSE to assess the economic consequences of their health and safety proposals; an instruction which the HSC publicly pledged to honour (Wilson 1985: 118). However, it must be recognized that offshore this simply continued what had always been a feature of the offshore working environment.

The Piper Alpha disaster was to prove the catalyst for change in the offshore environment. The scale of the disaster was unprecedented and inevitably led to detailed scrutiny of the health and safety provisions in the UKCS. This scrutiny was carried out by the Cullen Inquiry and revealed a regulatory system which was heavily criticized for its 'over-conservatism, insularity and a lack of ability to look at the regime and themselves in a critical way', resulting in safety developments being 'hampered'. In addition, the DEn management was seen as being responsible for offshore safety management being 'a number of years behind the approach onshore' (Cm 1310 1990: 382). The transfer of responsibility for offshore health and safety was the inevitable consequence of such criticism.

The establishment of the Offshore Safety Division (OSD) of the HSE put into practice a number of the 106 recommendations made by the Cullen Report (HSE 1993). The 'cornerstone' of the HSE involvement was, and remains, the Safety Case system (HSE 1993). The Safety Case system is largely based upon onshore regulatory controls such as the Control of Industrial Major Hazard Regulations (CIMAH) and requires the operator on a fixed, or mobile installation to submit a detailed plan for the different stages of exploration and production (HSE 1992: vii–viii).

The Safety Case regulations require that the HSE receive a safety case for each offshore installation before the deadline in November 1995. The safety case involves the detailing of an effective safety system to manage health and safety on offshore installations. This system must have arrangements for an independent audit identifying all potential hazards and ensuring all potential risks are kept to a 'level that is as low as is reasonably practicable'.

The HSE has begun what it terms the 'third phase of offshore legislation reform', the first two being the transfer of authority to the HSE and the introduction of the Safety Case. There are three components to these reforms: the application offshore of *new* across-the-board safety regulations including EC health and safety directives; the extension offshore of key existing onshore regulations; and the reform of *offshore-specific* regulations.

With the HSE taking over responsibility for offshore health and safety inspection only recently, and the transitional period of reform still in its infancy, it is difficult to assess the extent of interaction and the characteristics of relationships within the policy formulation process. What is certain is that the activities of the HSE contrast with those of its predecessor. Institutions, particularly trade unions, which were previously excluded from the consultation process are now in direct and regular contact with the HSE. However, it is too early to talk of any stable relationships developing. The extent to which consultation can be equated with influence is, at least, problematic; approximately 100 organizations submitted responses to the HSC Safety Case draft proposals (HSE 1993).

It is significant that the workforce and organized labour have entered into some form of relationship with the primary state actor in the policy issue area for the first time. However, at the same time, the interests of the oil industry still dominate the policy network. This was clearly demonstrated by the success of the United Kingdom Offshore Operators' Association's opposition to Cullen's recommendations relating to the temporary safe refuge (TSR) (Cm 1310: 394). Between December 1991 and March 1992 UKOOA had made strong representations concerning the TSR proposals, criticizing the proposal for the mandatory installation of TSRs on all rigs, including those normally unmanned. The drafting of the regulations altered, resulting in the HSE suggesting that exemptions for unmanned installations would be made available. UKOOA were not satisfied with the HSE concessions and continued their opposition (Foster and Woolfson 1992: 18). The HSE responded to further pressure by conceding that the regulations pertaining to TSRs needed to be flexible. The minimum period which a TSR has to be able to withstand a major fire was to remain at one hour, but by late November 1992, the HSC announced that 'the [TSR] Regulations now recognise that exceptionally a shorter minimum period may be appropriate for certain small installations with few personnel' (HSE 1993). In addition, UKOOA have successfully rationalized four supplementary regulations introduced to enhance the Safety Case Regulations and appear to have won the argument that the industry itself should develop the technical Guidance used to accompany Regulations; Guidance which would normally be provided by the regulatory agency. UKOOA continue to argue against the adoption of an Approved Code of Practice (ACoP) on the grounds that it would result in a rigid safety system which would not allow for industry generated developments (Hughes 1994: 3–4). Indeed, Woolfson and Beck (1995: 3) argue that the HSE has taken an 'accommodatory stance' towards the industry and has a common concern for the continued economic viability of the industry and an acceptance of the need for the current cost–cutting programme.

The success of UKOOA in influencing the policy process contrasts with submission of the labour organization, the Offshore Industry Liaison Committee (OILC), to the Safety Case Regulations. The OILC advocated meaningful workforce involvement in the creation and maintenance of the offshore safety regime. They have also called for the recognition of trade unions offshore and the use of secret ballots to allow the workforce to accept or reject trade union membership. Additionally, the OILC have called for the protection of trade union members' rights and the statutory protection of safety representatives' rights in line with onshore regulation (OILC 1992). The regulations introduced do not reflect any of the OILC proposals. This is unsurprising given that the HSE perform a regulatory function for a government which introduced the

Offshore Safety Act 1992 in order to provide the legislative framework for the implementation of all but one of Lord Cullen's recommendations: the protection against victimization of safety representatives. This omission was justified by government on the grounds that it was an employment issue not suited to inclusion in safety legislation. It took a Private Member's Bill, eventually supported by the government (after earlier criticism), to provide the Offshore Safety (Protection Against Victimisation) Act, 1992 (Foster and Woolfson 1992: 21; HSE 1993). This legislation has subsequently been incorporated into the Offshore Safety Act (1992).

The role of the HSE in fostering relationships with labour organizations is a new development. However, there is clearly conflict within the HSE. One senior official, Tony Barrell, claimed that labour organizations were becoming redundant in safety matters. In contrast, elsewhere both Barrell and John Rimington, another senior official, argued that workforce involvement in the safety regime is vital (HC 343 1991: 94; *Blowout*, the OILC magazine, February 1992: 7; Foster and Woolfson 1992: 23). There is also confusion concerning the nature of workforce involvement. Definitions of it are contradictory; the oil companies have an interpretation of workforce involvement as an alternative to involvement by organized labour – a view unlikely to find favour among the trade unions (Foster and Woolfson 1992: 21).

In addition, the workforce have accused the oil companies of pursuing a policy of suppressing any independent form of organization. The oil companies have been accused of actively discouraging union membership through various tactics such as bribery, 'fear, intimidation and victimisation' (Foster and Woolfson 1992: 11). It has also been claimed that oil companies in the UKCS limit dissent from contracted workers by pressurizing contractor companies to terminate the employment of workers who raise the issue of trade union recognition (OILC 1991: 41, 18; Foster and Woolfson 1992: 11). Unsurprisingly the oil companies have denied these allegations.

Norway

On 31 March 1963, Norway declared sovereignty over its continental shelf for the purpose of exploiting its natural resources and the Act Relating to Exploration for and Exploitation of Submarine Natural Resources was passed in June 1963. The Act claimed the state's rights over the Norwegian Continental Shelf (NCS). It also served as an enabling provision for future regulations. In November 1963, a committee was established to develop regulations concerning oil-related activity, but as '[r]egards safety related aspects, th[ese] regulations contained only general provisions which enabled the Department [of Industry] to stipulate further regulations'.

The Regulations Relating to Safety etc. for [the] Exploration and Exploitation of Petroleum were passed by Royal Decree in August 1967. These regulations were the substance of the early enabling provisions and resulted in the recommendation that a working group be established to review government regulatory activities, the attitudes of the oil companies and their willingness to comply with the regulations. The recommendations of the working group were accepted by the Department of Industry, which in July 1969 delegated regulatory authority to eight separate government agencies. The powers retained by these agencies included: supervisory activities; the stipulation of regulations; the authority to grant dispensations; and the authority to seize operations if safety was considered to be jeopardized.

The regulatory system was similar to that in the UK; both countries seem to have had no credible sanctions at their disposal. The capacity to issue regulations was common to both regimes, as was the lack of any real power of enforcement. However, in Norway the situation was more complex and focused on the initial declaration of sovereignty over the NCS. This declaration did not specify any geographic limits and, thus, it was accepted that the Norwegian Penal Code was applicable to the NCS just as it was to Norway itself (Barrett *et al.* 1987: 42). In addition, the foundation of relationships in Norway are somewhat different from that of Britain and elsewhere. In Norway the licence to extract resources is not 'sold'. The implication is that the licensee can be regarded as a contractor to the state. This was significant for health and safety policy as it is not the subject of negotiation in its application. As such, there was a general acceptance of the fact that offshore activities should conform to onshore norms. This point is emphasized by the attitudes of government and the trade unions to working conditions and rights, and the fact that no-one in the Norwegian establishment expected such rights to be questioned by the oil companies (Andersen 1984: 18).

In 1973 the Norwegian Petroleum Directorate (NPD) and the state oil company, Statoil, were created to impose greater control upon the oil companies. Statoil was established to enable Norway to capture a larger share of the oil revenues than would otherwise be possible. However, the need to increase native expertise was also stressed in order to increase 'the state's capacity to fully participate in all aspects of the industry' (Visher and Remoe 1984: 328).

In contrast to the British regime, any exclusion of organized labour from policy discussions, or even discussions on company strategy was, and remains, highly controversial. The traditional emphasis on tripartite consultation was 'a system [which] is founded on mutual respect and observance of the "rules of the game" ' (Andersen 1984: 19). This was in stark contrast to the attitudes of the oil companies, who adhered to what Andersen (1984: 19) refers to as the 'American tradition'. The Norwegian system was, and remains, one which involves the creation of long-term strategies for the benefit of all concerned. This system was directly challenged by the oil companies who were concerned with the short-term advantage and held a deep-rooted antipathy towards independently organized labour.

Until 1977 the Employment Protection Act, 1956 had served as the basis for securing workers' rights. However, it became increasingly obvious that the Act was insufficient to deal with the intransigence of elements of the onshore and offshore industry. The introduction of the Working Environment Act (WEA) was meant to rectify this deficiency and is crucial to an understanding of the operation of policy networks and offshore health and safety in Norway.

The WEA illustrates the basic contrast with the British system (although not with the original spirit of the HASAWA), in that it focuses attention on the creation of conditions within which the health and safety regime can be dealt with by the industry itself. Section 1 of the Act states its objective to create 'a secure working environment' with 'sound contract conditions' and an environment in which employer and employee organizations can resolve any problems under the supervision and guidance of the public authorities.

Therefore, the issue of workforce involvement is a central tenet in the system and is reflected in the approach to the system of regulatory control onshore and offshore. The NPD illustrate the importance of workforce involvement by regarding it as one of the 'foundations' of the Norwegian safety culture. They view the representatives of the workforce as serious, legitimate and responsible participants (Wahlen and Rydning 1993: 55).

The Norwegian Government has played a dominant role in determining, rather than just shaping, the structural relationships within policy networks relating to the offshore oil industry. The statutory basis of structural interaction reflects the central guiding role of the NPD in deciding who should be involved in any 'network' and the distribution (or redistribution) of resources within it. The relationship is one which is not subject to negotiation, a fact which influences behaviour and encourages a more stable, long-term basis for interaction.

The initial period saw the Norwegian Government struggle to cope with the strategy adopted by the oil companies. The tradition in Norway had been for industry to comply with the letter of the law. The clash of cultures resulted in the government being temporarily without solutions. They lacked the strategy to enable proper implementation of safety-related regulations and the experience of detailed inspection and enforcement which this involved. However, in contrast to the UK Government, the Norwegian Government and its agencies proved able to act once attention had been drawn to conditions and a viable policy response had been formulated.

The Ekofisk 'blowout' did not result in any fatalities yet stimulated a rapid rethinking of the structure of regulation and safety management offshore before the capsize of the Alexander L. Keilland in 1980 (PAPI 1990: 25, 9). This suggests that the Norwegian policy network had the capacity (or willingness) to react to a major exogenous shock; relationships are less conservative, with a degree of flexibility not often associated with policy networks.

The 'internal control' system was the result of the re-evaluation and has been in operation since 1985. With the legislative provision of the Petroleum Act the regulatory system was rationalized by making the NPD the sole regulatory agency (Ministry of Local Government and Labour 1992: 2). The NPD have a very clear role in offshore activities and exist within a system in which policy is defined by government/ministries. The NPD look after the participants' performance, and the industry gets on with its commercial activities.

The relative ease with which the Norwegian Government introduced such change suggests that it has been the dominant partner within the policy network. The structure has maintained the characteristics which prevail today; the rationalization of regulatory functions has served to increase the effectiveness of government intervention and to encourage a more proactive approach to health and safety.

The main legislative provisions in offshore health and safety matters are the Petroleum Act and the WEA. These Acts determine the nature of relationships, at both the shop floor level and in the policy network (PAPI 1990: 5); '[t]he Act not only protected the workers' rights, but also *forced* a general process of cooperation between the supervising authorities, the oil companies and the unions' (Wahlen and Rydning 1993: 55; emphasis added).

The Norwegian health and safety regime has two elements; the 'top-down' and the 'bottom-up' systems. The latter involves the cooperation of the workforce, which distinguishes Norway from Britain. Involvement is achieved through the WEA, the Petroleum Act and accompanying regulations, which specify the involvement of the workforce in the formation and implementation of the safety regime. The most important aspects of this system are the roles of the safety delegate and the Working Environment Committee (WEC). The WECs are the meeting point within the 'top-down' system which comprises the management, line-management and professional safety officers.

Safety delegates and the WECs are not token positions; they hold substantial statutory powers. The safety delegate has the authority to halt production if it is felt that continuing could result in serious injury or the loss of life. The safety delegate is given special protection from dismissal so that, even if such dangers were later discovered to be unfounded, the safety delegate is granted immunity provided his/her decision had no ulterior motive. In addition, safety delegates are involved in the inspection and implementation of any aspects related to the working environment. This involves the operator and the NPD keeping the senior safety delegate informed of any new proposals related to health and safety.

The structure of the WECs is very revealing with respect to the parallel it has with the relationships involved in the policy network. WECs are a statutory requirement for any business with 50 or more employees. The structure of the committees is formally determined by the WEA; it stipulates an employer–employee parity, with the chair, and thus the casting vote, alternating every two years. This system has not resulted in the advantage swinging from one interest to the other; the two groups have instead opted for a long-term, mutually-beneficial relationship where advantage is left largely unexploited (Wahlen and Rydning 1993: 56–7).

It is argued here that the relationships at the level of the WECs reflect structural relationships involved in the development of legislation and regulations concerned with health and safety. The main forum for interaction is that concerned with 'the external reference group regulations' (ERR). The forum comprises the employers, Norwegian Oil Industry Association (OLF), trade unions, Norwegian TUC main LO affiliated offshore union; independent offshore union (LO/Nopef; OFS) and the NPD, as hosts. This policy forum meets twice-yearly and is the means whereby the NPD can discuss future proposals and can hear the views of the industry (Wahlen and Rydning 1993; PAPI 1990: 10).

As well as coordinating the structure of relationships within the policy network, the NPD are also concerned with the collection of technological data. They have a database which is supplied by the oil companies and is distributed to research institutions after the information has been desensitized to protect business interests (Andresen 1992: 9). Thus, the NPD, far from being at a technological disadvantage, actually play a central role in encouraging technological development.

The Norwegian approach to the policy process, like the safety and health regime itself, is structured by government activity. The relationships are a statutory requirement. This suggests that the government and its agency are the dominant force, deciding on the membership of the policy network. The close contacts between the safety delegates, organized labour, the OLF and the NPD are certainly evidence of a policy network. The main characteristics of it are the long-term, positive-sum approach adopted as well as the strong leadership role played by the state in both its inclusionary approach to the membership of the network and its central role in coordinating technical information and setting the agenda for future policy objectives.

Diversity in British and Norwegian policy networks

The difference between policy network structures in Britain and Norway is 'explained' by several exogenous factors: economic considerations; political issues; and cultural differences in the public perceptions of organized labour.

One of the most striking influences on policy networks in Britain and Norway is the status of labour organizations. Since 1935 Norway has been characterized by tripartite arrangements in which trade unions have been accepted as credible partners in consultation with capital and the state (Sunde 1996: 2). Legislative provisions offshore reflect 'visions and ideas representing certain traditions in Norwegian culture and industrial practice' (Andresen 1992: 2–3). Certainly, workforce involvement in the offshore health and safety regime is a crucial feature of a policy network, which in this case has a clear impact upon policy outcomes. The broader social and political context has a far-reaching influence upon the relative status of actors and the form of ritual interaction between them. Put simply, it is impossible to understand the difference between the policy networks identified in Britain and Norway without first acknowledging the existence of contrasting systems of industrial relations and the differences in the status and expected involvement of organized labour.

The policy networks here are clearly influenced by political factors. As Ognedal admits, although it is often hard for the regulatory agency to accept it, safety policy is defined by 'signals' sent by politicians. However, these 'signals' are themselves influenced by macro-level concerns which are not simply political. The political, social and economic cannot be neatly separated; they are involved in a continuing interaction where each is influenced and influences in a symbiotic manner. These interactions form the broader structural constraints which shape the membership and outcomes of sectoral and sub-sectoral policy networks.

The importance of economic structural constraints has been evident since the mid-1960s. The different economic conditions experienced by Britain and Norway played a vital role in determining the structure of future policy networks concerned with offshore health and safety. Norway had enjoyed a consistently high rate of economic growth in the post-1945 period, while the UK had suffered from an erratic and lower rate which, in conjunction with the serious balance of payments deficit and an increasing dependence on imported oil, served to make the potential of domestic oil extremely attractive (Noreng 1980: 41). Put simply, at a crucial stage in the relationship between government and the oil companies, the UK Government needed the cooperation of the oil industry to extract the maximum possible reserves in order to cope with the domestic economic situation. In contrast, the Norwegian Government did not have the same urgency and could afford to wait. This meant that the UK Government had a weak negotiating hand when dealing with the oil companies and other countries, in large part because its short-term needs were consistent with those of the oil companies; rapid exploitation maximizing taxation revenue and minimizing British balance of payment deficits.

In formulating an approach to regulation in the oil industry, the UK was heavily influenced by the demands of the financial sector. The balance of payments problem was regarded as a priority and largely determined UK oil policy when, prior to the first licensing round in 1964, an interdepartmental committee, drawn from the Treasury, the Ministry of Power, and the Cabinet Office, met and committed the UK to a rapid depletion rate policy 'in order to meet the "overriding need" for a balance of payments' (Carson 1982: 91). This commitment to the rapid development of activities and exploitation of resources was reasserted first by the Labour Government in 1967, during the fiscal crisis which resulted in devaluation, and again during the Conservative administration between 1970 and 1974.

The weak position of the UK, exemplified in its need for a high depletion rate policy, was based on its capacity to absorb the benefits of future oil and gas discoveries. In this respect, the UK and Norway differed greatly. The UK wanted a rapid exploitation rate of any hydrocarbon reserves in order to combat the effects of long-term economic decline. In contrast, the Norwegians wanted to counter any unwelcome effects that oil and gas discoveries might bring to a stable and prosperous economy (Noreng 1980: 112).

The oil companies always favoured high depletion rates, partly because production and exploration costs invariably increase (Noreng 1980: 113). In this respect, their position was close to that of successive UK Governments; an important factor when observing the structural relationship and shared values between the DEn, the PED and UKOOA.

So, what are the consequences of different depletion rate policies on the structure of policy networks? Noreng argues that the relationship between government and the oil companies is one which is interdependent; the oil companies lack the ownership of the resources and the legitimacy with which to carry out their activities, while government lacks the expertise and know-ledge associated with the industry and is unwilling to risk capital in such an uncertain venture (Noreng 1980: 19). Within such a relationship, the depletion rate policy is a 'key element' in determining the balance of power. This directly influences the options open to government with respect to those issues peripheral to economic priorities. Carson (1982: 116) argues that the relation-ship between the industry and the regulatory agency favoured the demands of the industry as a result of the urgency of legislative activity and the priority given to rapid exploration and production. The implication is that the deple-tion rate policy, and the rushed legislative process, were responsible for the subordination of non-priority areas (such as health and safety), significantly influencing their long-term development. Therefore, the macroeconomic in-fluences on government and its departmental agencies resulted in safety being neglected, certainly in so far as it would reduce production. The political response to macroeconomic pressures was to define the membership and focus of the policy network, thereby affecting the range of viable outcomes.

The influences were similar in Norway, despite the obvious contrasts in policy objectives. The adoption of a moderate depletion rate policy reflected the relative buoyancy of the economy and meant that the macroeconomic problem concerned how to regulate the oil industry. As Ognedal (6–7) ob-serves, not only were the oil companies viewed with suspicion, they were also regarded as having interests which ran counter to those of the Norwegian state. The response was to ensure that the depletion rate and working conditions and rights were monitored and that 'petroleum activities would become of max-imum benefit to the nation as a whole'.

Conclusion

Policy networks can be seen to affect policy outcomes through their exclusion-ary or inclusionary nature which ensures that certain groups and policy options are either suppressed or guaranteed a voice in the policy formulation and implementation process. The degree of integration within the policy networks is crucial to understanding the nature of relationships and the impact this has upon policy formulation and policy outcomes. In Britain, offshore health and safety policy networks have undergone some changes over the period of oil and gas activity. However, exclusivity has been an enduring characteristic, as has the rather tight relationship between the oil companies and the regulatory agencies. In particular, the 'cosy' relationship, involving the PED (and its predecessors) and the oil companies, displays the characteristics of a network at the policy community end of the Marsh and Rhodes continuum (see above p. 16); demonstrating close formal and informal interaction and a high level of mutuality. This relationship, based upon long-term mutually beneficial interaction, involved the exclusion of 'alternative' interests, such as those representing organized labour. Therefore, the policy community identified was highly conservative and this led to the limited development of safety noted by Lord Cullen in his inquiry. In addition, the post-Piper Alpha period of HSE regulatory control still involves a close-knit core relationship with UKOOA. However, this is less to do with shared values between the two principal actors and more to do with pressures being placed on the HSE to stress the economic viability of safety offshore.

Norwegian offshore health and safety networks have had a very different development. The initial period of offshore activity saw a highly fragmented regulatory regime involving a wide range of governmental bodies. The prevailing approach to offshore safety was one in which the state actors and Norwegian interests expected the international oil companies involved to conform to the Norwegian 'model' of tripartite consultation and comply with the laws and regulations as they existed onshore. The inability or unwillingness on the part of the oil companies to adjust to this approach resulted in the creation of a highly formalized policy network where an inclusionary policy resulted in the membership being relatively open. No obvious exclusions exist, but the level of interaction is high and there is an institutionalized framework which has created a long-term mutuality and recognized rules of the game. In this case advantage is left unexploited in favour of the continuation of the existing relationships. Therefore, the Norwegian case is in one sense towards the looser 'issue network' end of the Marsh and Rhodes continuum, while the level of interaction and the resources within the network demonstrate a tightly knit level of interaction more associated with the 'policy community' end.

In both Britain and Norway the dominant member or interest within the network has been the state, playing a crucial role in shaping the membership and agenda of the policy networks. The state appears to be of prime importance and the networks tend to reflect its chosen policies at the macroeconomic level. In large part this is because the oil companies cannot exploit offshore reserves without the legal backing of the state concerned. The relationship in Britain could be argued to be a classic example of agency capture, but the policy of the oil companies in relation to the rate of exploration and production is consistent with that of successive British Governments and major economic interests. As such, it is difficult to see a major state dependence upon the oil companies, although the relative dependence on technical expertise is an enduring feature of relationships in the UKCS.

The Norwegian case is a more obvious example of state dominance. The creation of the WEA and the Petroleum Act and the institutionalization of rules and basic relationships demonstrates the central role of the Norwegian state. Through the use of Statoil and the NPD the Norwegian state has successfully made itself the centre of technical and specialized knowledge. Similarly, the promotion of meaningful workforce involvement has resulted in the resources of trade unions being enhanced as they perform crucial duties related to the recruitment and training of safety delegates and members of WECs. This suggests that the oil companies are in a weaker position than those in the UKCS – a factor which is visible because the state and oil companies do not have the same level of common interest evident in the British example.

It is also clear from the case study that the sectoral level networks dealing with broad oil policies have been largely responsible for shaping both the membership of, and policies adopted by, the sub-sectoral networks dealing with offshore health and safety. As Tables 6.1 and 6.2 illustrate, for most of the period from the early 1960s until the 1980s offshore health and safety was highly fragmented at the sub-sectoral level and most decisions regarding policy were taken at the sector level, mostly in relation to general oil policy. Obviously, it is an empirical question whether policy outcomes are more likely to be shaped at the sectoral or sub-sectoral levels. What is clear is that more attention should be paid towards the relationship between sectoral and sub-sectoral activity. The claim in the policy network literature that the sub-sectoral networks are more important (see Jordan et al. 1995) is based upon a view that policy making is so disaggregated that little or no sectoral activity is viable.

In both Britain and Norway, the evidence suggests that sectoral concerns with production and exploration crucially influenced the membership and agenda of subsequent sub-sectoral policy networks. In Britain, the economic necessity for rapid exploration and exploitation meant that health and safety was never going to be prioritized. The relationships between the oil companies and successive regulatory bodies was characterized by the strong emphasis placed upon production-related issues within the sponsoring Department. Even with the advent of the HSE responsibility for offshore health and safety, the emphasis on cost effectiveness and the economic viability of future developments is having an important influence on the pace of safety improvements.

The Norwegian case study is even more pronounced, with strong pressures emanating for a tightening-up of safety provisions and a general policy of

Table 6.1   Policy networks in Norwegian health and safety policy related to offshore oil activities 1964–95

Area	Actors		
	1964–73	1973–85	1985–95
Policy sector (oil policy)	Ministry of Industry and other relevant Departments		
Policy sub-sector (offshore health and safety policy)		NPD, other regulatory agencies, operators and labour organizations	NPD, LO/Nopef, OFS, OLF

Table 6.2 Policy networks in British health and safety policy related to off-shore oil activities 1964–95

Area	Actors		
	1964–71	*1971–90*	*1990–95*
Policy sector (oil policy)	Ministry of Power, the operators	DEn, PED (or predecessors), the operators	
Policy sub-sector (offshore health and safety policy)			HSE, UKOOA, other employer groups, TUC and OILC

control on oil company activities. The Norwegian approach has been one of initial mistrust of the oil companies. This relationship emerged from the realization at the sectoral level that Norwegian 'national interests' and oil company policies were not compatible. In particular, the need to manage the pace of developments offshore and monitor the impacts of oil and gas revenue on the stable Norwegian economy proved a crucial sectoral pressure on the emerging rationalized sub-sectoral policy network.

The relationship between the sectoral and sub-sectoral levels is relevant to the question of why networks take the forms that they do. Crucial to this process is the role of the state and, in particular, its identification of a definite interest. The importance to the state of any given issue will have a profound influence upon any subsequent policy networks which emerge, or will have an effect on the transformation of existing networks. The study demonstrates how the adoption of an exclusionary policy in Britain had the effect of limiting the extent to which safety was allowed to improve at the expense of production. In contrast, the Norwegian case was characterized by an inclusionary approach which undermined the position of the oil companies and left them as one voice among many in an institutionalized relationship based upon parity. In both cases the sub-sectoral networks that emerged were a reflection of broader considerations, both political and economic.

Perhaps the most important question which needs to be asked of policy networks is the extent to which they 'explain' the different outcomes in the two countries. The influence of economic factors as well as the issue of workforce involvement are two exogenous factors which constitute the broader context for any consideration of policy network activity. However, although the networks do reflect these influences it is the relationships between members within the network that shape policy. In particular, the characteristics of any relationships within policy networks will have an obvious impact on subsequent policy outcomes. The exclusive relationships which have been evident in the British case have had the effect of giving a disproportionate influence to production and exploration matters. Health and safety have been

affected as a result of the exclusion of those interests which ha'
which contrast with those of the oil companies and those state int.
nating the sectoral level. In contrast, the Norwegian policy networks have
more open and relationships have been formalized and institutionalized to
ensure that certain issues cannot be neglected. The formal powers and status of
organized labour, as well as the compulsory nature of network participation,
have had the effect of ensuring that a wide range of considerations are on the
agenda and that production cannot be prioritized in either the consultation or
implementation processes.

Therefore, policy networks can 'explain' policy outcomes to the extent
that, when viewed alongside the broader constraints which exist upon them,
they enhance our understanding of the processes adopted to achieve broader
policy objectives. With more attention given to comparative studies which
contextualize network activity, and due attention to both the relationships
between networks and between the sectoral and sub-sectoral levels, our understanding of the complexity of the state and state interest relations can only
increase.

7

Policing policy and policy networks in Britain and New Zealand

Elizabeth McLeay

Together with the protection of the state against external threats to security, the maintenance of internal order through coercion and political socialization is a primary state function, although rarely studied by political scientists (see Ritchie 1992). Whether wealthy or poor, authoritarian or liberal–democratic, governments devote substantial resources to policing, although the ratio between state coercion and citizen consent differs according to regime type. Do liberal–democratic states, with their representative party systems, active interest groups and need to legitimate policy decisions through consultation and negotiation, demonstrate similar structural and policy-making characteristics in policing? This chapter takes two liberal-democratic states with very similar political cultures, Britain and New Zealand, and analyses their policing policy networks. It examines the role that the policy networks play in policing policy in the two countries and identifies the extent, and reasons for, the changes which have occurred in these networks over the past two decades.

There is very little published work on policing policy networks (see Benyon *et al.* 1994; Den Boer 1994), so there are no basic maps of the pattern of policing decisions at the central level in these two states. Thus, this paper concentrates primarily on empirical analysis. The language of policy networks is employed to pose the questions and help structure the material, but debates about the use of terminology and usefulness of the policy network framework have been largely ignored.

Despite the enormous disparity between their two populations, Britain and New Zealand provide appropriate examples for comparison. They share similar political structures and there are also similarities in recent policy trends, with each state undergoing considerable social and economic change, influenced by monetarism, neo-liberal economic theory and the exigencies of fiscal crisis.

The Westminster 'model', which enables a clear choice of governments with relatively unfettered powers, makes change easier. Governing parties do not need to negotiate with coalition partners or with their informal parliamentary party supporters in order to legislate and budget. Because of the relative weaknesses of the two parliaments, the attention of organized interests has been primarily on bureaucrats and ministers with 'insider groups' relying primarily upon their structural and personal links with government and 'outsider' groups attending to public opinion (Grant 1978). However, the governments of both Britain and New Zealand, influenced by experience and public choice doctrine, have been increasingly wary of the influence of 'special interests' since the heyday of tripartism and integration of groups into the policy process during the 1970s.

As 'law and order' has been a salient political issue in both polities, given rising crime rates, and because the police inhabit hierarchical organizations upon which it is theoretically straightforward to impose change, it might be hypothesized that the governing parties, influenced by public opinion, would exert their political will and legislative dominance and strongly influence policy making in areas relating to the police. On the contrary, in both states governing parties have only recently sought to shape policing policy; before the mid-1980s policing policy was dominated by the practitioners themselves. New Zealand and Britain were states where, in the past: 'the character of governments change but police structure appears very durable' (Bayley 1979: 127). In this policy area the question was not so much whether the policy network included groups and organizations beyond the state, but whether elected governments had any substantial input into how policing policy was made. The structural and ideological characteristics of the two policing systems as they had developed during the twentieth century created a situation in which it was difficult for governments to influence policy.

From the mid-1980s, however, the governments of both states sought to assert themselves in police policy making. Although there were differences between Britain and New Zealand in the changes attempted by the respective governments, there were also striking similarities: in order to improve police efficiency the policy mechanisms of the New Public Management philosophy fashionable in each country were employed; and in order to improve police effectiveness in the face of rising crime, the policing policy network was expanded. This paper asks what these initiatives tell us about the policy networks in this area of public policy. First, however, a distinctive feature of policing as a policy issue needs to be explained – the ideology of constabular independence.

Policing ideology

Although the two states demonstrate contrasting organizational characteristics, as explained below, the two policing sectors share the operating doctrine of the independence of the constabulary. The dominance of this doctrine in policing distinguishes it from all other policy sectors. Its strength and pervasiveness complicates and limits policy formulation and implementation. 'It is said that because the constable's powers are inherent in his office and possessed by the office holder alone – "original and not delegated" was the phrase used by the 1962 Royal Commission – he enjoys a freedom from control by elected representatives unique in public law' (Lustgarten 1986: 25). This gives police officers enormous discretion in terms of operational independence, both at street level and at the top level of Chief Constable (Britain) or Commissioner of Police (New Zealand). Police officers, it is said, are primarily responsible to the law, not to elected representatives; and this protects the police, and therefore society, from discriminatory or biased decision making by individual police constables and from the threat of politicization of senior decision makers.

Britain demonstrates a more elaborate version of police ideology than does New Zealand. This difference goes back to the different origins of the two policing systems. The origins of the British police lie in the village constable. The police, it has been generalized, were to create and retain order, particularly between the social classes, and to balance the rights and autonomy of the local community against central state authority. This latter aspect, if not the former, has become part of the ideology of British policing; it plays a rhetorical role in the conflict between centralization and decentralization that has been part of policing for most of its history. For example, George Bundred, at the time Chair of the Police Committee of the Association of Metropolitan Authorities, said in 1989: 'Every time someone demands fewer police forces, every time someone ignores the legitimate interests of police authorities, this delicate partnership is put at risk. And with it our individual freedoms are being put in danger' (Press Release, Summer Conference of Association of Chief Constables [ACPO]). In short, decentralization reinforces the doctrine of operational independence.

In New Zealand, the proper role of the colonial state was seen as principally developmental (McLeay 1992). The creation of the New Zealand police took place when the country was a series of dispersed settlements, some disrupted by the wars born out of the settlers' greed for Maori land. Until the national, unified, police force was created in 1876–7, there were police systems of 'a bewildering diversity and changeability' (Fairburn 1989: 243). However, lack of resources and regional rivalries soon led to the centralization of power generally and policing particularly. A centralized force was established and has endured ever since. Although important, the doctrine of operational independence never gained the prominence in New Zealand that it did in Britain, partly because of the newer state's centralized policing structure.

There have been many criticisms in both countries of the doctrine of constabulary independence; not least because the hierarchical disciplined structures in practice effectively work against individual constabulary discretion, as decisions to arrest are subject to overview by senior officers (Lustgarten 1986: 12), and because it is notoriously difficult to distinguish policy from operational decisions. Moreover, complete operational independence precludes large areas of political accountability (Morgan 1989). Nevertheless, constabulary independence is part of the ideology of policing; it affects police practices and, moreover, the expectations of politicians and bureaucrats about the limits of governmental control of the police. It affects the construction of policing policy agendas (McLeay 1990). Thus, it is an essential component of the ideological and structural nature of the sectoral policy network because it influences perceptions of power parameters and accountability limits. It has also protected the police from 'political interference' and, in so doing, sets police policy in almost an insulated world of its own. Before the recent structural and policy framework changes in policing are analysed, the parameters of this world – its main structural and sectoral characteristics – need to be understood.

Public policy and the police: structural characteristics

No policy network can be analysed without understanding the main structural characteristics of the formal governmental and sectoral organizations. Hence, the following section compares the two policy systems in terms of the following factors: the formal organization of policing; the formally prescribed roles of the elected politicians; the state agencies involved in policing; and the organization of the sectoral interests.

Organizational characteristics

There are wide variations in the organizational structures and numbers of police organizations even within the four English-speaking, Westminster-influenced states of Canada, Australia, Britain and New Zealand. So, Britain and New Zealand provide examples of a decentralized and a centralized policing system.

There are 43 autonomous police forces in England and Wales, with (in 1992) an approximate total of 128,000 sworn police plus about 50,000 civilians. There are also regional crime squads and some shared common services (police colleges, the Forensic Science Service, Drugs Intelligence). Scotland, with eight forces (until 1996 when the number was reduced) and approximately 14,200 sworn police and several thousand civilians, has its own police college, its Scottish Criminal Records Office and Crime Squad and various regional services, such as the forensic services. Scottish forces also share resources available to the rest of Britain, such as the National Identification Bureau and the relatively new and controversial National Criminal Intelligence Service. The police in Northern Ireland, which have a different history, structure and role are excluded from this analysis. There are huge differences in size amongst British forces, ranging from Dumfries and Galloway, with under 400 in 1992, to London with (in 1996) about 28,000 police officers and 14,000 civilian staff.

Chief Constables are appointed by their police authorities (see below), with approval required from the Home Secretary and Secretary of State for

Scotland respectively. In effect, the Chief Constables, not the local authorities, make the decisions about policing their areas under central guidelines. Robert Reiner reported that his interviews with Chief Constables showed clearly that 'their conception of a good local authority is one which acts as a sounding-board for local opinion, but one which does not ultimately question the chief's decisions' (1991: 251; and see Jones *et al.* 1994: 220–78). Clearly, where the statutory powers of controlling agencies impose minimal requirements on operational organization, power is asymmetrically distributed, and much will depend then on personal relationships and habitual behavioural norms. There is considerable anecdotal evidence indicating that the relationship between police chiefs and the authorities (not the topic of this chapter) depends greatly on personality and personal discretion and trust.

The contemporary New Zealand Police is headed by the Commissioner who is in overall charge of five police regions (reduced from six in 1996), each headed by an assistant commissioner. In mid-1996 there were 6912 sworn establishment positions, and 1839 non-sworn full-time positions (New Zealand Police 1996: 90). The Commissioner of Police and Deputy Commissioner are appointed by the Governor-General on the advice of the government (Police Act 1958). The Police Regulations state that: '(i) The Commissioner shall be responsible to the Minister for the general administration and control of the Police'; and '(ii) He shall cause all members of the Police to discharge their duties to the Government and the public satisfactorily and efficiently.' There has been debate about whether the second requirement implies that there is ministerial control over police enforcement duties (Cameron 1986: 18–19; Orr 1986: 50–5; Strategos 1989: 42–50; Beckett 1991). Although there is a degree of regional and local autonomy as to how resources are employed and policy is implemented, the objectives are defined centrally. The central policy-making group is called the Police Executive Committee, chaired by the Commissioner, comprising key individuals in police headquarters and also the regional commanders. The Commissioner appoints sworn and non-sworn members of the police under the level of Deputy Commissioner. The Commissioner must be a 'good employer' under the relevant sections of the State Sector Act 1988.

In common with most other liberal–democratic states (Goldsmith 1991), the British and New Zealand police are subject to the investigation of an independent Police Complaints Authority, bodies which are not part of the regular policy network although their reports can affect policing practices. The prosecution of offenders is carried out by the Procurator Fiscal in Scotland and the Crown Prosecution Service in England and Wales. In New Zealand the police continue to carry out the prosecuting role. It might also be added that the New Zealand Police are subject to New Zealand's liberal Official Information Act 1982, although the instructions issued to police in the *Police Gazette* constitute protected information.

Despite their similar political structures and legal systems, Britain and New Zealand exhibit contrasting organizational characteristics concerning the police: 'National structures of policing reflect decisions about the geographic distribution of political power. They emerge early in national histories, and they change very little subsequently' (Bayley 1992: 531). When it comes to the internal organization of the regional and local police in both states, however, there are few differences between Britain and New Zealand, reflecting two factors: the common tasks of these single-level, all-purpose forces; and the impact of the internationalization of police knowledge and views.

Elected politicians and the police

At the local level in England and Wales the police authorities are required under the Police Act 1964, s.4(a) to 'secure the maintenance of an adequate and efficient police force'. It is the duty of Chief Constables to 'direct and control their forces', to enforce the law and to report once a year in writing to their police authorities and to the Home Secretary. The authorities have had no power to require changes to practices and policies disclosed in the reports. The responsibilities in Scotland are similar under the Police (Scotland) Act 1967 (National Audit Office 1992: 8–9). Neither the police authorities nor the Secretary of State have had the power to direct a Chief Constable on the 'enforcement of the law or on the deployment of police officers' (National Audit Office 1992: 9). In Scotland, however, Chief Constables have a duty to comply with instructions from 'the Lord Advocate, the Sheriff Principal or the appropriate prosecutor in relation to offences and prosecutions' (National Audit Office 1992: 9).

At the central level, the Home Secretary is responsible to parliament for the Metropolitan Police for whom there has been no police authority. In 1995, however, a non-statutory Metropolitan Police Committee was created to act as a link between the Metropolitan Police Service and the Home Secretary. The Home Secretary has had no direct responsibility for the adequacy and efficiency of the provincial forces, although again there have been some recent changes. The Scottish Home Secretary is in an analogous position. Because under the relevant legislation these two ministers have had no statutory responsibility for what police actually do, they answer questions in the House of Commons on a narrow range of issues only, mainly concerning such issues as statistical information about force numbers. Questions about force policies and operations are excluded. Despite the lack of parliamentary accountability, however, the Secretaries of State have possessed (potentially) significant resource allocation powers since the bulk of police funding, about three-quarters (including both the local allocations and funding for regional and central services), comes from central government. The two Secretaries of State are also responsible for the Inspectorates of Constabulary, who establish and maintain standards across the forces, and the Home and Scottish Office. This blurred situation set the scene, and provided some of the rationalization, for the systemic changes of the 1990s.

In New Zealand, unlike Britain and most of the rest of the democratic world, there is a Minister of Police as well as a Minister of Justice. The role of the latter 'corresponds broadly to those of the Lord Chancellor (in his or her executive capacity) and Home Secretary in England. However, many of the Home Secretary's functions have their New Zealand counterpart in the Department of Internal Affairs, whose Minister is the successor of the Colonial Secretary' (Department of Justice 1993: 65). There is also an Attorney-General who sits in Cabinet. The Minister of Police is accountable to parliament for the police, answering on a wider range of parliamentary questions than his or her counterparts in Britain. Particular incidents involving police are discussed in the New Zealand Parliament. The Minister pays formal lip service to the doctrine of operational independence by only rarely becoming directly involved in the application of law enforcement, although there have been a few notable exceptions; for example, over an immigration issue in 1976 (the notoriously heavy-handed rounding up of Pacific Island 'Overstayers') and over the policing of the controversial Springbok (rugby) Tour of 1981 (Orr 1986: 55–8; McGill 1992: 151–70). The relationship between the Minister and the Commissioner, however, is so direct that policy suggestions are quite freely made in private and, indeed, there are institutionalized links between the Minister's Office and the Commissioner's Office, with weekly meetings between the two (Interview, Minister of Police 1997): 'Police policies and procedures are often the subject of discussion between Commissioner and Minister' (New Zealand Police 1989: Paper 15: 4).

The central state agencies

Despite the decentralized organization of English and Scottish policing, the Home Office and the Scottish Office are central actors in the distribution of resources. These agencies, using complex formulae, advise on the allocation of finance to all the forces, within the Treasury's budgetary allocation (House of Commons Committee of Public Accounts 1991). Further, they have 'eyes and ears' in the shape of the HM Inspectorate of Constabulary (HMIC). Thus, these central agencies possess information, plus potential sanctions, and their circulars to the forces have to be taken seriously by Chief Constables. Furthermore, the relatively new science of policing (furthered in the Home Office and elsewhere) has hastened centralization by its focus on central government.

On the other hand, an activist Home or Scottish Secretary, despite the persuasive powers of the Home Office, cannot depend upon corporatist-style adherence by Chief Constables. Institutionalized decentralization, police professionalism and the doctrine of constabulary independence have worked together to legitimize the autonomy of individual Chief Constables. This is why the relationship between the Home Office and the chief police officers 'tends to be cooperative rather than confrontational'. Besides, 'Its guidance as expressed in circulars is normally the product of prior consultation with the Association of Chief Police Officers [ACPO, discussed below] and other expressions of professional opinion, aimed at achieving a consensus about appropriate policies' (Reiner 1993: 18).

The HMIC has worked with the Home Office to improve standards of policing and the deployment of policing resources. The National Audit Office, which has worked closely with the HMIC, has become a vociferous critic of the police, and an increasingly active participant in the policing policy network. Its reports have influenced the use of police resources.

At the heart of the policy process of the New Zealand Police is a group of senior police officers led by the Commissioner. They formulate priorities, working within the overall governmental strategy and budgetary allocation. The Treasury is a significant actor, especially regarding the specification of outputs. The Audit Office, too, reviews the corporate and strategic planning of the police and has indeed been critical in the past of the lack of clarity of those outputs.

New Zealand's *Cabinet Office Manual* (Cabinet Office 1996) provides an excellent insight into the inner state policy circles of policing policy making. The *Manual* states that 'Departments preparing submissions must ensure that they consider all the implications for other government agencies and consult them at the earliest possible stage' (p. 42) and an appendix is helpfully provided which summarizes the key interests of government departments.

The police must be consulted on: 'statute and regulation changes where policing will be required; general law and order issues; border control; and criminal law and sentencing' (p. 116). The list of 'Justice' issues includes Corrections, Courts, Education Review Office, Health, Justice, Maori Development, Pacific Island Affairs, Police, Research, Science and Technology, Serious Fraud Office, Social Welfare, Women's Affairs, and Youth Affairs (Cabinet Office 1996: 119). Of course, this latter list reflects the wider reaches of justice issues, from Maori rights to truancy and domestic violence.

Members of the police regularly appear before interdepartmental committees on legislation. In 1987, for example, police officers (not in their capacity as police unionists) appeared before committees on the following issues: children and young persons' legislation, violent offences, international terrorism and riot law reform. They appeared before parliamentary committees considering issues such as the protection of undercover police officers and homosexual law reform; and also appeared before committees of inquiry on the sale of liquor and violence in the community (New Zealand Police 1987: 7).

The sectoral interests

The policing sectoral interests in Britain are: representing the ranks, the Police Federation, England and Wales, the Scottish Police Federation, and the Police Federation, Northern Ireland; then there are the Association of Scottish Police Superintendents, the Superintendents' Association of Northern Ireland and the Superintendents' Association, England and Wales; and the final level consists of the Association of Chief Police Officers (England, Wales and Northern Ireland) and the Association of Chief Police Officers in Scotland. Given this lack of sectoral vertical cohesion it is not surprising that there have been repeated calls for amalgamation to try to achieve a unified front when dealing with central and local government.

The Police Federations and the Superintendents' Associations are only partly integrated into the regular sectoral decision-making processes, as the later parts of this chapter show. Repeated complaints from these bodies about their lack of representation appear in journals such as the *Police Review*. The perceived legitimacy of the Police Federations and Superintendents' Associations depends on the issue: they are regularly consulted, for instance, on staffing and wages issues and are represented on the Police Advisory Board (with ACPO) which deals with the conditions of service of all officers, and also the Police Training Council. The Police Federations, and more recently the Superintendents' Associations, are much more likely than ACPO to attempt to use the mass media to target politicians and the public. For some years they have had parliamentary advisers amongst MPs to monitor police interests in the House of Commons. They have been particularly vocal on issues such as police numbers, resisting privatization along with ACPO (Johnston 1992: 346) and legal limitations on police powers.

All police officers holding substantial positions above that of Chief Superintendent are eligible to be members of the two ACPOs. Presidents take office for one year. The crucial ACPO (England, Wales and Northern Ireland) committee has been the Steering Committee (Interview, former Chief Constable 1989). Also there has been an executive committee comprised of representatives from the eight regions, mainly concerned with negotiable matters, and a Chief Constables' Council. Three important coordinating committees are International Affairs, Finance and Quality of Service. In 1994, the principal specialist committees, comprising representatives from each of the eight ACPO regions, were the Crime, General Purposes, Personnel and Training, Technical and Research, Terrorism and Allied Matters, and Traffic committees. These committees have been the 'policy powerhouses' (Interview, former President 1989) which advise on specific issues. There is a small Secretariat which has its costs met from the common police service fund (jointly provided from central and local government). There is a full-time General Secretary, a Policy Analysis Unit and a Public Relations Officer. According to its *Constitution and Rules* (Association of Chief Police Officers in Scotland 1994), the structure of the Scottish body is similar.

The ACPOs, like the other police sectoral organizations, act as orthodox trade unions concerned with training, pay and conditions. Members pay to join. Their second role is that of a coordinating body, bringing together the views and experiences of the constituent organizations. In that sense, they are umbrella organizations which try to control the actions of subordinate units. Third, each ACPO socializes senior police officers by training individuals for higher office. Fourth, and most germane for the purposes of this article, these bodies are important in the policy process. They are thoroughly integrated into state decision making. In 1994 ACPO (England, Wales and Northern Ireland) was represented on over 60 groups chaired by government Departments.

Moreover, members of ACPO (or its nominees) are frequently seconded to the Home Office (in 1989 to the Science and Technology Group and the Police Requirements Support Unit). ACPO is represented on the Home Office Standing Committee on Crime and on the Police Training Committee. The Central Conference of Chief Constables meets twice yearly with Home Office civil servants to discuss 'issues of common concern to the police service'. This secret meeting is chaired by the Permanent Secretary of the Home Office. The committees of ACPO present evidence to the Home Affairs Committee of the House of Commons (for example to the Home Affairs Committee on Organised Crime). Members of ACPO have worked with the HMIC and the Audit Commission to produce coordinated strategies on crime. The ACPOs have played a major part on European border issues. The Scottish Office Home and Health Department similarly integrates representatives from ACPO into its decision-making processes.

ACPO has demonstrated key weaknesses over the years. There is a limited notion of organizational hierarchy, largely because Chief Constables head their own forces, armed with the doctrine of constabulary independence plus the statutory powers outlined above. This means that the ACPO leadership cannot invariably deliver the acquiescence and cooperation of all the other Chiefs. The circulation of the presidency, moreover, has not helped provide continuity of political representation in state decision-making fora. Further, in comparison with other lobby organizations, particularly business and professional ones, ACPO is poorly resourced in terms of finance and independent resource capabilities, although some improvements have been made in recent years – in 1992 it had a budget of £390,000. Agreement between the Home Office and ACPO is certainly not automatic, and ACPO can and does lose policy debates: ACPO's unsuccessful advocacy of a national identity card system in 1989 provides an example (Kirby 1989: 3). The campaign for identity cards continued to be fought by ACPO in the 1990s. A further problem has been the uncertain relationship between the ACPOs' two key functions: acting as a trade union; and advising government. Thus, in 1994 there were discussions concerning creating a new body to act for the police 'as the Law Society does for lawyers and the British Medical Association does for doctors' (Campbell 1994: 2).

ACPO has undoubtedly been a key body in directing policing policies. It occupies a strategic position, providing the organizational linkage between the central and the local state. Its credibility lies in its professional status (less equivocal than the lower ranks), its legitimate claims to representativeness and its organizational structure. A comment from an official report in 1979 sums up the essence of ACPO's longstanding superior position:

> We accept that the relationship between the Home Departments and the ACPOs has [a] . . . dimension which reflects the final operational responsibility of the Chief Constables and their position as part of the management triangle of the Secretary of State, the police authorities, and the Chief Constables. Thus, the contact between the Home Departments

and the ACPO is different both in volume and kind from that with the other staff associations.

(Edmund-Davies 1979)

The local authority associations are also involved in the policy process on some issues, mainly related to wages and conditions. Publicity is given to the views of the police authorities through these associations, and their views are expressed directly in the annual Summer Conference which senior police officers and police authority and association representatives attend. This occasion also provides an opportunity for the informal exchange of views on national and local issues (Personal observation, Summer Conference 1989).

After a struggle to be permitted to be unionized, the New Zealand Police Association was formed in 1936. It represents all police officers up to and including senior sergeants. Membership is voluntary but only a handful of members do not belong (McGill 1992: 1). Apart from wage and conditions issues, one of the functions of the organization is 'To constitute the official channel of communication between its members as a body and: (i) The Minister of Police; (ii) The Commissioner of Police' (McGill 1992: 1). Rather a quiescent body for a long while, from the mid-1980s the Association became increasingly outspoken, tracking its counterpart organization in Britain. For example, it fervently objected to the creation of the Police Complaints Authority. Like its British counterparts, the New Zealand Police Association campaigned vociferously on police numbers. It was also critical of the Bill of Rights Act 1990 which restrained police powers.

The New Zealand Police Officers' Guild was created in 1955 for the ranks of inspector up to and including deputy commissioner. In 1992, 240 officers belonged (McGill 1992: 1). This body is poorly resourced – there was no paid officer until 1989 (*New Zealand Herald*, 25 February 1989). It is much quieter than the Association, taking a low profile politically. The Guild does not play much of a role in police decision making and policy making as an organization.

Policing policy: the key structural characteristics

It can be seen from this brief outline that the political core of these two policy-making systems are very different. The smaller state possesses an appropriately small group of actors in control of the police; and the vastly more populous state has a complex, diffused organizational structure, involving intergovernmental relationships, regulatory mechanisms and territorial foci. In addition, there is the subtle but important difference in the role of the respective responsible ministers, despite the prevalence of the doctrine of operational independence that defines policing ideology in both jurisdictions. Structure, here, cuts across legal and constitutional beliefs.

In order to develop this comparison and establish the nature of the policy networks themselves, I now discuss the broad initiatives that have forced the police in both states to change their policies and practices.

Changing policies and behaviour and the nature of the policing policy network

In both states discussed here, governments have been faced with rising crime figures, public discontent about 'law and order' and fiscal constraints. One governmental response (not the focus here) has been to try to persuade individuals to become involved in defending themselves against crime, for example, in 'neighbourhood watch' schemes.

The second main response of the two governments has been to change policing behaviour to make the police become more efficient and cost-effective through a two-pronged strategy: increased state monitoring of the police, a project that had much to do with the 'New Public Management' favoured by the two countries' governments; and the expansion of 'policing' into a wider policy framework that might be called 'criminal justice'. Because these attempts represent severe challenges to the autonomy of the practitioners of policing, not least because they impact on 'operations', they provide interesting examples of the nature of the two policy networks.

Changing policing practices

Since the mid-1980s, British central government has been attempting to standardize police practices in order to improve effectiveness and efficiency, a campaign that has involved the Home Office, the Scottish Office, the HMIC and the Audit Office. On the whole the development of these initiatives has involved ACPO. For example, in 1991 the HMIC issued guidelines on the monitoring of ACPO's *Statement of Common Purpose and Values* and its *Strategic Policy Documents*, to be followed by Home Office Circulars (HMIC 1992: 12–13). When Robert Reiner asked 40 Chief Constables about the influence of central bodies on police decision making, they responded that the Home Office was most important. Seventy per cent felt that the Home Office had 'a lot' of influence and 30 per cent 'fair' influence. In comparison, Her Majesty's Inspectorate of Constabulary (HMIC) attracted 35 per cent choosing 'a lot' and 52.5 per cent 'a fair amount' of influence. When asked about the Association of Chief Police Officers (ACPO), 32.5 per cent felt that it had 'a lot' of influence, and 37.5 per cent 'fair' influence (Reiner 1991: 268). Reiner wrote: 'The Home Office is seen as a powerful, increasingly interventionist body, which can be disregarded only at the chief's peril' (p. 267). Indeed, a Chief Inspector examined Home Office Circulars in 1973/4, 1983/4 and 1988/9, finding little alteration in number but changes to language and tone, with the Circulars becoming more prescriptive and centralist (Clark 1991: 121).

A major British Government initiative was to attempt to alter the career structure of the police. The Sheehy Report on wages, ranking and conditions recommended extensive changes (Sheehy 1993). The police associations were incensed at what they saw as attacks on their careers and their professionalism. The Scottish Police Federation, for example, conducted public opinion surveys, wrote to every MP, saw the Home Secretary and 'attended all four

Scottish political party conferences to ensure that our views were held'. With the other associations it held a rally of 23,000 police officers (Scottish Police Federation 1993: Foreword). The government bowed to the pressure and many recommendations were rejected, although three management ranks were abolished and fixed-term contracts introduced for ACPO-level officers (Benyon 1993: 53–4).

The police organizations were consulted, both in the course of the inquiry and when its findings were implemented. The report itself included a 'List of those Organisations *Specifically Invited* to Submit Evidence' (my italics) and a list headed 'Submission of Evidence from Organisations' (Sheehy 1993). Of course, invitations to submit evidence serve the primary purposes of validating the process and legitimating the outcomes. Nevertheless, it is worth noting that the police sectoral organizations take their place amongst the bodies and individuals in the first list (as do the local authority associations). And their hostility to the report certainly affected its implementation.

Resource allocation was also an issue during the 1990s. Dissent between the sectoral interests (especially ACPO) and the governmental agencies in Britain rose steeply during the 1990s when a new funding formula was proposed. The proposed formula was fiercely contested, both inside official circles and publicly.

By the mid-1990s, the frustrations felt by the British Conservative Government concerning the difficulties of implementing policing policies and, especially, controlling expenditure and establishing priorities were being publicly expressed; for example in the Police Reform White Paper which preceded the controversial Police and Magistrates' Court Act 1994 (Home Office 1993).

The Police and Magistrates' Court Act 1994 gave new power to the Home Secretary to set objectives across the police forces. These are announced annually. Now, each police force sets out its objectives, within the national objectives, and sets out performance indicators which enable achievements to be monitored. Force amalgamations were simplified. Also, the Home Secretary is now able to appoint some members of police authorities. These changes constituted an historic challenge to how police priorities and structures had been established. The Act itself, however, was the culmination of a series of moves by government to control and influence policing. As mentioned earlier, the Home Office had become more assertive and the Audit Office had played an increasingly active role in attempting to gain value for money in policing. To some extent the police had responded to criticisms of unclear objectives and inefficient use of resources with internal reforms. For example, the British police, like their colleagues in New Zealand and elsewhere, had implemented Policing by Objectives, including the development of performance indicators (Robinson *et al.* 1989: 31–7). But the 1994 legislation went much further in the imposition of centralized priorities and practices.

The passage of the 1994 legislation illustrated all the problems of shifting the decision-making arena away from Whitehall – where the majority of reforms had been worked out and disseminated through Circulars – to West-minster, for it created much publicity for the government's actions: both the ACPO and the Police Federation (PF) objected to its provisions. Further, the Act was slightly weakened during its passage through the Lords.

In yet another move to change the practices of policing, the Home Office attempted to clarify police tasks in the Core and Ancillary Tasks Review (1995), widely viewed by police as a step towards the privatization of certain functions but in the event not influential. This initiative did not go far, proba-bly due to police lobbying, but also because many measures might have stimu-lated public opposition.

By 1994 tension was so great concerning the perceived increased asser-tiveness of the Home Office, central government demands on the police and the problem of diminishing resources, that: 'In an unprecedented wholesale abandonment of the gentlemanly conventions that have for so long governed relations between ACPO and the Home Office, various chiefs went on the record to criticise Home Office policy and the Home Secretary personally' (Waddington 1994: 28).

Thus, the British police have been the objects of wide-ranging changes. All of them were the initiatives of central government, although all, also, involved some degree of input from the police themselves. The reasons for the involvement of the various sectoral groups were encapsulated by a recent statement by a senior F1 division Home Office official discussing who should be consulted over a planned Circular:

> Usually ACPO have to be brought in because they are responsible for actually making it happen. The police authorities . . . ought to be in-volved if expenditure is involved because they would provide 49 per cent. If it had a direct impact on the actual work of police officers then there would be a case for involving the Police Federation and Superin-tendents Association.
>
> (Jones et al. 1994: 203)

It should be emphasized that not all the recent changes were opposed by the police. The Criminal Justice and Public Order Act 1994 which, among other provisions, controversially strengthened the public order power of the police and altered the nature of the 'right to silence' (a long-time ACPO goal) was influenced by, among other groups and actors, ACPO. Here, however, the authority and autonomy of the police were not being threatened.

There were no special major legislative initiatives in New Zealand to encompass the police under the New Public Management agenda. The public sector reforms there were marked by the introduction of generic pieces of legislation which included all relevant bodies. As such, the police were merely included in the State Sector Act 1988 (relating primarily to employment and contractual issues) and the Public Finance Act 1989. However, entirely with-out parliamentary and public debate, some concessions were made to the particular constitutional position of the police. The New Zealand Police is not one of the core departments listed under the State Sector Act, reflecting its 'arms-length' distancing from the accountability arrangements under the Act between public servants and ministers. The Commissioner of Police, as a 'statutory officer' along with the Solicitor-General, the State Services Commissioner and the Controller and Auditor-General, is exempt from the employment provisions of the State Sector Act. Nevertheless, the Commissioner enters into a 'Memorandum of Understanding' with the Minister of Police which gives the Commissioner operational independence on issues relating to the 'rule of law', but also sets out the mutually agreed outputs and performance criteria that are to be found in the performance agreements between 'ordinary' chief executives and their ministers (Kay 1996: 24).

The New Zealand Police Association opposed aspects of Labour's state restructuring programme and, in general, there were tensions between the police administration and the Association. It has lobbied the Minister of Police for its favoured candidate for appointment to Commissioner and in 1990 it organized a march on Parliament against the superannuation provisions of the State Sector Restructuring Bill 1989 (McGill 1992: 183).

In 1989, the police themselves were the target of an inquiry. The Cabinet Expenditure Review Committee (see McLeay 1995: 92–101) set up a review of the 'organizational requirements of the New Zealand Police' (Strategos 1989: 6). The key issue was the efficient use of resources. The recommendations included the absorption by the police of the Traffic Department, hitherto part of the Ministry of Transport – not a decision backed by many police. The National Government which won the 1990 election implemented this change in 1992. Strategos criticized the strategic planning and financial management of the police (and there were some changes after report's publication), and advocated some privatization (generally not heeded). It observed that between 1979/80 and 1988/89 expenditure on the police had risen in real terms by 61 per cent (Strategos 1989: 20), a figure challenged publicly by the police. Strategos argued that, in accordance with the public sector reforms, 'policy and advisory roles as a general rule ought to be separate from administrative and operational roles' (p. 29). After observing that there were particular constitutional difficulties in treating the police in exactly the same way as other state agencies, the report concluded that there should be a Ministry of Police: 'Clearly . . . a Minister with no policy-making backup outside the police hierarchy may be at a serious disadvantage in seeking to assume a policy-making role' (Strategos 1989: 45). It noted that the then Department of Justice evidently did not contribute to police policy: '[W]e were told that "the appropriate role for the Police is not a matter to which the [Justice] department has given any detailed consideration" ' (Strategos 1989: 45). Accountability between Minister and Commissioner should be clarified and a Law Enforcement Committee (relevant ministers and chief executives) on the lines of the Australian Commonwealth government should be created. None of the latter three structural and constitutional changes were implemented.

The New Zealand Police also fall within the ambit of the Public Finance Act 1989, one of the defining pieces of legislation of the New Public Management revolution in New Zealand. Government was seen as a purchaser of outputs from the public sector appropriate for the fulfilment of government's specified outcomes. The New Zealand Police, like nearly all other public sector agencies, is in a contractual relationship with government, and has worked out its budgeted outputs with the responsible Minister. Like all other parts of the public sector, the police specify performance measures. All these agreements are carefully monitored by New Zealand's powerful Treasury.

The Police Association objected to many of the recent changes. One complaint was that the police, particularly the Commissioner, had become increasingly identified with government under the new public sector rules. A former President, Steve Hinds, said of the then Commissioner that: 'Instead of heading a team he would never rat on, the commissioner now qualified any commitment with comment about his responsibility to government, to saving money, to being efficient and effective; his contract made him accountable' (McGill 1992: 187).

The New Zealand Police have also been part of an overall governmental agenda-setting design. For the 1993 general election the National Government published a document entitled *Path to 2010*. After the return of National to office, the State Services Commission, building on that document, developed a series of Strategic Result Areas for the period 1994–7. The Department of Prime Minister and Cabinet has also had a key role in this process (Boston *et al.* 1996: 282–3). Under the area of 'Community Security' there are six objectives relevant to police (Department of Prime Minister and Cabinet 1995b: 8). Chief executives in New Zealand include Key Result Areas (relevant and specific to their portfolios) in their performance contracts and they are also reflected in the departmental corporate plans. The police have a strategic plan which specifies values, goals, objectives, strategies and programmes. These now fit into the rather vaguer SRAs. The National Steering Committee of the Police identified in 1995 seven strategies that defined priorities for the next two years and which are contained in the corporate plan. Therefore, there is now input from ministers through the performance agreement, the specification of outputs and the budgetary allocations.

Such new goals and mechanisms have placed the responsible ministers in both states in more proactive roles. State fiscal problems, the reformulated priorities that have been the product of the New Public Management, and rising crime rates have all facilitated governments to assume greater control of the police. But, although the recent legal and management changes have grasped back a measure of policy initiative to central government and, in so doing, given the responsible ministers a greater role in directing policy objectives, this role change has not been accompanied by the ministers assuming full ministerial responsibility for their actions in the parliamentary and public arenas. In a sense, it was a more extensive bureaucratic control that was being sought and exercised over the police, a control that actually served to expand the state policy network on policing issues. It may be also that 'Bureaucratic control of the police may impel political intrusion . . . as much as political control. Politicians are not the only politically interested persons' (Bayley 1979: 135).

The crucial decisions outlined above were all made by state actors, with some input by advisory commissions or private sector advisers. They were the product of both governmental frustration with policing – especially the case in Britain – and the changing fashions of public management. In both states the policy networks that these decisions revealed were confined to central government bureaucrats and top police officers; the rank and file had only limited access to the decision-making processes and even more limited impact on the direction of the decisions themselves. Except on issues relating to civil liberties, non-state groups had no influence whatsoever, a point I return to later. Before then, however, another series of central state initiatives, relevant to the changing scope of the policing policy network, needs to be discussed.

Policing and criminal justice

In Britain since the late 1980s, some central government initiatives developed, aimed at controlling crime, which have involved state agencies other than the Home Office and ACPO. In 1990 the National Criminal Intelligence Service, accountable to the Home Secretary, was formed against the wishes of the police sectoral groups, and the creation of the Crime Prevention Agency was announced in 1995, bringing together 'the three main organizations involved in crime prevention – the Home Office, the Association of Chief Police Officers and Crime Concern, in partnership with business and others' (Home Office 1996). ACPO unsuccessfully opposed the 1992 creation of the National Criminal Intelligence Service, especially its operational functions, perhaps thereby reducing its effectiveness (Hilliard 1994).

In 1991, a Criminal Justice Consultative Council was based in the Home Office, chaired by a Lord Justice, and comprising members from the criminal justice system, government departments, the police and social services. This was described recently by a Chief Constable as a substantial new development which provides 'a national forum in which progress can be made, a mechanism for sorting out the "rubbing points" in the system'; a means, along with the Area Criminal Justice Liaison Committees and Local Court Users' Groups, 'for policy makers and practitioners to come together' (Hoddinott 1994: 2). A Scottish Crime Council was also established. These agencies can be seen as efforts of the state to cope with rising levels of crime by moving towards a more integrated criminal justice policy.

The Law Commission in New Zealand, established in 1985, became involved in the research and advocacy of legislation or legal processes, often relating to the work of the police. (In 1996, for example, the Law Commission was leading research on women and the law, an area which involves the police.) In addition, against police views (New Zealand Police 1989: Paper 21), a Serious Fraud Office was established. In the mid-1990s, New Zealand policing policy began to involve quite extensively the Ministry of Justice which, rather like the Home Office, leads by commissioning research and developing policy. The Department of Prime Minister and Cabinet had housed several major policy reform initiatives after National took office in 1990. A Crime Prevention Unit was situated there after National's 1993 election win and was still there in 1997, partly because of disagreements on where it should be permanently stationed. The Unit advised the government on the strategic development of crime prevention and established a network of 'safer communities' (Department of Prime Minister and Cabinet 1995a). Furthermore, in 1995 the restructuring of the Department of Justice was announced. The Department was replaced with a Department of Courts, a Department of Corrections and a Ministry of Justice. The press release made it clear that the government was pursuing an integrated criminal justice strategy, with better use of law enforcement information and a Ministry with an improved policy capacity, capable of leading policy development and providing advice on desired outputs and results across the relevant agencies, including the police (Eckhoff 1995). The Ministry included a Criminal Justice Group and a Strategic Responses to Crime concentration within the Strategic Assessment Group. Thus, the policing policy network within the state was expanded. Further confirmation of this trend was the announcement of the Justice Sector Information Strategy to encourage agencies such as the Police, Transport, Social Welfare, Corrections and Justice to take a common approach on data definition and protocols for communications between computer systems (King 1996: 2). (Note that New Zealand has a Privacy Act to protect citizens' confidentiality.)

Both countries, therefore, show that the central state has recently expanded the agencies concerned with policing policies, attempts which can be construed as efforts to widen the regular policy network of policing and provide contestability to practitioners' views and advice. In the case of Britain, this expanded the policy network of policing whilst, at the same time, reinforcing the centralizing New Public Management trends. In the case of New Zealand, the changes widened slightly the number of agencies involved in the policy network without affecting that country's highly centralized policy-making processes.

The policy networks

There is no doubt that there are established networks in the policing policy sectors of both New Zealand and Britain. As the preceding analysis indicates, they comprise inner arenas of state bureaucrats and senior police officers and outer circles comprised of sporadic and issue-related sectoral pressure groups. The core participants are drawn from a very narrow set of groups and institutions who have 'frequent, high-quality interaction' on 'all matters related to the policy issue' (Marsh and Rhodes 1992: 251, Table 11:1). These tight policy networks are predominantly state employees, albeit from different bureaucracies and political groupings; elected representatives are only occasionally involved. The imposition of New Public Management reforms on the police, and the expansion of the number of state agencies involved in policing, was at least in part a response to the atrophy of the policing policy networks. The agencies involved in implementing these changes again confirmed the narrowness of the policy network, although the examples given showed a new exercise of political will over policy practitioners, a reversal of the comparative power relationships.

The core participants – top police officers and bureaucrats – certainly do not always agree with one another. They may share common basic values but they also disagree on the ways to pursue certain (often agreed) ends. They share interests, but their working policy environments are different. One group lives in the world of government agencies where they must both listen to the elected government and, at the same time, negotiate with other central governmental agencies and protect their own careers and bureaucratic strength. The other group lives in the world of policing practitioners and local and regional responsibilities. But they have a common interest in maintaining a stable policy environment.

A marked feature of the radical changes outlined above was the absence of non-state actors in the policy formulation process. This really only becomes obvious when other policy areas that have undergone structural change are compared to policing. When the Thatcher Government implemented its policy on the sale of state houses, for example, housing pressure groups lobbied government and used the media to put their case. When the Lange Government implemented its policy of local control of schools in New Zealand, a wide-ranging group of interests expressed their views to the government. In one case the non-state actors had no perceptible impact on the decision and in the other their impact was limited, demonstrating that the determined political will of single-party majority governments is difficult to thwart. But the involvement of non-state actors in these other issues showed that there was a pattern of expectations about how the policy network normally operated. In the case of the policing structural changes, the only participants in the policy debates were the state actors themselves and a smattering of interested lawyers.

The evidence has been in both Britain and New Zealand that, as far as national, rather than local, policing policy is concerned, it is difficult for non-governmental actors to have a real impact on police decisions and actions. It appears that actors and groups beyond the bureaucratic and sectoral organizations appear as influential players only on some issues and occasions.

At the national level, the identity of non-state players who have influenced policy has depended on the issue concerned. When key actors attract attention by their behaviour they stimulate public attention on the police. Police corruption of all sorts has gained the attention of civil rights and lawyers' organizations and police violence has attracted the notice of similar sorts of voluntary and sectional groups. This happened with the policing of the controversial Springbok Tour in New Zealand in 1981 and the miners' strike in Britain in 1984. Also, trends in public opinion and ideological shifts have brought new groups with an interest in policing into public focus. The outstanding example is the role played by the women's movement on violence to women, especially Rape Crisis Centres and the Women's Refuge organizations. In each of the two states women have lobbied both to improve the law (and its interpretation and practices) and to improve policing attitudes and practices towards women. In parts of Britain and in New Zealand generally women associated with these issues now regularly address police recruits and have close links with police. Furthermore, policing policy (although not always the practice and culture of policing) on these issues has been profoundly affected by women's political involvement. Another, different, sort of example is that of roads and traffic, where the transport lobbies have had some sporadic input into policing.

But, in general, pressure group involvement has been a limited phenomenon in policing policy; the public's role is generally passive and group involvement tends to be irregular and related to specific, fairly narrowly defined issues. There was no evidence that, during the change processes discussed above, non-state groups such as single-issue groups played any part whatsoever in the policy formation process. There are pressure groups such as civil liberties groups who have a continuing interest in criminal justice as broadly conceived, including policing, but there is no regular network comparable with, for example, those which exist in both countries on environmental, housing and welfare issues.

Non-state groups have become involved when there is disagreement between the police sectoral groups and government. The issue of the 'right to silence', for example, much criticized by the police, involved the legal profession and civil liberties groups. Sometimes policy failure has involved non-state organizations whose ideas and/or support are seen as politically necessary. An example was when the National Association for the Care and Resettlement of Offenders (NACRO) was involved in influencing crime prevention policies during the 1980s and was regularly consulted on this issue (Jones et al. 1994). But there are no non-state pressure groups involved in policing policy on a regular basis.

Thus, it appears that the wider issue networks that appear in policing, as Rhodes and Marsh observe about issue networks generally, are unstable, have large numbers of members and have limited vertical interdependence (1992: 14). As a generalization:

> the consumers of the policy – the citizens – are not organised and do not influence policy outcomes except in a general way through the ballot box . . . In contrast to other policy areas such as social minorities, there are no distinct groups representing the 'users' or the 'beneficiaries' of the policy.
> (Ritchie 1992: 203)

Conclusions: institutions, issues and networks

Despite the different police structures in Britain and New Zealand, policing policy in each of these two states is characterized by a very narrow policy network exhibiting professional and bureaucratic dominance and weak inputs from citizens, whether in their roles as representatives or lobbyists. Both states have had some, not all, of the elements of full-scale policy communities (Rhodes and Marsh 1992: 13).

Until the changes of the late 1980s and the 1990s, policing demonstrated stability in relationships, relationships derived from actors' structural positions regarding state coercion and regulation. Policing policy networks had continuity of membership; and they had vertical interdependence based on shared service delivery and responsibilities. Overall, there has been a high degree of consensus relating to the primary values of policing. Nevertheless, policing policy networks are not wholly insulated from other networks and the general public as the examples of violence to women and the tendency towards forms of community policing and involvement have shown. Furthermore, because the policing sector is closely connected with the broader criminal justice policy area, and is reliant on the legal system, policing issues overlay with these other aspects of public policy and the sectoral independence of policing is thus compromised. The policing sector exhibits the characteristics of a policy network that is dominated by a core of state employees: policy makers, regulators, and practitioners. It is not, however, a policy community.

A further point about this comparison relates to how sectoral ideology underpins the shape and nature of policing policy. The doctrine of constabular independence has acted as a defence against policy expansion, even within government (legislature and executive) and especially against citizens' organizations. This ideological feature, so characteristic of the politics of the police, is not to be found in other policy areas. The construction and perpetuation of an inner policy arena was enabled by the doctrine of constabulary independence. Moreover, policing has been characterized by soft-edged policy definition, allowing the key actors to compress and expand policies to suit their own purposes. It is not surprising then, that in order for elected politicians to have more influence on policing, the structures themselves have had to be challenged.

There might be a case for arguing that New Zealand's small size, plus its centralized police force, combine to create a policy network that is markedly more reliant on interpersonal influence than on structural forces, more similar perhaps to the police regions than the central policing network of Britain. Nevertheless, it is the structure of policing itself in relation to the state in both our examples that is the predominant determining characteristic of policing policy. Structure, in the future, might change substantially as a result of the internationalization of policing (across borders and through modern communications systems) and the breaking down of state sovereignty (McLaughlin 1992). These developments will impact more on European Britain than New Zealand, isolated in the South Pacific.

The contrasting organizational structures, however, do affect the potential, legitimate policy participants within the overall structural similarities. The British devolved system expands the policy network; simple centralization as in the New Zealand case keeps the policy network very small and elite-dominated. To some extent this has affected public debate and political argument about the police. Because in Britain there are other actors in policing with legitimate and legal, if ill-defined, roles, there has been a public debate about accountability. This debate is absent in New Zealand. However, in Britain, the decentralized structure has actually tended to enhance professional influence against political control, cementing the influence in particular of the senior police officers working through ACPO. This has also meant, as the comparison of the implementation of government's recent objectives has shown, that it has been more difficult to implement change in Britain than in New Zealand.

In both states, however, politicians, working though bureaucratic mechanisms, have sought to control and influence the direction of policing. This has had the effect of expanding the number of state bureaucracies with a legitimate and continuing interest in policing. Simultaneously, the autonomy of the traditional policing policy state network has been challenged; 'policing' has increasingly been subsumed into the broader sector of 'criminal justice', introducing further influential agencies and, moreover, groups outside the state. It might be that policing policy in future becomes part of this wider sectoral network.

Historically, legislative influence on the police has been limited. Political debate about policing alternatives has been scarcely productive, concentrating on police numbers. Is there something about Westminster systems of government that not only depoliticizes policing but also removes it almost altogether from within the ambit of representative political systems? Perhaps dominantly two-party systems, because they are divided mainly by socio-economic differences, deal inadequately with social values and issues relating to civil and criminal rights. Or perhaps, conversely, it is because democratic states in general are aware of the potential dangers of politicizing policing. But the evidence presented in this chapter is limited indeed. We need to look also at policing in multi-party systems. New Zealand in the future will provide a fascinating case study. The evidence of this chapter, however, is that the nature of policing itself tends to limit citizen involvement in this issue.

8

Sociometric mapping techniques and the comparison of policy networks: economic decision making in Leeds and Lille

Peter John and Alistair Cole

Political scientists frequently deploy the network metaphor. In particular, students of public policy utilize the idea to illuminate the complexity of contemporary decision making. The concepts of 'issue network' and 'policy community' are useful simplifications of the complex relationships between the many organizations involved in policy making and implementation. Whether the policy sector is health, education or transport, decision makers are just as likely to be in interest groups, agencies and parastatal bodies as well as from traditional bureaucracies and political parties. The network idea captures neatly the phenomenon of shared decision making and the way in which organizations exchange resources to achieve their goals.

Yet, at the end of the 1990s, disillusion has set in. As discussed in Chapter 1, critics such as Dowding (1995) believe that policy networks is a descriptive concept and does not explain why decision making takes a particular course at a particular time. When applied by the case study researcher, the ascription of a type of network in a policy sector oversimplifies rather than enlightens. The lack of precision can undermine even the modest claims of the research approach. How does the researcher know that policy making in agriculture is a closed community? The very ease of applying networks suggests they are just another name for political action. Policy networks is an approach that disguises the conflicts and bargains at the centre of political relationships.

In the UK at least, the debate about policy networks has largely side-stepped the long tradition of social network or sociometric analysis that a generation of scholars have applied to anthropological and sociological research problems. Political scientists in the US and in the rest of Europe have recently used sociometric analysis. Yet political scientists in the UK and elsewhere often believe the proposal to map networks is quirky or misguided. How can drawing the 'stars' and shapes of networks tell researchers much about decision making? Are not lines and graphs a fruitless attempt to quantify the unquantifiable? To add to the cynicism, some notable commentators criticize the method. Rod Rhodes, in his study of intergovernmental relations in the UK, regards case studies and 'thick' descriptions as superior to the mapping of the relationships (1986: 4, 358). Rhodes argues elsewhere that 'definitional and theoretical proliferation prevail and social network analysis tends to be preoccupied with description and the measurement of linkages' (1990: 295). Keith Dowding is also sceptical about how much insight formal analysis can deliver when he writes that 'network analysis has proved inadequate in providing fully determined causal analysis of particular networks in structural terms' (1995: 158).

In response to both the criticisms of case study-driven policy network accounts and formal analysis, this chapter examines the application and utility of sociometric mapping techniques for policy-orientated research. The argument of the chapter is that sociometric network analysis supplies a kit of research tools to assist the understanding of the structure and functioning of networks. In particular, the method usefully assists the comparison of policy networks in different contexts, particularly between nation states. The confirmation and rejection of hypotheses of network structure advances knowledge as a supplement though not as a replacement for case study methods.

Formal network analysis can help solve one of the classic questions in comparative politics – whether the nature of the policy sector drives decision making or whether national institutions and cultures are the factors. In the former approach, it is policy that determines politics (as in Lowi's (1972) famous formulation); in the latter, state traditions and cultures make policy unique to each national context (Dyson 1980). To find this out the chapter compares and contrasts the structure of urban economic policy networks in one large city in England – Leeds, and another in France – Lille.

Network analysis

Formal network analysis is a method of measuring and analysing relationships among a group of actors. After ascertaining who or which bodies are in the network, researchers count the occurrence or frequency of interactions between the participants and derive measures of the structure of the network. There are two main types of network. The first is an *egocentric* network which is the personal relationships of an actor perceived by her or him, and is extensively used in anthropological and sociological studies (e.g. Wellman 1979).

The second is the whole network of relationships. Political scientists are generally interested in the latter type so they can understand the properties of policy-making systems, though it would be interesting to know more about the contrasting personal networks of each actor.

The most common unit of measurement in a network is contact – either whether a contact takes place between an actor or not, or its frequency measured in units of time. There is, however, no intellectual restriction on what constitutes a relationship in a network. Indeed, the many sociological studies use a variety of measures (see Scott 1991 and Wasserman and Faust 1994 for reviews of the large literature). Examples include exchanges of resources (Baker 1990), memberships of company boards (Mariolis 1983; Mintz and Swartz 1985; Scott 1986) and marriages between families (Padgett and Ansell 1993). Sociometric analysis only measures relationships; it is up to the investigator to determine which ones are important and what they mean.

Political scientists use a similar set of relationships to sociologists, such as resource flows between organizations or overlapping memberships; though the most frequently used measure is the frequency of contacts. Contacts can be formal records of links between bodies, examining, for example, the ones that give evidence together to a legislative committee, or can be divined by questionnaires, structured interviews or diaries. Whatever the measure and the means of acquiring information, researchers can code the relationships between key actors and create a matrix where the actors are both rows and columns. This is called a graph if the relationships are binary, i.e. 1 or 0, or a value graph if there are frequencies of interaction, say between 0 and 5. Researchers usually enter the graph into a text editor and then import it into one of the commonly used network analysis computer programmes, such as UCINET IV, GRADAP or STRUCTURE, which then produce the measures of network structure (see Scott 1991: 176–82 for a review of the software packages).

Underlying the analysis of network structure, there is a substantial body of mathematics called graph theory. The social scientist can proceed without a detailed knowledge of this literature except to understand how the computer programmes produce the sociometric measures (see Wasserman and Faust 1994 for a review). The difficulty emerges in trying to interpret what types of political phenomena these measures capture. The most commonly used measure is *density* which measures the ratio of the number of interactions in a network with the total possible ties. In value graphs, density is the frequency of interaction as a proportion of the total possible ties. The concept is simple, and researchers deploy it to understand the extent to which actors interact. It gives an idea about the closeness of relationships and their importance to network participants. The problem is that it is difficult to compare network density because the score tends to decrease with network size (Scott 1991: 76). Because the relationship between network density and size is non-linear, Scott recommends a complex formula to compensate. However, the solution requires information on the circumference of the network which is hard to calculate.

Another common measure is network *centrality* which tries to capture the property of actors in terms of their links with others (Freeman 1979). In common-sense terms this measures the extent to which communication within a network passes through an actor. For example, the middle point in a 'star' of relationships has a high centrality score. Political scientists are interested in centrality because researchers can deduce what kind of policy network it is from whether the network is dominated by bureaucratic, political or private sector decision makers (see John and Cole 1995; John forthcoming). It is the people who have high centrality scores in the network who have important decisional and meditative roles, and who are the key to understanding the circulation of ideas and decisions to act collectively, particularly when the individuals are in different organizations.

There are various measures of centrality. The simplest is *degree* centrality which is derived from counting the number of adjacent links between an actor and the others. The measure is of limited use because it does not capture the property of a network as a whole. *Closeness* calculates centrality for both direct and indirect links. It is a score calculated by measuring the extent to which an actor can most easily reach others through the shortest number of jumps across the network. *Betweenness* measures the extent to which actors fall between pairs of other actors showing the extent to which they intermediate between others in the network. Finally, the *Bonacich* (1987) measure of centrality is the actor's summed connections in the network weighted by the centrality of other actors. The score captures the idea that it is not just centrality on its own that is important but the relationships between central points, a global concept, and based on the idea that actors have more power if they are connected to other points that are not central.

Centrality is a useful measure when attempting to understand the structure of the network. However, it is less useful for the rigorous comparison of networks. It is here that measures of *structural equivalence* are relevant. Structural equivalence identifies common positions among actors based on their linkages. It is a mathematical property of subsets of actors in a network. Actors are structurally equivalent if they have identical ties to and from all other actors in the network. What the analysis does is to pick out groups of actors who have similar relationships to others, often by applying clustering techniques.

There are several methods of calculating structural equivalence. One is to factor analyse the correlations of the rows of a graph to create groups of actors who are equivalent. The procedure can be done hierarchically through the CONCOR iterative algorithm. CONCOR produces a tree map of groups of actors: a *dendogram*. Though social network researchers frequently deploy CONCOR, network theorists criticize it because the subdividing procedure distorts the selection of the actors in each group (Scott 1991: 135–41). Less problematically, other iterative procedures, such as the TABU search (Glover 1989, 1990) and the CATJI routines (Kilsworth and Bernard 1974), produce non-hierarchically derived groups of structurally equivalent actors. Finally, it is possible to create visual representations of the distances between actors to compare networks, a method the empirical section of this chapter uses.

As well as density, centrality and structural equivalence, there are a battery of other measures. For example, there are *cliques*, subgroups within networks; *blockmodels*, which are partitions of actors into subsets; and *regular equivalence* which is a measure of the extent to which actors are similar rather than identical. To become familiar with these measures, the reader should once again consult Scott (1991) and Wasserman and Faust (1994) as well as the host of articles in the *Journal of Mathematical Sociology, Social Networks, American Journal of Sociology, Psychometrika* and other journals.

Political scientists have applied many of these techniques (see Knoke 1990 and Dowding 1995: 150–8 for reviews). The earliest is the classic community power study of Atlanta carried out by Floyd Hunter (1953) who draws sociograms of the elite – visual representations of the linkages between key actors. He uses these maps of relationships to support the idea that close-knit elites rule cities. The community power studies of German and US towns, carried out by Laumann, Pappi and others in the 1970s, employ the measures of centrality, density and cliques (Laumann and Pappi 1973, 1976; Galaskiewicz 1979). A later study examines the differences in policy networks in US energy and health (Laumann and Knoke 1987) which deploys an array of network measures, such as multidimensional scaling of the distances between actors. In contrast, Heinz and his colleagues find the absence of a core to a network in their study of Washington elites (Heinz *et al.* 1993). Another group of researchers explore the similarities and differences in labour policy networks between the US, Germany and Japan (Knoke *et al.* 1996). The comparative research discovers that state traditions and histories of government intervention in the economy are important sources of variation in network structure.

Criticisms of formal network analysis

There are a number of criticisms of the utility of network analysis for the study of public policy. First, it is not clear what networks measure. What do the respondents mean when they specify their contacts? Some political relationships are symbolic or ceremonial; some interactions may be operational or to do with implementing policy; and others may be about policy choices. Is the research to incorporate all these interactions or only some of them? It is possible that networks merely reflect the ephemera of politics rather than show important relationships or illuminate political power. The response to this criticism is that interviewers may make clear to respondents what their contacts involve. At the same time, contacts are important over and above power relationships because actors seek to engage in networking for information, friendship and trust, all of which are important in ensuring cooperation and effective policy making. That relationships do not reduce to a series of short-term instrumental exchanges between actors is a testament to the importance of networks in contemporary governance.

Second, the boundaries of networks are unclear (Laumann *et al*. 1992). On the one hand, network measures require a precise graph; on the other, policy networks are by definition diffuse and shade into each other. It would seem that the precise measures used in network analysis impose an arbitrary simplicity onto a complex world. The response is that it is possible to find boundaries to networks because research usually finds that, while there are a small number of core actors (e.g. Laumann and Knoke 1987), network members are much less involved if the policy sector is not their main concern. The arbitrariness of the network boundary does not greatly affect the network scores as the marginal actors have few links to the core membership. Thus, for example, the decision whether to include a middle-ranking economic development officer or not does not make much difference to the analysis. Also some sampling techniques, such as the 'snowball' (Goodman 1961), where the researcher gradually acquires the network sample, are sensitive to network boundaries (see Wasserman and Faust 1994: 34–5).

The third criticism is that network analysis is usually cross-sectional and only provides a snapshot of very fluid sets of relationships. If networks change rapidly, it is hard to generalize precisely about what set of relationships the network measures capture. The response is again to be careful in collecting the data. Interviewers may ask respondents to specify the time period over which the contacts occurred. At the same time, the rigorous comparison of networks, as shown later in this chapter, can remedy some of the limitations of cross-sectional data. In addition, some recent studies have begun to measure change over time (e.g. König 1997).

Fourth, it is not possible to decide who or what are the actors. Many, if not most, policy network accounts assume that organizations form the networks (Rhodes 1988; Marsh and Rhodes 1992) as they have the ability to exchange resources. In sociological analysis, however, individuals are the building blocks. It is very hard to summarize the relationships in terms of frequency of contact between organizations because the relationships are complex and made up of a multitude of different contacts. On the other hand, individuals act in an organizational capacity. However, it is possible to overcome some of the ambiguity by assuming that the networks are the property of individuals while being aware of their organizational roles.

Finally, as the quotations by Rhodes and Dowding at the beginning of this chapter indicate, many researchers believe the considerable effort spent collecting and analysing network data yields only the obvious or very little. There is precious little value added by an approach that produces such unsurprising findings as the fact that there is a core to a network (e.g. Laumann and Knoke 1987) or that network centrality is correlated with power (Brass and Burkhardt 1992). It is true that the results from formal network analysis are not always staggering. However, there are important findings and debates. For example, Laumann and Knoke (1987) identify differences in network structures between policy sectors. There is a fruitful discussion about whether networks have a core or not (Knoke *et al*. 1996: 121) which shows that it is not

ous that networks are structured in a particular way. The progress of the
...rch programme so far shows that researchers are in the process of develop-
...theories, refining empirical tests and debating the multifarious results. Network analysis is not an empirical dead end.

Economic policy in Leeds and Lille

The research project investigated economic policy networks in Leeds and Lille
using both network analysis and qualitative methods. The latter involved interviewing decision makers and collecting primary and secondary documents. A
subsequent section describes the method of generating the sociometric data.
This section gives a brief description of the character of the two cities so as to
understand their similarities and differences (for further details see John and
Cole forthcoming).

Leeds

Leeds is one of the major provincial English cities alongside Birmingham,
Manchester and Newcastle. It has a population of about 800,000 with a dynamic economy and is the administrative centre for the region of Yorkshire
and Humberside. Leeds City Council dominates the local government scene.
Its area is physically large, 213 square miles, extending far into the rural hinter-
land and beyond. The council employs about 36,000 people, has a budget
of about £500m and is a major landowner in the city. Even apart from its
statutory functions, it is a powerful economic player. The other public sector
economic organizations in Leeds at the time of the research were the Urban
Development Corporation (UDC) (wound up at the end of March 1995) and a
Training and Enterprise Council (TEC) set up in 1989 to run government
training and to give business leadership to local enterprise policies. The former
organization was a short-life central government redevelopment body, with
responsibility for planning and housing in two smaller areas of the city; the
latter agency signalled the greater importance of central government in local
decisions which disrupted local networks. Leeds and Bradford Chamber of
Commerce and Industry represents a good deal of the private sector. At the
regional level, called Yorkshire and Humberside, there is an integrated government office for the region, created in April 1994, unifying the four central
government departments of state with regional organizations.

Since 1980 Leeds has had two Labour leaders. The first was George
Mudie between 1980 and 1989, now MP for Leeds East, a former union
official, a very able administrator and political operator; the second was Jon
Trickett from 1989 to 1996. Trickett was an interesting blend of old and new.
He adopted new ideas, for example on transport, women's and green issues and
on local economic development policy. There was a new direction in local
economic development policy initiated when Trickett came to power. Trickett believed in an integrated approach, involving partnership with other actors.

He sought to persuade leading people of Leeds's vitality as a competitive and European city, an attribute that could be enhanced through marketing, by creating a high technology and service centre and by competing for government programmes. The leader hoped to forge a problem-solving network by creating a consensus among the key elites. The result was the Leeds Initiative, a public–private economic development partnership body, formed in 1990. The network was based on an alliance between the city and the chamber, with the TEC, UDC and universities playing a lesser role.

The key factor that affects local economic policy in Leeds is its unique economy. Leeds is a compact urban regional centre with thriving financial, insurance and legal service sectors that grew rapidly during the 1980s. The dynamism of the private sector gives it a more prominent role in driving policy than in other northern cities. Though business is diversified, it often comes together to promote Leeds as a centre. There is a natural culture of cooperation in the city that has its expression in public decisions whether it is about contributing to causes or joining public–private partnerships.

Lille

Lille is the principal city in northern France, a densely populated urban area similar to British northern cities with their manufacturing traditions and problems of industrial decline. It is a metropolitan area with several centres. The Lille urban community has almost 1,200,000 inhabitants spread across 85 communes. Because of its size and importance in the metropole, Lille is the principal commune, but the urban area is not an integrated city like Leeds. The former textile towns of Roubaix (100,000) and Tourcoing (90,000) retain a spirit of independence from Lille while the new town of Villeneuve d'Ascq (65,000) is a competitor for service provision and higher education facilities.

The complex local and central government structures in the Lille area have an impact on the way the networks function. In France the spatial extent of the economic policy network is less clear than in the UK as there is an overlap of communal, intercommunal, departmental and regional networks; and each have some of the same powerful individuals in them. The Lille commune network is at the core of decision making. The leading figure is the mayor, Pierre Mauroy, a former prime minister who personally promoted major economic development projects in Lille, such as the international rail link, the new train station and Euralille (the commercial and shopping complex attached to the new station). As a traditional *notable*, Mauroy not only holds two elected offices (mayor of Lille and senator), but presides over a broad range of para-public agencies (in particular several mixed economy societies, the French version of the public–private partnership). Within the Lille metropolitan area, important institutional roles are also performed by the other subnational authorities: by the Lille Urban Community responsible for much urban policy (CUDL), by the Nord Department and by the Nord/Pas-de-Calais Region. Apart from a greater number of local authorities, the power of local agencies of the state sets the French system apart from the UK, the two main ones being the DRIRE (the industry ministry) and the SGAR (the regional prefecture). The DRIRE distributes and determines the most central government grants to firms; the SGAR administers European union grants and negotiates the state–region planning contracts.

Other elected actors also play a role in urban policy. There exists a long tradition of business organization in Lille, manifested in a powerful and original regional employers' union, and in an integrated and effective chamber of commerce covering Lille, Roubaix and Tourcoing. A range of other public, semi-public and private actors input directly or indirectly into local economic development policy. Large firms and employers' organizations were reluctant to participate in the development of local economic development networks. Representatives of large firms and the employers' federations tend to place more importance on lobbying in Paris and the European Commission.

The comparative method and Franco-British urban studies

Network research thrives on the single case study. The sheer complexity of networks encourages investigators to examine one policy in one country. However, the number of generalizations that can be adduced from one example are small. The comparative method, on the other hand, allows the researcher to test hypotheses even with a small number of cases (Collier 1993; Berg-Schlosser and De Meur 1994). By comparing carefully selected cases across nations the investigator can ascertain the relative effect of country institutions and political cultures on the policy process. The contrasts between the history, institutions, culture and economies of Leeds and Lille suggests the deployment of the 'most different' systems design (Przeworski and Teune 1970). By selecting contrasting cases, the investigator can make inferences about the importance of the similarities that do occur whereas in similar cases the researcher can only focus on the differences which may have a number of causes. In effect, if contrasting political institutions operating in their unique political cultures have similar relationships to each other in policy networks it is possible to infer that it is the nature of the policy sector that determines politics as much as political institutions and traditions.

Indeed, comparative studies of British and French local politics generally deploy the argument that policy-making relationships, and by implication networks, differ because the institutional framework, embedded political dependencies and national cultures vary (Lagrove and Wright 1979; Ashford 1982; Page and Goldsmith 1987; Page 1991). The UK is traditionally thought to be a local government-dominated subnational system with centralized local political parties and senior bureaucrats administering a wide range of services in large, democratically elected authorities. Networks are strong between the political leadership and the senior officer cadre, but public sector actors are weakly linked into the local community and into national parties and government. In France, the classic studies of centre–periphery relations emphasized the interpenetration of the centre and the localities by the practice of multiple office holding and found that *notables* (especially mayors of large cities) were able to rely on national political contacts to override resistance from prefects and ministerial field officials (Dupuy and Thoenig 1983). There is bureaucratic competition between the prefectures and the decentralized field services (representatives of the spending ministries). The French system of negotiation between the prefect and leading mayors could, in many senses, be seen as a form of semi-institutionalized bargaining. The 1980s decentralization reforms solidified rather than disrupted this distribution of power (Mabileau 1991).

Traditional portrayals are based in part on historical stereotypes. The portraits derive from only a few studies which, when they are examined closely, reveal a much more complex pattern of relationships than the 'dual elite' of politicians and bureaucrats. For example, Saunders's (1980) account of Croydon shows the proximity of the business elite to the council's leadership. Dunleavy's (1981) study of mass housing reveals the close connections between local political leaders and business interests within the nationalized professional policy communities. Newton's (1976) study of Birmingham reveals there were 4264 pressure groups in the city that had close links with the city council. Similarly, Stoker and Wilson (1986) argue that beneath the ruling facade are the highly complex networks of intraorganizational politics.

Nevertheless, whatever qualifications can be added to the traditional account, the picture of national difference up until the 1970s is consistent with the development of nation states around clear political and constitutional traditions that affected the process of politics at all territorial levels. The question to ask is whether, under the influence of the internationalization of local and national economies and the Europeanization of public policies, this account of nationally different patterns of local decision making has been overtaken by a more open structure in which negotiation takes place in a more trusting public space in wider networks of public and private actors. The hypothesis to be examined here is that recent social, economic and managerial changes have restructured distinct decision-making systems, particularly in sectors like economic development, so that they resemble local governance. Traditional forms of politics, orientated around the formal powers and role of key people in locally elected institutions, have altered toward a more flexible, negotiated and decentred institutional and policy environment that incorporates a wide variety of decision makers including those from the private sector (Cole and John 1995). While Leeds and Lille remain different institutionally, culturally and geographically, the hypothesis is that their role as large metropolitan cities in the new competitive urban governance means they have a similar structure to their networks.

Research methods

The research team ascertained the structure of the network by personally interviewing the key actors and mapping the relationships between them. The research period in each city lasted about six months – Leeds: October 1994 to March 1995 and Lille: July 1994 to January 1995. The researchers drew the first wave of the sample from a local academic expert in each city who listed who were the key actors in economic policy. The researchers then contacted each actor by a letter which asked for a personal interview. If individuals did not reply to the letter, the researchers sent a second letter or made a telephone call repeating the request. If respondents refused to give an interview, excluded themselves or failed to respond, the researchers excluded them from the network unless they were nominated as being in contact on policy issues with at least one other person in the network. This adapts the reputational approach used in most elite studies (see Laumann and Pappi 1973). The researchers created a further wave of respondents by asking interviewees at the end of the interview to suggest other people to include and by noting during the interview the people with whom interviewees said they were in regular contact on economic policy issues, following the well-known snow-balling approach. In addition, to ensure the network was based on the cities rather than on ever-extending numbers of subnational actors, the interviewers excluded second- and subsequent-wave interviewees if they were not nominated as a contact by at least one member of the original list. From this procedure the study identified 64 economic policy actors in Leeds and 73 in Lille.

As an opening question, posed prior to the qualitative semi-structured questions, the interviewers asked each respondent: 'Who are you in regular contact with on local economic development policy issues and how frequent are your contacts?' The interviewer explained that contacts should involve discussions or decisions about policy issues and that contacts include meetings, telephone conversations, personalized letters and electronic mails. The researchers coded responses as: (5) daily/every other day; (4) weekly/fortnightly; (3) monthly; (2) two/three monthly; and (1) six monthly or more. The interviewers gave respondents a two-page questionnaire to complete and send back to the research team after the interview. The questionnaire also asked respondents to specify their contacts in policy on a scale of one to five and the results were cross-checked with the responses in the interviews. The researchers averaged the scores between the interviews and questionnaires in the few cases where the responses were not consistent. Where actors' contacts with each other did not tally the researcher either averaged the frequencies (see Lazer 1995) or, if the scores were adjacent, took the one of the more senior policy maker on the grounds that people on the outside of a policy network are more likely to exaggerate their contacts than those on the inside. Where actors said they were in contact with others but these policy makers did not mention them, the nomination was accepted as were the nominations of someone who refused an interview. The researchers entered these scores into a DOS text editor and imported them as a value graph into SPSS 7.5 for windows to create the distance matrix and to perform the multidimensional scaling.

Derived stimulus configuration
Euclidean distance model

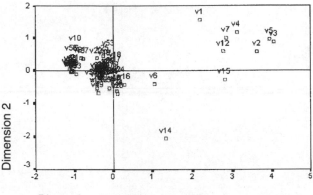

Dimension 1

Stress = .12122   R-squared = .96995

Selected actor key:
v1   F. Hamilton, Chair, Economic Development Committee, Leeds City Council
v2   J. Trickett, Leader, Leeds City Council
v3   E. Anderson, Executive Director of Development, Leeds City Council
v4   P. Smith, Chief Executive Officer, Leeds City Council
v5   J. Siddall, Director, Leeds Initiative, Leeds City Council
v6   B. Walker, Deputy Leader, Leeds City Council
v7   D. Pearce, Chief Executive, Leeds TEC
v10 Representative of Regional Trades Union Congress
v12 P. Coles-Johnson, Director, Leeds and Bradford Chamber of Commerce and
     Industry
v14 D. Richardson, former President, Leeds and Bradford Chamber of Commerce
     and Industry
v15 J. Walker, Regional Director, Government Office for Yorkshire and
     Humberside
v16 E. Holroyd, President, Leeds and Bradford Chamber of Commerce and Industry

Figure 8.1   Spatial distribution of Leeds' economic policy network

Analysis

The analysis investigates whether similar groups of actors are structurally
equivalent in the two cities. Rather than use algorithms to produce dendo-
grams of actors who are structurally equivalent, the results here are a visual
display which is easier to understand, and replicates the method of explanation
used by Knoke *et al.* (1996: 87–100) and other researchers. Such analyses
follow Burt's (1976) use of Euclidean distance to measure structural equivalence. Euclidean distance is the square root of the sum of the squares of the

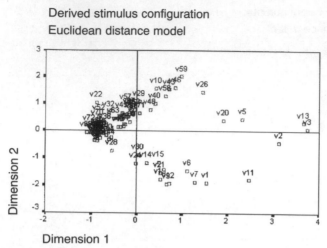

Derived stimulus configuration
Euclidean distance model

Stress = .16300   RSQ = .92214

Selected actor key:

v1   P. Mauroy, Senator-mayor of Lille; President, Lille Urban Community
v2   R. Vandierendonck, Mayor of Roubaix
v3   B. Roman, Economic *adjoint*, Municipality of Lille
v5   R. Caillau, Assistant General-Secretary for Economic Affairs, Municipality of Lille
v6   G. Caudron, Deputy-mayor of Villeneuve d'Ascq
v7   J.-P. Balduyck, Mayor of Tourcoing
v9   M. Hacené, Regional Prefect
v11 R. Thuau, SGAR, Nord/Pas-de-Calais Regional Prefecture
v13 G. Tiébot, President, Lille, Roubaix, Tourcoing Chamber of Commerce 1986–95
v14 P. Delnatte, Vice-president, Departmental Council
v20 F. Ampe, Director, Lille Urban Development Agency
v26 B. Haesebroueck, Director of Strategies and Development, Lille Urban Community

Figure 8.2   Spatial distribution of Lille's economic policy network

added differences between the value of a tie between two actors in its column and row and then its row and column. More formally if x_{ik} is the value of the link between actor i to actor k then

$$d_{ij} = \sqrt[g]{\sum_{k=1}^{g} [(x_{ik} - x_{jk})^2 + (x_{ki} - x_{kj})^2]}$$

for i ≠ k j ≠ k

If actors i and j are structurally equivalent then their entries in the rows and columns are identical and thus the Euclidean distance is zero.

To see the resulting sociomatrix of Euclidean values spatially, it is possible to scale the data on two dimensions. In SPSS, the ALSCAL programme iterates a solution on two dimensions and plots the variables accordingly. Figures 8.1and 8.2 display the Leeds and Lille networks respectively. In general, the smaller the distance between the actors the greater their structural equivalence. Thus, it is the groups of actors in the two-dimensional space who show the property of the network. Each routine creates a stress value. The closer it is to zero the better the fit of the data. There is also an r-squared and stress value that shows the extent to which the plots converge on each other.

Discussion

The mapping in two-dimensional space shows both differences and similarities in the structure of the networks. The main difference is that in Leeds most actors are structurally equivalent to each other with a separate small group of actors quite distinct from the others occupying a more dispersed group. In Lille, there is marginally more dispersion overall. The actors spread out to resemble slightly the 'hollow core' discovered by Heinz and his colleagues. The results suggest more concentration of actors and relationships in the simple unitary local government system in Leeds whereas Lille has more open and dispersed relationships reflecting its complex pattern of subnational governance (the 85 communes, the CUDL, the department and region as well as the layers of the central state). However, in spite of these differences, the networks are quite similar. There is a high concentration in one main group of the less important actors whereas the leading actors are in another group. Both maps show a division between a core of key actors and the rest. Scaling in both cases produces similar stress values and r-square scores. Indeed, the actors in the leading group are similar in each city and comprise the elected leaders, key local government bureaucrats, representatives of the chamber of commerce and key state bureaucrats suggesting the existence of a coalition of actors in economic development based on the private sector and various elements of the local and central state.

Conclusion

Far from being over-technical and too preoccupied with formal issues, sociometric mapping techniques show their worth by being an essential tool to compare networks. Rather than relying just on the impressions gained from the case study method, the researcher can test hypotheses derived from theory and the comparative method by examining similarities and differences in the structure of networks. On the surface Lille and Leeds appear diametrically opposed: Lille has a polycentric urban geography, a fragmented institutional structure and acute economic problems; Leeds has a distinct urban identity, a unitary local government structure and a buoyant economy. The two cities operate in vastly different central–local political systems: the UK with its vast local authorities and separated central state; France with its myriad of powerful communes but with an all-present central state. Yet in governing the local economy, the structures of the networks are surprisingly similar, even though there are a few differences. The results give some modified support to the idea that public and private sector elites are involved in governing large European cities rather than just the representatives of the main institutions – what may be called a European version of regime politics (Harding 1997) – and complement the qualitative findings (John and Cole 1998).

Researchers can trust the results because they apply the same method to collecting the data in each context rather than solely relying on the culture-laden method of interviews and the formal and legal account of decision making conveyed in written documentation. In measuring the contacts between individuals in a network the comparativist is able to ascertain the relative importance of political institutions and cultures as against the ubiquity of policy sectors like economic development in a more competitive international economic context. As such, researchers can weigh up accounts of network relationships in the light of the results from sociometric data analysis.

Acknowledgements

This chapter draws from an Economic and Social Research Council-funded project comparing networks of local decision makers in education and local economic policy in four cities in Britain and France – Leeds, Lille, Southampton and Rennes, part of the Council's local governance programme (grant number L311253047). We are grateful to the ESRC for its support.

Part three

Policy networks at the European level

9

Transnational local authority networking within the European Union: passing fashion or new paradigm?

John Benington and Janet Harvey

Transnational networks are now a key part of the policy development process within the EU, with increasing numbers of local authorities becoming involved. This is reflected in the recent emergence of transnational networks and cross-national networking as fashionable concepts in a wide range of different academic discourses and policy debates. Such debates have, however, largely been framed in terms of transnational networks as abstract concepts or ideal types and there has been little empirical research in this area. There is a need, therefore, for detailed case studies of transnational networks (as institutions) and transnational networking (as a process), located within the wider political economic context.

In this chapter we begin by outlining our research methods and then the changing political economic context for local government in the UK, which has led to an upsurge in transnational networking, particularly in the context of the emerging European Union. We go on to describe the empirical findings from our ESRC case study research into transnational local authority networks. We subsequently focus on the distinctive characteristics of transnational networks and networking which we have identified. We conclude with a discussion of the significance of transnational local authority networks and networking for the policy-making process. We argue that transnational networking is emerging as an additional arena and pattern of politics for UK local authorities, leading to a new politics of horizontal spheres of participation, in addition to the traditional politics of vertical tiers of representation.

Research methods

We have chosen to proceed by way of contextualized case studies, since we share Greenwood's belief that generalization from political theory has done little to date to illuminate the policy-making process in the EU: '[W]ithout a grounding in case studies, theoretical propositions which are based on no more than speculation, however exotic, run a greater risk of misleading' (Greenwood 1994). Similarly, we concur with Greenwood's view that case studies can prove a useful means of studying both collective action and the involvement of private interests in public policy formation.

In view of the fact that transnational local authority networking provides new territory for empirical research, we have focused on the first three stages of Greenwood's five-stage typology for case study methodology: generating description; identifying the issues; and formulating hypotheses. Conducting plausibility probes for candidate theories and full theory assertion constitute the remaining two stages (Greenwood 1994).

The data have been collected by means of in-depth semi-structured interviews, observation and 'shadowing' techniques and the analysis of documentary evidence. We employed a multi-case study approach to maximize the opportunities for comparison and contrast, but, given the complexity of the issues involved in transnational networks, we limited ourselves to a small number of cases (eight). This enabled us to trace the processes in depth, over time and from multiple stakeholder perspectives.

Transnational networks are not a homogeneous category, although it is possible to describe ideal-typical networks and even ideal-typical features of networking. Transnational networks vary in terms of their legal status, composition of governing bodies, accountability mechanisms, relationships to local interest groups/local and regional authorities/the nation state and the supranational state. The form and content of a particular network therefore is shaped within a particular historical, ideological and structural context (Benson 1982; Smith 1993). In arguing for the need for historical, contextualized accounts, Smith (1993) calls for a consideration of the 'wider historical and political context and the examination of particular issue areas' (Smith 1993: 50). Our case studies are, therefore, set in a political economic context, based upon our perspective on the nature of the restructuring of the European market, state and civil society.

We now turn to the specific political economic and social context within which UK local authorities and networks operate.

The changing political, economic and social context for local government in the UK

The relationship between local and central government in the UK has undergone considerable transformation in recent years in the context of structural and ideological changes in both the national and the European state. It may be useful to outline some of these changes.

A fundamental ambiguity surrounds the constitutional basis of local government in the UK. Unlike most continental European countries, Britain does not have a written constitution. This leaves UK local government without a clear constitutionally rooted mandate; instead it is dependent for its legal powers and financial resources upon a sovereign national parliament (see Sanderson 1995). In addition, until 1998 the UK refused to sign the European Charter of Local Self Government, endorsing the value of relative autonomy for local government. The scope of UK local government competence is therefore limited by central government legislation and policy.

Since at least the mid–1970s local government has been the subject of public expenditure cuts and controls. This trend intensified during the 1980s with the increased politicization in central/local governmental relations. Ideologically driven change led to fundamental changes in practice (for example, privatization of services, compulsory competitive tendering and the increased use of legislation to structure local authority action), with central government intervening in local government with greater frequency and force (see, for example, Loughlin 1986; Benington and Stoker 1989).

In addition, there have been simultaneous changes in the European context of local government. First, the economic context for many UK local authorities has been sharply affected by the restructuring of the European economy, in response to the crisis of 'over-production' in several key industrial sectors (e.g. steel, coal, automobiles, agriculture). This has been associated with takeovers, mergers, plant closures, relocations and redundancies, concentrating control over key sectors of European industry in the hands of a smaller number of larger, more powerful, multinational firms (Benington and Taylor 1993). This has been related to a further spatial concentration of European industry, investment, technology and employment, roughly within a golden triangle based on Paris, Frankfurt and Milan.

Second, the social policy context for UK local authorities is changing as a result of the EU's growing involvement and intervention and UK local authorities are increasingly feeling the impact of the spate of new European legislation and initiatives in this area. Furthermore, the Commission's Green and White Papers on Social Policy, and the Medium Term Social Action Plan, suggest that the Commission is now gearing up for a new phase of more active intervention in social policy development. A large number of local authorities also derive benefit from the European structural funds, especially the Social Fund for training projects and the Regional Development Fund for infrastructural projects, to develop new social initiatives. A growing number of local authorities are appointing European officers or setting up European units and sometimes establishing a Brussels office.

Third, the political context for local government has been influenced by the gradual development and integration of the European policy-making process. The creation of the Committee of the Regions (COR) has given regional and local authorities a formal channel of representation and consultation within the EU.

In addition, the EU seems to be developing a distinctive style of politics and policy making, which differs markedly from the recent UK central government tradition. As well as its formal vertical relationships with the member states through the Council of Ministers and national governments, the European Commission is also actively cultivating horizontal relationships with regional and local authorities, and also with voluntary and community organizations (Baine *et al.* 1992).

Against this backcloth, over the past decade many UK local authorities have come to see Strasbourg and Brussels as more sympathetic to their cause than Westminster and Whitehall and there has been much talk of using the EU as a Whitehall bypass.

Contextualized case studies of transnational networking

Given the pressures and incentives for greater involvement of UK local authorities in European activity described above, we were concerned to assess the significance of transnational local authority networking for politics and the policy-making process in UK local authorities. We were interested to explore the rationales of various actors for their involvement in such activity, and its implications, spin-offs, outcomes and significance for different stakeholders in the policy-making process.

Are transnational local authority networks a passing fashion or a lasting phenomenon? Are they merely 'Euro-chic', or do they have a more substantial significance for local politics and policy making? What are the dynamics of the development of transnational networks? What holds some networks together? What pulls others apart? What are their sources of strength and limitation? How much influence are networks able to exercise on eventual outcomes in the policy areas they are seeking to address? In order to consider these and other aspects of European transnational networking, we will review data from two contrasting case studies, drawn from our total of eight case studies.

In selecting case studies, we chose those European transnational networks which involved local authorities as central, although not necessarily exclusive, actors. Our background assumption is that 'governance' can no longer be seen exclusively in terms of the activities of public authorities alone. The governance of local communities now includes partnerships and networks of other actors and agencies (from the public, private, voluntary and community sectors).

Our case studies fell into three broad categories:

● **sectoral networks** which draw together local authorities concerned with the impact on their regional and local economies of the global and European restructuring of key industrial sectors e.g. the Coalfields Communities Campaign (CCC/EURACOM); Motor Industry Local Authority Network (MILAN/CAR); Aerospace Industry Regional and Local Authority Network (AIRLINE); Fashion Industry Network (FINE);

- **spatial/territorial networks** representing the interests of cities and communities in different European member states, with common interests based upon place/space e.g. EuroCities, Middle Sized Cities, Atlantic Arc;
- **thematic networks** organized around specific policy issues, often in the field of social welfare e.g. ELAINE concerned with race, EuroLinkAge concerned with ageing and older people, the European Anti-Poverty Network and Quartiers en Crise concerned with poverty.

The discussion that follows examines the similarities and differences between two of our case studies deriving from different and contrasting categories: European Action for Mining Communities (EURACOM) – a sectoral transnational network, and EuroCities – a spatial network.

European Action for Mining Communities (EURACOM)

The restructuring of the coal and steel industries has been central to the project of European integration since the formation of the European Coal and Steel Community. The problem in both sectors has been defined in terms of overproduction and over-pricing compared with other energy sources. The solution has been presented in terms of a planned reduction in coal mining and steel-making capacity, the removal of national protection and subsidies and the establishment of a more market-like regime. The European Community has been seen as refereeing the processes of restructuring and capacity reduction between the various nation states and providing a framework of compensation for producers and member states.

Coal mining communities around Europe have thus suffered disinvestment, decline and uncertainty. However, a strong self-identity as 'mining communities' persists in some coal mining areas and provides fertile territory for cooperation (Fothergill 1992). In the UK, in local authority terms, this history of collective action first took the form of the Coalfield Communities Campaign (CCC) and later led to the formation of its transnational counterpart, European Action for Mining Communities (EURACOM); the CCC remains the Secretariat of this transnational network.

Coal production in the UK had declined gradually from its height in 1913 with over one million miners to 226,000 at the beginning of the 1984 coal strike. By 1991, with the onset of systematic pit closures, the number of miners had fallen dramatically to 65,000. Oil, natural gas and nuclear power were replacing coal. In addition, cheap imported coal (from countries such as Colombia, South Africa and Australia) and higher productivity gains from new technology also served to undercut demand for labour in the UK industry. Average EU coal production costs are much higher than world prices, so there is little likelihood of market forces saving the European coal industry (Daniel and Jamieson 1992).

It is within this context that the CCC and EURACOM sought to protect existing jobs in European coal mines and pressed for funding to regenerate the coal mining and former coal mining areas. The CCC now has more than 90 member local authorities in the UK and has provided the blueprint for similar associations in six other European mining areas (Belgium, France, Germany, Portugal, Spain and the Netherlands) involving in total 450 local authorities as members; it is these that constitute EURACOM.

It had become apparent in the late 1980s that the EU would respond more positively to a European-wide cross-national initiative rather than to separate national or regional lobbies. Early in 1988, members of the European Parliament from mining areas had established an international group to discuss common issues and, associated with this, EURACOM was formed later that same year, gaining formal constitutional status in 1991. EURACOM argued for an EU Initiative for the European coal mining areas. There had already been European Community Initiatives for steel industry areas affected by job loss (RESIDER) and for those affected by a declining shipbuilding industry (RENAVAL). In 1989, RECHAR was established for the regeneration of coal mining and former coal mining areas.

RECHAR is administered by DGXVI of the European Commission as part of the EU's regional policy. The then Commissioner for Regional Affairs, Bruce Millan, had previously been a Labour MP in a shipbuilding area of Scotland, and was not unfamiliar with, nor unsympathetic to, the problems of areas in industrial decline. Britain was the main beneficiary of the first round of RECHAR grants, since the criteria for receiving funding were based on job loss. Problems over the delivery of funding led to a dispute in the UK concerning additionality. The CCC joined forces with DGXVI and succeeded in gaining more transparency and accountability in this area (Bache 1992; Bache et al. 1996). The capping of local authority expenditure also led to problems of raising matched funding to facilitate the take-up of RECHAR grants.

Bruce Millan publicly argued that finance should come direct to the local and regional authorities, bypassing national governments. However, member states seem unlikely to agree to forego this control mechanism. This illustrates a more general dilemma which the European Commission faces of how best to ensure effective implementation of EU policy at regional and local level, when member states oppose its intervention (Mazey and Richardson 1993). From this case study it is clear that the European Commission, under its then British Labour Commissioner for Regional Affairs, proved willing to pursue a test case, challenging the British Government on the issue of subsidiarity, with the support of a cross-national coalition of regional and local authorities. EURACOM and CCC were equally positive about entering into this alliance to oppose national government.

More generally, EURACOM provides a platform for presenting a united cross-national front for lobbying the EU on coalfield issues. In the British context, the prime benefit has been obtaining RECHAR funding. However, other members have had other priorities. For example, Spain has used EURACOM to argue against the reduction of coal industry subsidies (still operative in that country). In the interests of coherence, EURACOM has chosen to remain highly focused and only attempts to influence policy on a few fronts at any one time, believing that to spread itself too thinly might fragment an organization already challenged by language barriers, geographical distance and so on. Fragmentation has also been avoided by fighting issues whose successful outcome benefits all individual members to some degree. For example, Britain has gained disproportionately from RECHAR funding, but Spain and Germany have benefited from the fight to retain coal subsidies (the British coal industry is, of course, not subsidized). Maintaining cohesion within transnational networks where there may be a variety of different and sometimes conflicting national interests, therefore, seems to depend upon developing a degree of solidarity and reciprocity, rather than necessarily trying to establish complete uniformity between all partners on all issues.

The CCC Secretariat, both in its services to the British CCC and to EURACOM, acts as a specialized, expert, lobbying organization, geared towards influencing policy decisions on issues affecting its members. EURACOM has gradually widened its range of concerns from its early focus on compensation for job loss. This, the organization believes, has added to its credibility with the Commission as an expert voice speaking on behalf of all the European coalfields. For example, DGXVI has actively canvassed the opinion of EURACOM on occasions, and the present Director of the CCC acted as an adviser to the Commission on the design of RECHAR II, a second programme of support for coal mining areas. In certain areas, however, they have been unable to extend their remit. For example, the CCC, through EURACOM, tried to encourage the Commission to censure the British Government over pit closures but were referred to the principle of subsidiarity.

The CCC through its involvement in EURACOM has been able to deal directly with the Commission, and thereby to some extent bypass national government. Rhodes (1988) suggests that the UK Conservative Government never accepted the Commission's goal of adjusting regional imbalances, seeing receipts from the European Regional Development Fund (ERDF) merely as compensation for the UK's contribution to the EU's budget. The then Conservative UK Government was viewed by the CCC as the main opponent in its negotiations with the Commission for a second stage programme of assistance, RECHAR II, while EURACOM was seen as a crucial vehicle for pursuing this aim. EURACOM's large European-wide membership indicated that visible and widespread support for RECHAR II existed throughout the European coalfields. EURACOM derives credibility from being representative of the majority of coalfields in Europe and from being an all-party organization.

However, while EURACOM has been very successful in influencing EU policy on issues affecting mining and ex-mining areas, there are limits to the ability of transnational networks to bypass national governments. National governments have powers to decide when and how EU policy measures are to be implemented. With RECHAR, this concerned the delivery mechanisms for European funding. This case study suggests that, even where transnational governmental coalitions have successfully influenced the formulation of

European policies, and secured favourable decisions in principle from the EU, these are still open to intervention and influence by national governments at the implementation stage (Keohane and Nye 1974; Bache 1992; Bache *et al.* 1996).

EuroCities

The Coalfields Community Campaign network is organized around the interests of a common industrial sector. EuroCities, by contrast, is an example of a network organized around a common spatial or territorial interest.

Three quarters of EU citizens live in urban areas – this makes Europe the most urbanized subcontinent in the world. Despite this, a high proportion of the European Commission's budget has gone to rural areas through the Common Agricultural Policy. This has led to calls from regional and local authorities for the EU to begin to address urban problems through the development of an urban policy for Europe.

These demands are rooted in a number of wider political, economic and social forces and processes. Over the past 15 to 20 years, deep inequalities have opened up both between and within cities in the UK and in continental Europe. Several commentators have concluded that a more competitive and integrated European market will widen existing disparities between regions and cities (Neuberger 1989; Rajan 1990; Cameron *et al.* 1991). New investment, technology and jobs have tended to concentrate within the so-called 'golden triangle' between Paris, Frankfurt and Milan.

Cities, whilst often manifesting the worst concentrations of social disadvantage, also contain concentrations of resources, for example, new technologies, wealth and expertise. Several cities have begun to promote their potential as growth poles for advanced economic development in the new Europe and to boost their identity as technological or cultural capitals. Cities are likely, therefore, to be in the vanguard of economic and social regeneration.

The European Treaty does not make any specific reference to urban areas and therefore does not give the EU a specific legal competence for developing urban policy. Nevertheless, in recent years the EU has agreed several cross-national programmes with an urban dimension, including: the URBAN Initiative; urban pilot projects under Article 10 of the European Regional Development Fund; and secondary criteria under the same Fund which allow the possibility of cities gaining access to regional aid. At the same time, many areas of policy development contain urban dimensions, for example DGXI (the Environmental Directorate) issued a Green Paper in 1990 on the urban environment; and DGV (the Social Affairs Directorate) runs programmes to combat social exclusion and poverty in disadvantaged urban areas. The Green Paper targeted the unemployed, homeless and ethnic minority people, the majority of whom are concentrated in inner city areas. In this sense a specific urban dimension to policy has been recognized by the EU but the thrust of its initiatives remains fragmented and resides at the level of individual programmes and projects. However, the fact that an urban dimension is emerging incrementally is symbolically and politically important.

The European Commission has undoubtedly acted as a catalyst to facilitate the rapid growth in cross-national networking between cities and regions that has arisen in response to these pressures and opportunities (Parkinson Report to DGXVI). For example, the Commission launched the RECITE programme (1992) to promote such links. However, the regions and cities have not simply been reactive to Commission initiatives. Several networks and associations have been proactive in pursuing greater prioritization of urban issues within the EU, the most prominent being EuroCities.

EuroCities was founded in 1986 from a conference initiated by Rotterdam City Council called 'Cities: The Engine for Economic Recovery'. Its original constituency was largely the 'second' cities within the European member states (e.g. Birmingham, Barcelona, Bologna). However, its membership is now much broader, encompassing over 65 local authority members (UK cities account for about 20 per cent of overall membership). EuroCities arose from the frustrations of the local authorities of large cities that they were unable to raise urban issues effectively with the European Commission, the Council of Ministers or the European Parliament.

The EuroCities network is strongly led by senior local authority politicians (often mayors or leaders of councils with national or European status and aspirations), advised by officers and academics. Nine cities constitute the executive committee which develops and coordinates the overall strategy for the network. Sub-committees or commissions (led by particular cities) cover specific policy areas like social affairs, the environment, economic development and urban regeneration. For a time, EuroCities also had a policy advisory group of academics and other experts tasked with developing a blueprint for an urban policy for Europe. EuroCities emphasize the role of cities as centres of regional as well as local economic development. EuroCities also has aims to aid the integration and development of eastern European cities.

Part of EuroCities' strategy is to stage high-profile gatherings of member cities, whose delegates are often leading mayors and/or leading local politicians (who are often also prominent figures on the wider European political stage), to which European Commission members and other influential figures will be invited. These events are designed as a 'show of strength', to promote the credibility of the network with the Commission and also to establish the wide democratic constituency for the organization which such politicians represent. The corollary of this high-profile strategy is that such political elites are potentially able to use EuroCities as a springboard for their own particular European political ambitions. At times this may result in the promotion of individual rather than collective interests. Overall, however, EuroCities' leadership believe that their elite strategy has given them a direct and influential route to leading figures in the European Commission and Parliament.

EuroCities also pursues wider lobbying activities. For example, a statement putting forward an agenda for cities was sent to all Members of the European Parliament (MEPs) during the last Euro-elections; a submission was made on urban issues to the 1996 Intergovernmental Conference; comments were submitted on the first draft of the EU's Community Initiatives proposals; and intensive lobbying took place for the inclusion of a Community Initiative on urban issues (URBAN). EuroCities claim that their intervention played a crucial part in the adoption of the latter. By lobbying the Commission directly they circumvented the UK Government (which opposed URBAN on the same grounds on which it opposed RECHAR).

Our research revealed several reasons for local authority involvement in EuroCities. Individual UK authorities often joined EuroCities to raise the profile of their city in the European policy arena. Profiling might also take an individualized form, with certain local politicians using EuroCities as a vehicle for profiling themselves on the European stage. Profiling was often to the fore when a city played a lead role in a EuroCities policy sub-committee. EuroCities membership also often served a strategic role in gaining policy competence in specific areas (for example, environmental or technology policy); policy borrowing and exchange of experience were, therefore, valued. Additionally, the network provided a source of potential partners for joint funding bids; since these 'partnerships' had developed over time, the likelihood of compatibility and reliability was greater. More generally, EuroCities participants felt a commonality of interests and experience as urban policy makers and managers; in contrast with the disjunctures they might feel with rural areas in the same country.

The ongoing challenge for EuroCities is how to construct and maintain a common interest between cities which, with the enlargement of the EU, are increasingly diverse. For example, there are considerable internal tensions within EuroCities between the needs and approaches of cities in developed and developing economies, characterized by some EuroCities members as differing not only in their political economic contexts but also in their cultural styles (typified as 'southern' and 'northern' European world-views and modes of working).

In addition to internal cleavages, EuroCities has also attracted external opposition. For example, territorial and competency disputes have arisen with other networks, such as the Council for European Municipalities and Regions (CEMR) and, on occasion, smaller cities or more rural regions have accused EuroCities of representing 'the big boys muscling up together'.

EuroCities has more diffuse aims and diverse membership than EURACOM and such a 'broad church' requires sustained effort to maintain a sense of common purpose and cohesion. Compared with EURACOM, it cannot easily unite around a common enemy or in opposition to specific governmental or EU policies. Its stance is more typically one of proposition and agenda-creating. EuroCities' emphasis is wider and longer-term than EURACOM. The emphasis is not merely to influence a specific policy or funding programme but to reorientate the whole balance and perspective of European policy, away from agriculture and towards urban priorities. Certain of its leading politicians may emphasize their own European political profile but the local authorities they represent are looking for direct material benefits from their membership of EuroCities. This concerns both tangible returns in terms of contacts made, access to European decision makers and grants won, but also less tangible results, such as gaining innovative ideas and benchmarking of good practice.

The growth of transnational networks

What has stimulated the growth in transnational networking among local authorities within the European Union? The factors are complex. The initiative in some cases (e.g. the Coalfields Communities Campaign and EuroCities) is predominantly bottom-up, from local authorities and other organizations keen to influence European policy. In other cases (e.g. the European Programmes to Combat Poverty, which we have also studied but not reported here), the initiative is mainly top-down, from the European Commission's attempt to 'ground' and legitimate its policy development in the regions and localities as well as in the nation states. In yet other cases, the initiative has come from local authorities but then been fostered and funded, almost in clientilist terms, by the Commission (for example, ELAINE, the transnational European networks for race relations advisors).

What is the EU's aim in fostering transnational networks? One aim is the need to promote a sense of integration and cohesion within the Union at a time of potential disintegration within several parts of Europe (e.g. Bosnia). The moves towards a more competitive European market have reinforced divisions between areas of prosperity and of underdevelopment within Europe, and necessitated the creation of policies to lessen the consequences. As divisions have deepened, several EU programmes have been designed to promote cohesion – with a discourse of integration, inclusion, solidarity, partnerships and networking. Several EU programmes and community initiatives thus prioritize cross-national networks linking more prosperous and less developed regions within Europe.

Reciprocal benefits

To what extent does the EU gain reciprocal benefits from its involvement with transnational local authority networks? The Commission in some cases actively fosters the formation of transnational networks to match or mirror its policy concerns. For example, high ranking officials in DGV stimulated and supported the formation of the European Anti-Poverty Network (EAPN), effectively encouraging it to represent the voice of the voluntary and community sectors at European level, to lobby for more comprehensive action against poverty, and to enter into a consultative relationship with the Commission. The Commission rapidly gains access to a great deal of information and intelligence from localities across the whole of the EU, with transnational networks acting as their antennae and early warning systems. In exchange local authorities gain privileged access to the policy formulation process.

Another example is ELAINE (a transnational network of local authority race relations officers) which was not financially supported by the EU from its inception, but now receives a grant to support its activities from Directorate General V. In return DGV has an input into steering ELAINE's activities, and the network provides the Commission with an important source of ideas, intelligence and advice. Given that the Commission bureaucracy is still relatively small, briefings and expert lobbying from local authorities and transnational networks provide valuable information and intelligence to the Commission officials, particularly concerning policy formulation (Mazey and Richardson 1993; see also Grant 1993). The Coalfield Communities Campaign in their role as Secretariat to EURACOM reported that the Commission appeared to have welcomed their expertise and input. Indeed, on occasions they were approached by the Commission to offer expert briefings in their area. Similar evidence was found in the European anti-poverty programmes and networks.

'Holding the ring'

What holds transnational networks together, given their often diverse membership? Transnational networks have to strive to coalition-build between elements which, traditionally, have negotiated separately or even in opposition to each other. Furthermore, cross-national networking often cuts across the conventional boundaries between public, private, voluntary and community sectors. Cohesion is aided if wider sentiments can be appealed to. For example, EURACOM have built their transnational coalition not simply upon common interest but also upon their solidarity as miners and ex-miners. By contrast, the Motor Industry Local Authority Network (MILAN) and the Aerospace Industry Regional and Local Authority Network (AIRLINE) both found it much harder to find and to develop unifying common concerns. Neither the automobile nor the aerospace industries are in general decline like the coal industry; they are experiencing instead a crisis of overproduction which is expected to lead to a further process of takeover, merger, plant closure or relocation. The different firms and localities involved are thus direct competitors. MILAN and AIRLINE have each managed to build successful network coalitions in the UK, but have found it much harder to sustain coalitions across the diverse regions of Europe. Transnational networking activity has thus largely been limited to conferences and information exchange, with only a broad-based lobby in support of the two industries.

Policy development

Each of the successful networks spent much time and effort in research and policy development work, often within the context of cross-national working groups and policy commissions. Alternatively, it was generated by a secretariat and staffed by experts, often from academic research backgrounds. For example, the secretary of the CCC in the UK is a well-established regional economist, with a distinguished record of academic publication. In some cases (e.g. MILAN and AIRLINE), additional research and advice was bought in from external academic advisers or consultants. The role and contribution of this new breed of 'organic intellectual' within transnational networks would repay further research.

The main benefits of European transnational networking

Transnational networks often provide useful 'economies of scale' in the resources which their members can access. For example, they gain from: the pooling of information, intelligence and expertise; sharing the costs of research, consultancy and lobbying; access to a shared secretariat and office facilities, often in Brussels; and 'on the ground' EU knowledge, and early warning of new policy initiatives. Some local authorities referred to transnational networks as part of their antennae and early warning systems in the European Union.

Are UK local authorities involved in transnational networks mainly for the money? A major part of UK local authority involvement in the EU has for many years taken the form of grant-seeking and an opportunity-cost orientation to participation. However, in many cases a wider perspective informs European transnational networking, typified by a more sustained, long-term attempt to influence policy formulation and outcomes. For example, EuroCities has sought to produce a blueprint for an urban policy for Europe. To this end it convened a Policy Advisory Group (now defunct) which acted as a 'think tank' for urban issues and included academics, practitioners and elected members. Similarly, the European Anti-Poverty Network has been motivated less by grant-seeking for its members than by endeavouring to put poverty and social exclusion more centrally on the EU's policy agenda.

A transnational network's influence on EU policy formulation may, of course, eventually be linked with gaining more funding (the EU's new Urban Community Initiative is a small symbolic start for EuroCities). In the case of the CCC, forming EURACOM was associated directly with attempting to obtain an EU Community Initiative under the Structural Funds for coal mining areas. However, the primary concern in many transnational networks is not to maximize grants but to influence policy in specific areas. Networks like EuroCities and the European Anti-Poverty Network also feed into broader EU policy processes like the Green Paper consultation exercise on the reform of social policy, make policy statements to MEPs about policy issues during European elections, and contribute to the policy lobbying process leading into the EU's Inter-Governmental Conference.

Many UK participants clearly felt that the European Commission was potentially more susceptible to policy influence than the then UK Government. The EU also represented an important source of funding, all the more important given the cutbacks in central government funding for local authorities. Part of

UK local authorities' involvement in European networks is, therefore, explicable as a response to a constraining and unsympathetic national government (Bache 1992; Bache *et al.* 1996). The imagery most often appealed to in our interviews was the 'open door' of Brussels, as opposed to the 'closed door' in Westminster and Whitehall. UK members of cross-national local authority networks also reported greater ease of direct access to Commission officials. The European Commission is still a relatively young organization. Richardson (1993) terms it an 'adolescent bureaucracy', implying that its procedures and cultural practices may be less entrenched than longer-established governmental bureaucracies. In addition, EU officials are obliged to find solutions to complex cross-national policy problems and are often glad of the opportunity to test out ideas and to get informal feedback and advice from the regional and local authorities which will be involved in implementing many of their programmes, beyond the formal responses from the member states and the Council of Ministers.

Advantages and disadvantages of transnational networking

Lobbying via a transnational network ensured that the EU was aware that views concerning a particular policy issue were not confined to a single local authority or national perspective. Transnational networking, therefore, gave local authorities added value in terms of legitimacy. The more widely representative a network could demonstrate itself to be, the greater its potential credibility within the EU policy-making process. For example, EURACOM comprises 450 local authorities representing the majority of coal mining or former coal mining areas in Europe and is an all-party organization. Both EURACOM and EuroCities maintain that certain transnational meetings were designed to be 'shows of strength' to the Commission. These high-profile meetings were held once a year or bi-annually and were distinct from the regular business meetings. As one leading figure in the EuroCities network said: '(EuroCities) can deliver up, to a meeting in Strasbourg or Brussels, 30 or so Mayors of major European cities. There were people in the Commission who actually sat up and paid attention because EuroCities were able to pull together in one room 30 or more of the major local political figures around Europe.' This source of credibility, however, was prone to a down-side and sometimes EuroCities found difficulty in 'keeping such major political figures in line' with corporate policy. In turn, consulting with representative transnational bodies also clearly reflects the Commission's need, as an unelected body with a contestable mandate, to legitimate its increasingly interventionist role within the member states (Benington and Harvey 1994). Other empirical studies have indicated that EC decision makers prefer to consult via such transnational federations rather than through single country representations (see Pryce 1973; Mazey and Richardson 1993).

Involvement in transnational networks was seen as giving local authorities opportunities for rapid cross-national learning and policy innovation. This was regarded as particularly valuable in a context of rapid political, economic, social and technological change. In industrial firms the benefits of technology transfer and policy borrowing are quantifiable in economic terms but transnational transfers of knowledge are much less well understood in the social policy field. Learning how counterparts in other countries were tackling similar policy issues was reported as one of the main benefits of involvement in the EuroCities working groups and in the European Anti-Poverty Network.

Some tensions surrounding transnational networks

Several positive benefits of belonging to a transnational network have been outlined above, but internal tensions are also apparent. First, there is some evidence of a northern European/southern European tension in some networks. Apart from the material differences in their political and economic contexts, and state of development/under-development, tensions were also apparent around cultural factors like language (e.g. the propensity to speak English as the dominant language in some networks unites those from northern Europe but may alienate many from southern Europe). Northern Europeans appeared to despair of the perceived lack of structure, concrete action and systematic timetabling from southern Europeans, while the latter derided 'northern pragmatism', bureaucracy and lack of deductive philosophical methods.

The question of network enlargement is another source of potential tension. Such tensions mirror those of the European Union itself. Enlargement may increase the diversity and complexity of interests to a point where sustaining a common purpose may be difficult. How are new members to be integrated into the existing organizations without creating a two-tier membership, or a distinction between core and periphery? Can the development of trust relations based on face-to-face contacts within the network be damaged by large numbers?

Size is not the only factor influencing participation and inclusion within transnational networks. Members of some transnational networks reported feeling that their organization lacked internal transparency, democracy and openness in decision making, with their executive committees perceived to be acting occasionally like 'self-perpetuating oligarchies'. In another case, tensions arose within a network when some members took information from network negotiations and worked the information up into bilateral bids for funding with other parties outside the network. This has led to a recognition of the importance of building not only an initial coalition of interest to give the network a common purpose, but also of nurturing and sustaining relationships of trust over time. At the same time, the skills involved in building cohesion, trust and solidarity are all the more complex and time-consuming in transnational organizations.

Tensions may also arise between the relative emphasis to be given to economic and social goals and priorities. It can be argued that social policy is

still subordinate to economic policy within the EU and local authority networks reflect these relative priorities. Examples include the EuroCities social
welfare committee which has found it difficult not to become the poor relation
of the much more powerful economic committee. Similarly, while some
members of the CCC felt that more social and community-based schemes
should be promoted for funding, the majority view was that they and the
Commission wanted 'schemes with coal dust on them'. In broad terms, it
appeared that women CCC delegates identified themselves with the former
position and male CCC delegates (often Councillors who were ex-miners)
with the latter.

The tension between economic and social priorities intersects with a
related tension between statutory and voluntary organizations. In their relationships with the EU, UK local authorities have tended to focus primarily
upon economic and regional development concerns, with perhaps less attention to social policy issues. Voluntary and grassroots community organizations
on the other hand have often concentrated on social welfare issues. This
sometimes presents itself in terms of voluntary and grassroots representatives in
networks taking a more radical stance than local authorities, for example on
issues like racism and equal opportunities. However, the involvement of voluntary and community organizations in European transnational networks is
often sponsored or subsidized by the European Commission in some way.
Paradoxically, they may therefore be more vulnerable to incorporation than
the local authorities, which derive much of their mandate and funding from
their local elected councils, and may therefore, theoretically at least, have a
greater degree of relative autonomy.

The main source of tension for many transnational local authority networks, however, was with their national governments. It became clear from
our research that there were many areas where UK local authorities (of all
political persuasions) perceived a higher degree of common interest with the
European Commission and other subnational authorities than with the then
UK central Government. Keohane and Nye (1974) make the point in relation
to transnational coalitions of sub-units of government that: 'transnational relations may make all states dependent on forces that none of them control'.

An alternative route of influence?

How far therefore is transnational networking providing an alternative route of
influence and to what extent is it possible to bypass UK national government by
this means? What are the limits to the effectiveness of transnational networks?
In obtaining RECHAR funding from the EU on two occasions the CCC/
EURACOM was able to pursue and achieve a policy opposed by UK central
Government. This suggests that sub-central government was exercising influence
in a supranational arena to secure an outcome seen as undesirable by national
government, using horizontal, cross-national channels in order to achieve its
goals. A detailed examination, however, reveals a greater degree of complexity.

The CCC and the British Government can be seen as engaged in a constantly shifting cat and mouse game. The CCC's aim at every stage is to maximize the position of the coalfields and, in particular, the British coalfields. In practice, this involved forming a series of shifting alliances, which at one point might involve working closely with members of the Commission and EURACOM, but at another point in the process teaming up with DTI officials, and then, once again, at the final implementation stage seeking alliances with the Commission. So the picture is not a straightforward unilinear bypassing of national government, or even a two steps forward/one step back mode, but an altogether more complex pattern of shifting alliances between the UK local authorities, the transnational network, the UK Government and the European Commission.

National government officials proved to be most powerful at the implementation stage and transnational networks more influential at the stage of policy formation. The UK Government was able to reassert its influence in implementation via its control over the delivery mechanisms relating to funding from the EU. The government may therefore be seen acting as a 'gatekeeper' resisting efforts by coalitions to usurp its role. Similarly (although in a slightly modified form), RECHAR II funding is being dispensed by regional bodies formed for that specific purpose. These are quango bodies without any elected representative members; UK government officials have told the CCC that what is required is 'experts' because of the 'technical' issues involved. Bruce Millan, former Commissioner of DGXVI, had argued that finance should go directly to local and regional authorities. However, it is unlikely that member states will relinquish their control over the allocation of funds. Clearly, local authority networks cannot be said to be bypassing the nation state if decisions about crucial resource allocation and implementation are shifted away from their control and back towards central government.

Some of the above limitations in the capacity of transnational networks to influence the implementation as well as the formulation of policy may be peculiar to the UK, and may be a symptom of a particular phase of conflictual central/local relations rather than a reflection of inherent limitations in the leverage which can be exercised by transnational networks. Cross-national comparison would be needed to explore this further, but the UK experience is a salutary reminder that the nation state is still the primary channel for resource allocation and policy implementation within the EU, whatever influence other layers of government may have on policy formulation.

Some concluding propositions

One of the hypotheses we are trying to test in our research is that the growth in the activity and influence of the European Union represents the emergence not just of a new supranational tier of government but also of a qualitatively different sphere of governance, based upon a horizontal policy-making process in which overlapping and cross-cutting networks of public, private, voluntary and community organizations participate in interest articulation and policy formulation.

A relatively limited number of UK local authorities are involved in transnational networks within the EU. Involvement is most evident in larger authorities, where participation appears to be intensifying and increasing rapidly. Nevertheless, even for those local authorities which are actively involved, it is still too early to draw firm conclusions about the significance of this involvement for their policy making. Most transnational networks are only in their early stages of development. It takes time to build coalitions and the trust relationships that this implies. Many networks, therefore, are at present in what may be considered an embryonic form and many local authorities have still to dip their toes into these uncharted waters.

Notwithstanding these provisos, two key questions emerge. First, do the apparently open pluralistic consultation processes involving a wide range of actors from public, private, voluntary and community networks in practice amount to little more than co-optation or clientilism by the Commission? Certainly the Commission actively promotes and supports the formation and development of transnational networks which match or mirror its policy concerns as we have seen, for example, in the case of EAPN and ELAINE. The picture, however, is more complex than simple incorporation, but rather represents a symbiotic relationship between the Commission and several of the networks. On the one hand, the network gains privileged access to the Commission's policy-making process and is able to promote its case directly to senior officials. On the other hand, the (unelected) Commission derives legitimacy, expert knowledge, intelligence, innovative capacity and early feedback on its policy initiatives from its consultations and partnerships with networks of locally-based organizations across the member states.

Second, are transnational networks more powerful in some policy areas than others, and more effective in some policy stages than others? Even in areas where transnational networks have effected a positive input into policy, when such policies and programmes come to be implemented and harder-edged questions of resource allocation and distribution are raised, member states remain the prime determinants of policy implementation (for example, this was clear in the case of EURACOM and RECHAR funding).

The conclusion seems to be that, during the process of policy formulation in this early stage of the formation of the European Union, transnational networking forms part of a relatively open pluralist political process, based as much upon overlapping and cross-cutting spheres of societal influence as upon traditional vertical tiers of governmental representation (and that this seems to serve the interests of the European Commission as well as networks of local authorities, voluntary and community organizations who get involved). However, when it comes to policy implementation and resource allocation the nation states reassert their predominance and competency within the political process and exercise their power through the traditional tiers and channels of vertical representation.

10

Issue networks and the environment: explaining European Union environmental policy

Elizabeth Bomberg

This chapter applies a policy networks approach to European Union (EU) decision making related to the environment. It argues that network analysis can help us explain the EU's environmental policy process, its outputs, and its interaction with other policy spheres. The chapter begins by outlining the basic components and variations of policy networks in national and EU settings. Next, the relatively loose environmental policy 'issue network' is described. This characterization is aided by two case studies on auto emissions and packaging waste legislation. The third section uses network analysis to help explain environmental policy outputs. The following section explores the interaction between environmental and other policy networks. The prospects for change within and among EU policy networks are examined in the next section, and finally the conclusion assesses the usefulness of policy network analysis in explaining EU environmental policies, and suggests areas for further research.

Policy networks

A policy network includes an identifiable and policy-concerned set of public and private actors who depend on one another for resources such as information, expertise, access and legitimacy. Most networks form up around functions (implementation, regulation) and/or specific policy sectors (agriculture, environment). Sub-networks might also emerge around sub-sectors of a policy domain. For instance, this chapter examines the case of auto emissions and packaging waste which are sub-sectors of environmental policy.

This chapter adopts the concept as refined by Rhodes (1988), Marsh and Rhodes (1992) and Peterson (1995). In the 'Rhodes model' the following factors are emphasized:

1 The relative insularity and autonomy of networks (i.e. the degree to which interests not directly involved in a certain policy area are effectively excluded from influence).
2 The relative stability of network membership.
3 Resource dependencies – the extent to which actors within the network depend on one another for resources such as information, access and legitimacy.

Working with these three variables we can construct a continuum of networks varying from tight policy communities to loose issue networks (see Table 1.1, this volume).

Policy networks emphasize the informal relationships surrounding policy making. Typically, bureaucrats from different levels of government, interest groups and committees of experts are intimately involved in setting policy agendas, defining policy problems, and setting out an acceptable range of options. As Richardson and Jordan argue (1979: 74) these informal factors may better account for policy outputs than do party stances, manifestos, political leadership or parliamentary influence. However, 'macro' power structures matter. The overarching structure of any political system – particularly how powers are distributed between different institutions – will set the parameters within which policy networks can operate (see Bomberg 1994 and Chapter 5, this volume).

Although the notion of policy networks emerged primarily to explain policy making in national settings, it also has been applied at the level of the European Union. Peterson employs the model to analyse aspects of the EU's agricultural policy (1989) and European technology policy (1991). Mazey and Richardson (1992) use the approach to help explain the strategies and effects of lobbying in the EU. The approach is particularly useful at the EU level because it recognizes the complexity of the EU policy-making system. The EU incorporates a wider set of interests than does any national system of policy making. Moreover, compared with national settings, power within the EU is highly situation-specific; there are few clear lines of authority or standard consultative patterns within the EU generally. The process of policy formation in the EU is multilayered and complex. The policy network approach can be used to highlight what is different about EU policy making in discrete sectors of policy. It draws attention to the varying strength of different actors in different policy sectors. Its emphasis on resource dependencies helps identify which actors' interests are decisive and why.

More specifically, the approach is a helpful tool in understanding the relatively new system of EU environmental policy making. Unlike more entrenched policy sectors such as those surrounding the regulation of the chemicals industry or agricultural policy, patterns of EU policy making in the environmental arena are still quite new and fluid. Actors are unable to exert much control over the policy agenda; the policy itself is characterized by rapid change and fierce struggles between competing institutions and actors. It it best understood as occurring within an issue network populated by a wide range of actors.

Environmental issue network

Two case studies or 'episodes' will be used to illustrate the issue network character of EU environmental policy. This section begins by outlining briefly the development of these two pieces of legislation. The first case relates to auto emissions and culminated in the 1989 directive setting emission standards for small cars (OJ L 226 3.8.89). The origins of the directive date back to earlier legislation regulating emissions for large and medium-sized automobiles (see Johnson and Corcelle 1989). Although this legislation aimed to promote environmental protection, its primary purpose was the removal of non-tariff barriers to trade in automobiles. Using earlier legislation as a guide, the Commission issued a draft directive in 1987 setting emission limits for small automobiles. The emission standards initially specified in the draft directive were far weaker than those standards enforced in the United States, and were weaker than standards advocated by environmentalists, the European Parliament (EP) and member states such as Denmark and the Netherlands. In its first opinion in September 1988 the European Parliament proposed far stricter ceilings and advocated the mandatory introduction of catalytic converters. The Council of Ministers ignored the first opinion of the EP. Voting by qualified majority (QMV) in November 1988, the Council adopted the weaker standards in its common position. The Netherlands, Denmark and Greece opposed the position but were outvoted.

The directive fell under Article 100a which meant the EP was granted a second reading of the common position as well as the right to reject the common position by majority vote. The EP threatened to reject the Council position at its April 1989 plenary session. Environmental pressure groups such as Greenpeace mounted a well-publicized campaign supporting stricter standards. Meanwhile, the outvoted Dutch Government acted unilaterally by introducing tax breaks on cars which met the stricter US standards. Under such pressure, the Commissioner for Environment, Carlo Ripa di Meana, was able to convince the Commission to recognize the EP's preference for stricter US standards and to revise the common position on the draft directive. In return, the EP's Environment Committee compromised by dropping two amendments unacceptable to the Commission (Judge 1993). The amended common position requiring more stringent standards was returned to the Council where it was adopted by QMV in June 1989.

The second case involves the formulation of a directive on packaging and packaging waste. The directive introduced a harmonized waste management policy designed to reduce the impact of packaging waste on the environment. Formal discussion within the Commission began in earnest in 1991, but a final agreement was not reached until December 1994 (EP and Council Directive 94/62/EC).

Following over a year of consultation, negotiations and several drafts, the Commission published a formal proposal for a Council Directive on Packaging and Packaging Waste (OJ 12.10.92: 92/C263/01) in October 1992. The proposed directive established for all packaging waste[1] quantified targets for recovering waste and minimizing its final disposal. It stipulated that 90 per cent of packaging be recovered within ten years, 60 per cent of which was to be recycled. This formal October draft was softer than drafts produced earlier in 1991 and 1992. *European Report* (18 July 1992, IV: 9) revealed that 'the lengthy consultations organised during the preparation of the proposal have induced the Commission to tone down its initial ambitions'. Although not as ambitious as drafts published earlier, the October 1992 proposal did represent a first attempt to regulate disposal of all types of packaging within the EU, and to do so with recycling targets which were well above the EU average.

At its first reading in June 1993 the EP adopted the Vertemati Report and several amendments which sought to strengthen the draft directive by, *inter alia*, introducing a hierarchy of treatment (prevention, reuse, recycling, incineration, landfill disposal), and measures to prevent production of unnecessary packaging. Although the Commission's amended proposal, presented in September 1993, adopted several of the EP's amendments, many of the EP's tougher amendments (including those listed above) were rejected by the Commission as inappropriate or incompatible with the aims of the single market.

Months later, and following further consultation and negotiations, the Environment Ministers adopted in December 1993 a Packaging Waste Directive which was considerably weaker in content and tone than the original drafts (OJ C 285 15.12.93). The Council agreed that within five years of the directive's implementation not less than 50 per cent, nor more than 65 per cent of packaging waste should be recovered rather than dumped. Minimum recycling targets were dropped to 25 per cent. Within ten years the council would have to agree a 'substantial increase' in these percentages. Several concessions were made to cohesion countries because of their peripheral status and comparatively low consumption of packaging. A final significant change in Article One stated that the purpose of the directive was not only to contribute to the functioning of the Internal Market, but to ensure its functioning. Although the Council's decision received cautious welcome from packaging organizations, it was harshly criticized as regressive by several non-governmental organisations (NGOs) and three member states (Germany, Belgium and the Netherlands). Indeed, Dutch Environment Minister Hans Alders complained the directive had been so weakened it had 'nothing to do with the environment' (quoted in the *Financial Times*, 29 December 1993).

The Council's decision on packaging waste was not final. Under the co-decision procedure established by the Treaty on European Union (TEU), the decision was subject to second reading by the EP in 1994. Whilst it was widely believed that the EP would insist on its earlier tougher amendments, including the imposition of a hierarchy and prevention of unnecessary packaging, environmentalists within the EP failed to secure the parliamentary majority (260 votes) needed to pass the more stringent amendments.

Continued disagreements among national, EP and non-governmental actors over the wording of one amendment (number 31) concerning the use of national economic instruments resulted in a decision to convene a conciliation committee to commence talks in September 1994. Following several subsequent meetings of the conciliation committee, the EP and Council gave their final approval to the directive in December 1994. The agreed directive differed only slightly from the common position of December 1993. It maintained the loose targets stipulated in the Council's common position. Amendment 31 was reworded to allow member states with 'appropriate capacities for recycling and recovery' to set higher targets provided they did not distort competition or the operation of the single market. Yet even this alteration did not significantly change the spirit or content of the common position.

A closer examination of these cases illustrates the loose issue network in which EU environmental policy making occurs. The first indicator of a network is its permeability or autonomy, i.e. the extent to which external pressures impinge on the network's policy-making process. Several factors render the environment network permeable. Growing public concern for the environment has 'politicized' environmental issues and rendered them susceptible to public pressures, debate and scrutiny. Moreover, the broad scope of several environmental issues means they have become increasingly intertwined with other sectoral issues, especially those surrounding agriculture, regional funding, transport and internal market policies. Pressures from these other sectors influence the scope and nature of environmental policy and blur the boundaries of the environmental issue network. Indeed, most environmental issues cross over several policy areas and EU Directorates-General (DGs). Extensive discussions must take place within the Commission itself to determine which policies should be allocated among which Directorates. In short, the network's permeability means that 'there is not only conflict regarding outcomes but about the definition of the problem' (Jordan and Schubert 1992: 13).

Network permeability is illustrated by both the cases of auto emission and packaging waste. Both issues generated widespread interest and conflict among the public, private groups, national governments and technical experts. Both involved issues which did not fit neatly into one DG's jurisdiction. Finally, both cases were permeated by developments on the domestic level of member states. Germany's controversial national recycling programme (DSD) served as an impetus for EU-wide policy, but it also politicized the issue by inciting widespread opposition to recycling targets among industry and national governments.[2]

Because of the wide and diverse scope of issues covered in the environmental network, membership tends to be unstable or fluid. The EU's environmental issue network can include actors from DG XI (the Directorate responsible for Environment, Nuclear Safety and Civil Protection), members of other DGs, national civil servants and representatives, scientific experts, Members of the European Parliament (MEPs), environmental and business interest groups. The Commission's formal monopoly on legislative initiative means that a small group of officials in DG XI provide some form of membership stability. Yet DG XI is one of many actors involved in the policy-making process.

Given the restricted size of its permanent staff, DG XI must rely on a wide array of participants from outside its department for technical and political advice. In particular, it depends on experts and officials on secondment from other EU institutions, from member state departments and from private organizations and foundations. One official in DG XI claimed that 'we have more officials on loan than any other DG' (Interview, 27 January 1993). The role of temporary scientific experts in particular was underscored by a member of the European Parliament's Environment Committee:

> [EU] policy-making in the environmental area is curious in that it is made up of the normal political folk but it's also made up scientists of various kinds. They might be biochemists, biologists, or physicists . . . but they're all mixed up with the political types and this makes for a very disparate network.
>
> (Interview, 26 February 1993)

Later in the policy formulation process other members may become involved, including national civil servants and experts serving on Council working groups, Commission committees or COREPER. All these various actors enter and exit the network depending on the issue under discussion, its stage in the policy-making process and the specific interests involved.

The policy-making process surrounding both auto emissions and waste packaging legislation featured a varied and fluid membership. In both cases, technical and scientific experts were involved at various stages of the policy-making process to help clarify technological uncertainty as to the most effective means of reducing emissions, or the 'cleanest' method of treating packaging waste. Several other non-technical actors moved in and out of the network during the formulation of these two directives. The drafting of the 1989 auto emissions directive involved advisory committees made up of representatives from the Commission, the auto industry, oil refining industry, environment and consumer groups. Later, new members such as the catalyst manufacturers joined the network (Arp 1991: 26).

The mobility of actors involved in packaging legislation was even more striking. Porter and Butt Philip (1993: 17) note that even within the Commission itself, 16 different DGs were involved in the progress of the proposal at different stages of its formulation. Moreover, over 50 Euro-level interest groups were active at different times during its development. Several dozen environmental NGOs from EU and eastern European countries lobbied separately or under the auspices of SPAN (Sustainable Packaging Action Network) which was set up by Friends of the Earth (FoE) in 1991. SPAN, FoE and the European Environmental Bureau (EEB) were especially active early on in the process. A plethora of trade and industry groups (such as INCPEN, ERRA and EU-ROPEN)[3] also became active early on to prevent unfavourable new packaging legislation on the national level or to push for quicker harmonized EU action.

The unstable and fluctuating membership of an issue network suggests a related characteristic of an issue network – its inclusion of a wide array of members with conflicting interests. First, an issue network usually reflects the competing interests expressed by representatives of 15 member states. For instance, national representatives from the Netherlands and Germany have taken a lead role in pushing the Commission to adopt at the EU level the same ambitious packaging waste policy practised at home. Conversely, representatives from UK and Spain took the view that the stringent recycling requirements would hinder economic growth and development (Perchard 1993).

Second, DG XI is generally considered to be more open to lobbyists than any other Commission service. The relatively open nature of DG XI allows unprecedented opportunities for environmental NGOs to lobby and exert influence on European environmental policies. Among the most active on the EU level are FoE and the EEB which represents over 150 environmental organizations. These NGOs, moreover, can have a decided impact on pushing issues onto the environmental agenda. An adviser to the former Environment Commissioner Iaonnis Paleokrassus observed that in areas related to auto emissions and waste, lobbying from environmental groups 'clearly has some impact on the formulation of EU legislation' (Interview, 28 January 1993, Brussels).

Third, whereas policy communities tend to exclude parliamentary influence and scrutiny, the EU's environmental issue network is distinctively open to influence from the European Parliament. Indeed, the Commission welcomes the Parliament's view precisely because the EP is democratically elected and thus can help legitimate EU environmental policy. The EP has taken advantage of the greater environmental awareness among its electorates, as well as its increased powers deriving from constitutional change as embodied in the Single European Act (SEA) and the Treaty on European Union (TEU) agreed in December 1991 at Maastricht. Pushed by a small but vocal Green group of MEPs and an active Environment Committee, the Parliament has promoted its own 'environmental agenda' by providing the Commission with extensively researched inputs into legislative proposals on both auto emissions and packaging waste (see Bomberg 1998).

In both cases examined here the role of the EP was significant. In particular, both directives initially fell under Article 100a which allows the Parliament to amend the common position of the Council of Ministers. In the case of the packaging waste directive, the EP's powers extended to 'co-decision' as stipulated under Article 189b of the TEU. The EP's expanded role greatly increased the number of actors interested and active in these networks. It also increased the variety of views and positions being expressed. On both these issues MEPs were divided on national and party lines.

Finally, the strength or weakness of resource dependencies represents a critical component of policy networks. All networks involve some exchange of resources such as information, expertise, legitimacy and cooperation. However, instead of a tight relationship underpinned by strong dependency relationships, the environmental network includes more informal, less standardized sharing of resources among a wide variety of members. Network members located in DG XI rely on a broad range of sources (environmental groups, business interests, national authorities etc.) for information, expertise and legitimacy and cooperation in the later implementation process. They thus are not dependent on a select few sources. The sharing of scientific expertise was especially diffuse before 1994 as the Commission had no central database or clearing house of environmental or technological information.[4] Conversely, interest groups concerned with environmental issues have several alternative access points located within the multiple EU institutions as well as those on the national level. In short, dependencies remain weak because they are variable and diffuse.

Our cases illustrate the varied and variable distribution of resources within an issue network. In the auto emissions sub-network, the exchange of resources between the Commission and pressure groups was facilitated by several *ad hoc* working groups, the membership of which changed over time (Arp 1991: 26). Environmentalist MEPs' main resource – public support and democratic legitimacy – was strengthened by the imminent 1989 EP elections and broad public support for environmental protection. Informal bargaining and impromptu 'muscle flexing' thus occurred among a wide variety of actors.

Resource exchange in the packaging waste network was equally informal and uninstitutionalized. The Commission did hold a series of official meetings with independent experts, representatives from trade and industry, consumers and environmentalists, NGOs and member states. But, as Porter and Butt Philip (1993: 18) observe: 'the number of informal contacts, letters, calls and personal meetings with above representatives as well as a whole range of other interested parties was far far greater.'

The exchange of resources in these two sub-networks was loose, informal and open. It was also uneven. In many instances, certain groups and actors commanded greater resources and, thus, more influence in shaping outcomes. For instance, in the case of packaging waste, manufacturers and industry interests clearly had a resource advantage in terms of more sophisticated lobbying techniques, more lobbyists and more extensive control of scientific and technical data. One Socialist MEP aide underscored the resource advantage of actors representing the packaging industry: 'They had consultants, scientists and lobbyists in every corridor . . . and that is where decisions are made' (Interview, 14 March 1994). In sum, EU environmental policies are subject to bargaining between a vast array of actors over the definition of the problem as well as the desired outcome. This process usually includes not only competing DGs and experts from various backgrounds, but also various EP committees and MEPs, representatives of national governments and a wide variety of interest groups.

Yet these cases illustrate that issue networks are not merely pluralist politics by another name; despite the issue network's 'looseness', there is a network which can be captured, even if the agenda is unpredictable.

Explaining outcomes

The outcomes from issue networks are as unpredictable and varied as the process that created them. However, several general points can be made about issue network outcomes: they reflect bargaining among a wide variety of actors; they thus remain unpredictable and often difficult to implement; and they cannot be fully understood without examining the network's wider inter-action with other networks.

The contradictory and confusing nature of environment legislation is widely documented (see Liberatore 1991; Collins and Earnshaw 1992; Mazey and Richardson 1992). The policy network model suggests that the varied outcome reflects bargaining and resource exchange among a wide variety of public and private actors who disagree about the nature of the problem as well as the solution. The consequence is often a 'policy mess' or a 'constantly changing policy as different actors gain the upper hand and attempt to imple-ment a policy that suits their goals' (Smith 1993: 71). Our two cases studies suggest that in certain sub-networks the output has been relatively stringent legislation. These policies tend to be those for which scientific evidence is uncertain or ambiguous; environmental NGOs and MEPs control valuable resources such as information and public legitimacy; and pressure from other networks or non-network actors is weak or contradictory.

The sub-network surrounding auto emissions policy fits this pattern. The decisive role of the EP and environmental NGOs is widely acknowledged in the case of small car emissions. Put simply, the Parliament, working with the EEB and other NGOs, was able to force the Council of Ministers to amend its earlier, less stringent standards on auto emissions (see Bomberg and Peterson 1993: 151–2). Auto emissions policy for small cars was characterized by tech-nological uncertainty as to the most effective means of reducing emissions (see Arp 1991: 5–7). It was further characterized by active, concerted participation by environmental NGOs and MEPs. These 'green actors' took advantage of public support and their role as representatives of the public consciousness. This source of legitimacy was not lost on the Commission. David Grant Lawrence, a member of the Environment Commissioner's cabinet, recalled: 'This was a turning point for the Commission. It came just before the Euro-pean elections. It was becoming clear that the Greens would do well every-where. No minister could afford to be seen to sabotage a good decision' (quoted in the *Independent*, 8 May 1990).

Finally, network actors keen to see stricter standards were able to exploit splits within the Council of Ministers between countries who favoured more stringent limits (Germany, the Netherlands) and those preferring other tech-nologies or earlier, laxer standards (France, Spain, Italy). The auto emissions case demonstrates the circumstances under which an issue network can produce strong and effective policies. In this case, the output did not reflect pluralist incrementalism; it produced an EU policy which set a minimum level of environmental protection which was higher than could have been achieved at a domestic level in most EU member states.

But the diversity and complexity of an issue network can render its outputs unpredictable, complex and sometimes contradictory. Whereas policy making in the auto emission case resulted in a gradual tightening of standards, the opposite is true in the case of packaging waste. This case illustrates the extent to which key characteristics of an issue network – its shifting, uneven balance of resources and permeability – can shape policy outcomes.

In the case of packaging waste, the significant weakening of the original draft reflects informal bargaining and compromise within the network and the shifting balance of resources over time. The earlier ambitious targets reflected the dominance of environment groups and representatives from 'greener' member states. Key actors early on were enthusiastic officials in DG XI, members of the EP's Environment Committee and environmental NGOs such as SPAN and FoE who had been promoting debate on the packaging issue for over 20 years (Southworth 1993: 7). Indeed, FoE's influence on the EP's first reading of the directive led one key parliamentary actor to claim that 'most of the EP's amendments were taken straight from FoE' (Interview, 14 March 1994).

However, in the process of formulation several other actors (especially professional and industry representatives) were able to gain the upper hand. To secure later support of those responsible for implementing the directive, DG XI courted business interests by softening the directive but also by providing industry with a key role in setting the specifications for packaging law. Parliamentary actors also required increasingly sophisticated information and data which was readily provided by industry lobbyists. The increased intensity of industry lobbying of EP before its second reading has become legendary. One younger lobbyist compared it to a rock concert, with lobbyists arriving the night before with their sleeping bags (Interview, 21 November 1995). This intense exchange of resources certainly helps explain the Parliament's failure to pass tougher amendments in its second reading. Whilst representatives from packaging organizations describe the Parliament's second reading as a 'victory of common sense over emotion' (Interview, 21 November 1995), green organizations charged industry lobbyists with 'brainwashing', and a campaign of misinformation and deception.

By the time of the conciliation committee meetings, the shift in power and the importance of informal bargaining was obvious. Bargaining within the conciliation committee was informal, consisting of trialogues between representatives from the Commission, the Council Presidency and the parliamentary delegation. The Germans held the Council Presidency and thus were to represent the Council's formally negotiated view. But a Council representative from another member state complained that 'the Germans didn't act according to brief . . . They went off in their trialogue and tried to push things through' (Interview, October 1995, Brussels). The EP delegation wanted to widen discussion to include the Parliament's 'tougher' amendments, but the Council refused, knowing the EP could not muster the necessary majority to veto the common position. Environmentalists within the EP and NGOs were 'shut out' at this stage.

Outcomes thus reflect informal bargaining and a growing imbalance of resources among actors. In the packaging case, the resources of environmental groups and MEPs were weaker than in the auto emission case described above. First, internal splits among environmentalists reduced their impact. SPAN was harmed by internal disagreements as to whether recycling was an adequate goal or whether prevention should be demanded. Environmentalists in the EP were even more divided. Indeed, an earlier loose alliance between the Greens and the Socialists crumbled as Green MEPs refused to vote for the Vertemati Report, complaining that it provided inadequate protection of the environment. In a press release of 5 May 1995 the Green Group in the EP made it clear that they 'deplore[d] this sell out which allows the trash mountains to keep growing' (Press Release, 5 May 1995). Finally, the green resource of public support for environmental protection had subsided somewhat in comparison to the situation in which the 1989 auto emissions decision was reached. In short, whereas the resources of industry cooperation and support had become more valuable in the packaging sub-network, that of public support had become less so.

The permeability of the waste packaging network is also reflected in its outcome. In particular, the policy process was permeated by domestic developments and pressures from other sectors. Difficulties with the German DSD system had raised doubts as to the feasibility or desirability of high recycling targets. Pressure from the internal market was even more pronounced. The dominance of internal market pressures was underscored in Environment Commissioner Paleokrassus's response to EP and FoE's demands for a hierarchy of waste treatment methods. Parliament's amendments on this issue could not be accepted 'because this amendment changes the delicate balance between environmental protection and the smooth functioning of the Internal Market' (quoted in *European Report*, 26 June 1991, IV: 10). In sum – issue network outcomes reflect the exchange of key resources, the shifting membership and balance of resources and the permeability of networks from outside forces. These factors resulted in a much-amended and much-compromised document.

The packaging case suggests the extent to which the outcome of issue networks remain unpredictable, even very late in the policy-making process. Shortly before EP's second reading one EP actor closely involved with the directive noted: 'I wouldn't hazard a guess [as to the] EP's final decision, to say nothing of the directive's ultimate outcome' (Interview, 14 March 1994). The implications of this confusion and uncertainty on successful policy implementation are substantial. Analysts such as Liberatore (1991) and Collins and Earnshaw (1992) cite policy incoherence as a key cause of lax implementation and outright non-compliance. Certain features of an issue network – its reliance on wide and varied interests and varying, sometimes conflicting, scientific advice – can result in policies which are difficult to follow and harder to implement.

The most oft-cited example is water quality (see Bomberg and Peterson 1993). But the packaging directive is also rich with incongruities and ambiguities. Precise figures concerning quantities of packaging produced in member states are essential if the targets are to have any significance, but such data are inconsistent and incomplete (*Financial Times*, 11 January 1995). Industry representatives complain of the directive's quota systems and unclear and unnecessary labelling requirement (The EU Committee of the American Chamber of Commerce in Belgium 1995). Environmentalists also criticize the directive as 'absurd' and 'incoherent' (Green Group in the European Parliament, 5 May 1994). Indeed, one Green closely involved with the legislation commented that 'The best thing about this directive is that it's stuck in a rut and not working' (Interview, 25 September 1995).

EU environmental policy can thus be understood by analysing the internal activities of the network in which it is made. However, to understand EU environmental policy fully, we must also examine the interaction between the environment network and other EU policy networks. Our cases have suggested that pressures from the single market impinged on the formulation of environmental policy making. But the opposite is not always true: integration of environment into other areas remains weak. The next section explores this point by examining the interaction of different policy networks.

Network interaction and integration

The need for integration of environmental policies into other spheres such as the internal market, agriculture or regional policy has become evident to many policy analysts and practitioners. Constitutionally and formally, the link is well established. The inclusion of environmental factors into other EU policies was first made explicit in the 1987 SEA which mandated that 'environmental protection requirements shall be a component of the Community's other policies'. The Fifth Action Programme, *Towards Sustainability*, expresses the need to integrate environmental policies more explicitly into other policy areas. It states that '[g]iven the goal of achieving sustainable development, it seems only logical, if not essential, to apply an assessment of the environmental implications of all relevant policies, plans and programmes . . .' (CEC 1992: 66). The packaging waste directive is an attempt to achieve this by addressing environment protection and internal market completion in the same directive.

Yet progress towards integrating environmental considerations in EU procedures has been slow and difficult (Baldock *et al.* 1992; Weale and Williams 1992). Whereas environmental policy has become more stringent in its own traditional domain (e.g. auto emissions), the impact of environmental policies on other areas of policies remains weak. Other networks produce policies which not only fail to incorporate environmental criteria; in many instances they contradict them.

The non-integration of environmental criteria into other policies is particularly visible in areas related to regional, agriculture and internal market policy. The conflict between EU environmental directives and decisions on EU regional funding for peripheral regions is widely documented (see Baldock and Wenning 1990; Court of Auditors 1992; Bomberg 1994). Several others have demonstrated the extent to which internal market policy, beginning with the framing of the 1992 initiative itself, ignores or contradicts environment considerations (see Weale and Williams 1992; Kamminga 1994).

Constitutional or formal changes, in other words, do not alone bring about change. While the SEA and Action Programmes mandate that environmental concerns need to be incorporated into all other areas of EU policy, network dynamics mitigate against such an integrated approach. In particular, three causes related to the structure and interaction of different policy networks help explain this lack of integration or coordination. First, the relationship between different kinds of networks tend to be unbalanced because of disparities in their coherency, stability and autonomy. The case studies above demonstrated the extent to which the environmental network remains permeable and open to influences from outside actors and networks. The packaging waste case in particular illustrated the extent to which environment policy is informed by internal market imperatives. Yet, the environment issue network is comparatively too weak to exercise influence in kind.

This is primarily because the issue network, as described above, is relatively new, less established, and poorly resourced. Weale and Williams (1992: 58) note that despite the growth in importance of the environmental portfolio in recent years, it is still relatively junior in comparison to other policy areas. In the case of internal market policy this imbalance 'makes it difficult to challenge a programme whose essential features had already been established by powerful actors within the policy-making system'. Moreover, an issue network's diversity and open character mean that its outputs or 'signals' to other actors may be ambivalent, incoherent or confusing. In short, its issue network characteristics disadvantage it in relation to other, better-established policy networks. Consequently, the relationship between networks is characterized by subordination rather than integration.

The second cause of the 'integration deficit' is the limited overlap between network membership. There is some overlap; business lobbyists who are most at home in the internal market network may join the loose issue network deciding environment policy. For instance, in the packaging waste case study described above, traditional internal market actors (such as the EU Committee of the American Chamber of Commerce, the Union of Industries in the European Community (UNICE), and trade groups from the packaging industry) joined the environment issue network to push for EU action which would help eradicate national barriers to the internal market, or preclude more rigorous action within some individual member states.

But this overlap is sporadic and issue-specific rather than an institutionalized overlap of members. Internal market actors may enter the environment network, but other environment network actors do not overlap as often. Most scientific or technical experts called in to participate in the environment network are not active in other networks. Similarly, the DGs remain tightly compartmentalized and often pursue their own bureaucratic mission in isolation from whatever the rest of the Commission is doing (see Mazey and Richardson 1992; Peters 1992). Finally, other network actors, such as the environmental NGOs, have tended to concentrate their lobbying efforts within the environmental network. The reasons for this are primarily resource limitations and 'ease of entry'. Issue networks are inclusive by definition. Gaining admission to more established and closed networks is obviously much more difficult.

This impermeability represents the third obstacle to closer coordination of environmental and other EU policies. Several other networks, particularly those surrounding internal market or agricultural policy, remain insular and more impervious to outside influences. For instance, in contrast to the loose issue network in which environmental policy is made, agricultural policy, including policy regarding the regulations of agrochemicals, is formulated within a tighter policy community which is defined by tight relationships between a few select actors (see Smith 1989). As one member of the Green Group in the EP working on this issue put it: 'well of course there's a problem of access . . . it's not as though folks in DG VI (Agriculture) are begging for Green opinions . . .' (Interview, 11 February 1994, Brussels). Taken together, these traditional patterns of network interaction preclude policy coordination or integration. The prospects for change in this dynamic will be discussed below.

Network change

Networks can change. They can become less or more structurally dependent, open, permeable or fluid. For instance, as the environmental network matures, it may become less diffuse and permeable. Indeed, the Fifth Action Programme provided opportunities for more routinized consultation of interests by establishing a 'consultative forum' which includes representatives of enterprise, consumers, professional organizations and other NGOs and local and regional authorities. The idea was to create more coherency and 'promote a greater sense of responsibility among the principal actors' within the network (CEC 1992). A DG XI official closely involved in the Forum notes how it has helped build consensus at an early stage and thus helped to avoid drawn-out disagreements such as those surrounding the proposed packaging waste directive (Interview, 3 October 1995).

Institutionalizing networks in this way may produce more coherent, effective environmental policies. It might also tighten and entrench the network, thereby limiting severely the participation of the public and environmental actors. For instance, it has already become clear that Commission officials are relying less on environmental NGOs, especially the more radical groups such as Greenpeace, than was the case in the early 1990s (Peterson and Bomberg 1996).

The interaction among networks is also subject to constant flux. There are some indications that a new network dynamic is underway, one which is more conducive to integration. The impetus for change has come from both external and internal forces. First, change might follow on from 'macro' institutional developments such as the Maastricht Treaty. Whereas the SEA simply stated that environmental protection requirements are 'a component of the Community's other policies', the Maastricht Treaty's Article 130 r(2) goes further, stipulating that these requirements 'must be integrated into the definition and implementation of other Community policies'. If nothing else, this provision gives advocates of integration a constitutional stick with which to enforce their arguments.

Closer coordination may also emerge 'from within', through actions taken by network actors themselves. First, DG XI is pushing hard for a more active meshing of networks. It has commenced discussions with several DGs to ensure that environmental impacts are included in future developments (Wilson 1993: 5). More ambitiously, it has asked all DGs to calculate aggregate totals for all EU spending on environmental measures and to inform DG XI of the full results from this exercise. Such assertiveness by DG XI officials may be made easier by a strengthening of its resource base. The historical imbalance of resources and clout between networks may be shifting in favour of the environmental network. Overall environmental expenditure levels have risen steeply (Court of Auditors 1992). Moreover, the long-awaited establishment of the EEA will provide a much-needed base of information and technical data. Clearly this strengthening of financial and informational resources will strengthen DG XI's coordinating role.

Second, environmental NGOs and MEPs are making more concerted efforts to penetrate networks responsible for the formulation of other Community policies. For instance, the World Wide Fund for Nature (WWF) has established lobbying strategies directed at policy makers involved in the formulation of a wider range of EU policies (Long 1995). Moreover, there is a growing recognition among Green MEPs of the need to involve themselves in other networks. As a co-President of the Green Group in the EP noted: 'We've now got to pay more attention to economic and internal market policies; this is where environmental policy is being made' (Interview, 8 February 1994, Strasbourg).

Third, there is evidence that some other networks may become looser, more transparent and more amenable to demands from outside or oppositional interests. Officials from DG XVI (Regional Policy) insist they now accept the need to incorporate environmental objectives into their multi-annual programmes and projects, as well as cohesion fund spending. Some business representatives closely involved in internal market legislation recognize the need to incorporate environment considerations. In reference to the packaging case, the President of EUROPEN conceded that environmental pressures need to be taken into account and that this can be done to benefit industry. 'For marketing reasons, in the past industry liked big packaging. Now I think . . . reduction of volume of packaging is no longer anti-marketing, but rather pro-marketing' (Braakman 1993: 3).

It is still too early to assess the applicability or durability of these good intentions. Efforts by other networks to incorporate environmental concerns may constitute fundamental change, or they may amount to little more than empty promises. It should be noted that past institutional or constitutional changes have not brought about the called-for policy integration. Moreover, the prospects of change within other networks seem less likely. Some networks, especially those surrounding agriculture policy, remain relatively unaffected by environmental concerns or calls for integration. In short, as every student of the EU knows, 'integration' is a buzzword easier to utter than implement.

Conclusion and further research

This chapter has presented the policy networks approach as a useful way of explaining EU environmental policy making. The approach helps us order evidence in novel ways and it provides clues to anticipate policy outcomes. In particular, it helps explain how decisions are made in different settings, which actors are decisive and why. For instance, an examination of the shifting balance of resources and permeability of a network goes some way towards explaining the conflicting, often contradictory outcomes of EU environment policy making. By analysing the shifting power of a variety of actors within networks, this approach complements studies which otherwise tend to overestimate the power of member states (see Pollack 1995; Golub 1996).

Beyond that, the approach encourages the exploration of the interaction among sectoral networks. This chapter examined the horizontal link between the environmental issue network and other EU policy networks. It indicated that such interaction can have significant consequences for environmental protection, but that obstacles to closer coordination or integration of networks remain formidable.

The policy network model requires further modification, research and testing on the EU level. First, the notion of issue networks needs to be clarified to incorporate two points. Previous analyses of issue networks (Heclo 1978; Jordan and Schubert 1992; Marsh and Rhodes 1992) suggest such networks exist only in policy areas of secondary interest, or 'only if there is no threat to the interest of either an economic/producer group or professional group' (Marsh and Rhodes 1992: 254). But this chapter illustrated that issue networks may indeed emerge in sub-sectors of primary economic importance. In the packaging waste case, 'threatened' economic and producer groups entered the environment network at any number of stages of the policy-making process and had a significant impact on policy outcome.

Second, it is easy to exaggerate the pluralist structure of issue networks. Some descriptions of environment policy making resemble a pluralist balancing game with varying interests enjoying similar access and influence. This tone is underlined by two DG XI officials quoted in Mazey and Richardson (1992: 111) who describe access to DG XI as something of a 'free for all' with the 'door open for any groups wishing to contact Commission officers . . .'. Compared to other networks, the environment is relatively accessible. But openness should not be confused with equal influence. Clearly, resource imbalances occur within even fairly accessible networks. A senior commission official responsible for waste management insisted that for DG XI, apart from contacts with national administration, '90 per cent of the contacts are with trade and industry' (Interview, 8 November 1995). The varying resource base of different actors within the packaging waste sub-network illustrate this point. In short, the EU's environment issue network is not a pluralist paradise.

At least three other aspects of the policy network model need further research and testing. First, the primary purpose of network analysis is to explain the way in which meso-level decision making affects policy outcomes. It is of limited use in explaining 'macro' developments which may impinge on the policy-making process and outcome. For instance, this chapter underlined the changes brought about by decisions taken by EU member states to revise the Treaty of Rome via the Single European Act and the Maastricht Treaty. These 'history making decisions' (Peterson 1995) impinge on environmental policy by altering the EU's legislative procedures, rebalancing the powers of different EU institutions, and expanding the EU's remit. The link between the everyday decisions and the larger, 'macro' developments needs to be examined.

Moreover, when applying the policy network model to the EU, more attention needs to be paid to the activities of sectoral networks on the national level and their impact on EU policy formulation. This chapter has treated domestic factors as part of the 'permeability' characteristic of an issue network. This only partially explains the complex interaction between domestic developments and EU policy making. The vertical interaction of networks needs further exploration.

A related issue deserving further research is the coordination among EU, national and sub-national networks responsible for implementing EU policies. National and regional authorities are increasingly responsible for the success of EU policies 'on the ground'. In short, further study is needed which makes explicit how decisions are coordinated not just across different policy sectors but between levels of government as well.

Acknowledgements

This chapter will form part of a larger collaborative project which examines decision making in different policy sectors within the EU. The completed study partially funded by an ESRC grant (R000235829), will appear under the title *Decision Making in the European Union*, by John Peterson and Elizabeth

Bomberg (Macmillan 1998). I am grateful to John Peterson, Rod Rhodes and Martin Smith for comments on earlier drafts. Thanks also to the numerous EU officials, parliamentarians and lobbyists who offered the non-attributable interviews cited in this study.

Notes

1 Previous EU legislation had dealt only with beverage containers.
2 Germany's national Duales System Deutschland (DSD) was established in 1991 and obliges manufacturers and retailers to 'reabsorb' packaging material. Problems emerged because the collected material far outstripped Germany's capacity to recycle it. Consequently large amounts were exported to other member states and, in the eyes of recipient member states, were inhibiting development of their own waste management programmes.
3 The Industry Council for Packaging and the Environment (INCPEN), European Recovery and Recycling Association (ERRA), Association of Plastics Manufacturers in Europe (APME), and the European Organisation for Packaging and the Environment (EUROPEN) were among the most active. In addition to individual lobbying, several packaging and producer groups groups joined forces under the Packaging Chain Forum (PCF) (see Porter and Butt Philip 1993).
4 The establishment of a European Environment Agency (EEA), agreed in 1991, was intended to provide such a database. But the EEA's inauguration was postponed for three years due to disputes as to where it should be sited. A final decision to base the Agency in Copenhagen was only agreed in October 1993.

11

The utility and future of policy network analysis

David Marsh

This conclusion is divided into two major sections. In the first section I shall return to the questions outlined in the introduction which the contributors to this volume were asked to address. In the second section I will examine some key issues for the future of policy network research, paying particular attention to the development of a dialectical approach to the study of networks.

Answering the questions

The chief questions raised in this volume are:

- Is the concept a useful tool with which to understand policy making?
- Does the existence and activities of a policy network affect policy outcomes?
- How do policy networks change?
- How important are interpersonal, as compared with structural, links within the network?
- Do certain groups dominate the network?
- What methods are appropriate to study policy networks?
- What evidence is there from the contributions to this book that policy networks can be viewed as a new, and increasingly important, mode of governance?

A useful tool?

In fact, there are three separate, but related questions here. First, the broadest one: is the concept useful? Here, the simple answer seems to be yes. All the contributors to this volume see the policy network concept as a useful tool for the analysis of public policy making. There is general agreement that, at the very least, it represents a useful heuristic device; a sensible way of analysing and categorizing relations between state actors and other interests. Second, we need to ask: at what level is it useful? The initial problem here is whether it can be utilized at both the sectoral and sub-sectoral level. Some like Jordan *et al.* (1995) have argued that it has most, perhaps even only, resonance at the sub-sectoral level. However, Cavanagh's case study in particular suggests both that networks can exist at both levels – in his case the sectoral level network deals with broad issues of oil policy while the sub-sectoral network deals with offshore health and safety issues – and also that the sectoral network may lay down the parameters within which the sub-sectoral network operates. At the same time, policy network analysis, although it was developed to look at national level policy making, may be applicable at the transnational and the sub-national level. So, Bomberg and Benington and Harvey defend its utility at the transnational level, in both cases at the EU level, and Cole and John use it to analyse local power structures. Third, it is also important to ask whether the schema for classifying networks, developed by Marsh and Rhodes and utilized here, is of use. Most of the authors here found the schema useful; so, McLeay identifies policy networks towards the policy community end of the Marsh and Rhodes continuum in policing policy in both Britain and New Zealand, while Bomberg describes a European environmental policy network which exhibits most of the characteristics of an issue network.

An explanatory role for networks?

This is the most fundamental question: do policy networks affect policy outcomes? Most of the authors here argue that they do have an effect. In the theoretical section, Peters argues that policy networks may affect policy outcomes, but not in the United States because: 'American politics remains more unstructured than that found in most European countries'. The approaches of Hay and Daugbjerg and Marsh are perhaps more typical. Both suggest that networks affect outcomes, but that they are only part of any explanation. Hay contends that, if networks are to have explanatory power, then more attention needs to be paid to the process of networking; to networks as sites of strategic action. Daugbjerg and Marsh argue that the policy network is a meso-level concept, a model of interest group intermediation which needs to be integrated with macro-level theory and analysis and micro-level theory and analysis if it is to contribute to an explanation of policy outcomes.

As such, there are differences in the positions adopted by the theoretical contributions to this volume. However, a number of the case studies present convincing evidence that networks affect outcomes. Daugbjerg's comparative analysis of the agricultural networks in Sweden and Denmark is particularly powerful. He argues that the Danish agricultural network is much more cohesive than its Swedish counterpart and, as such, the farmers have very close relations with the Ministry of Agriculture. He suggests that because of the existence of this tight policy community: 'Danish farmers were more successful in transferring the main principle of agricultural policy, the principle of state responsibility, to environmental policy making.'

Similarly, Cavanagh distinguishes between the policy networks dealing with offshore health and safety in Britain and Norway. Both were tight, towards the policy community end of the Marsh and Rhodes continuum, but the state was a more dominant actor in Norway and union interests were included in the network in Norway and excluded in Britain. The very close identification of interests between the oil companies and the government in Britain, together with the exclusion of union interests, has given 'a disproportionate influence to production and exploration matters' and, consequently, led to the relative neglect of safety issues. In contrast, in Norway the network has a strong union presence and state and oil company interest are not so identified. As such, much more attention is paid to safety issues.

Network change

So, many authors argue that network change is related to change in policy outcomes. At the same time, many have suggested that network change can be explained in terms of the context within which the network is located; or to put it another way that network change results from exogenous rather than endogenous factors. In contrast, I would suggest that the relationship between the network and its context is dialectical; that this dualism, like a number of others, needs to be transcended.

There is considerable evidence to support that argument from the case studies presented here. Clearly, exogenous factors do affect policy networks, but it is how that context is interpreted and negotiated by the members of the network which affects outcomes. So, Daugbjerg and Bomberg both show how other networks operate as a key aspect of the context within which a particular network operates. However, Daugbjerg's case study indicates that it was how the agricultural policy networks in Denmark and Sweden interpreted the challenge from the environmental network which played a key role; the extra resources which the Danish farmers had because they were part of a network which enjoyed a closer relationship with the Ministry of Agriculture allowed them to minimize the effect of the challenge from the environmentalists. In a similar vein, Cavanagh indicates how the differences between both the economic context and the industrial relations tradition in Britain and Norway affected the structures of the offshore health and safety policy networks in both countries. However, in both cases it was how the network members interpreted those contextual constraints which shaped outcomes; so, for example, it was the British Government's interpretation of the economic constraint it faced and, thus, their view that Britain needed high production at all costs from the North Sea oil industry, which led to the close relations in the network between the government and the industry and shaped the policy pursued on safety issues.

The actions of network actors, particularly, though not exclusively, the actions of government, can also affect the context within which the networks operate. The Cavanagh chapter again provides an example. It was the industrial relations policy pursued by the Conservative Government which created the context within which union involvement in the health and safety field became more marginalized.

Both McLeay and Daugbjerg also deal with the role of public opinion in shaping the context within which networks operate. In most cases closed policy communities attempt to ignore public opinion but McLeay indicates how it impinged on the policing policy network in both Britain and New Zealand. Media coverage of issues like police corruption and gender-related issues, such as rape, led to public debate and the extension of the policing policy network to include a broader range of interests when these policy issues were being discussed. However, the politicians' interpretation of public opinion was clearly crucial and, of course, politicians can manipulate, as well as respond to, public opinion.

Interpersonal or structural links?

There is considerable evidence from this book that both the structural and the interpersonal aspects are crucial when trying to explain outcomes. In the case studies, all the authors are aware of the importance of both structure and agents. However, most stress one aspect. So, Benington and Harvey pay considerable attention to the strategic judgements of the members of the transnational networks on which they focus. Similarly, Cole and John's focus is almost exclusively on the role of agents; although that is almost inevitable given their methodology. In contrast, Daugbjerg and Cavanagh stress the importance of structures. McLeay makes a particularly interesting observation; she suggests that interpersonal relations are most important in the network in New Zealand, and more important than in Britain, because of its comparatively small size, which means the network is numerically smaller. Clearly, the point which needs to be emphasized here is the one made strongly in the introduction and developed later in this conclusion; this dualism between the structure of the network and the interaction between the agents is another that needs to be transcended. As Hay argues very persuasively, we should see both as important and conceptualize the relationship as dialectical; I return to this question in the second section below.

A dominant interest?

As we have already seen, the case studies in this book present evidence of different types of networks, from fairly tight policy communities to relatively loose issue networks. However, there do appear to be some clear patterns which confirm the conclusions on this issue in Marsh and Rhodes's book. All the networks are dominated by economic and government interests; although of course the looser issue networks are more open to broader interests and, as we saw, sometimes subject to pressure from public opinion. So, Cavanagh identifies a British network which is dominated by the government and the oil industry, but a Norwegian network in which the trade unions play a more important role. Daugbjerg identifies two networks dominated by state and farming interests, although the Swedish network proved more permeable. Cole and John argue that the networks in Leeds and Lille are dominated by business and local political actors. McLeay emphasizes the importance of state and police actors in the networks in both Britain and New Zealand. Only Bomberg's treatment of EU environmental policy making presents a broader, more plural picture, with the involvement of a wide variety of governmental and non-governmental interests.

Overall, there is not much here which would naturally relate policy networks and pluralism, unless we accept a very weak notion of pluralism. Certainly, there is plurality in the sense that the particular interests which dominate in different policy areas are different. However, those involved in policy making are partial in both senses of the word; many interests are excluded from networks and the members of networks are primarily concerned to forward their own interests. There is perhaps more support here for a statist interpretation of the distribution of power. Indeed, a number of the contributors see their networks as dominated by government interests. In my view, the membership of policy networks usually reflects the pattern of structured inequality within society and the activities of the networks reflect the interests of that membership; although there is not one single basis of structured inequality.

Which method?

The majority of authors here use the case study approach, looking at networks within one policy area and often concentrating on the networks role in one particular, or a limited number of, policy decision(s). This is likely to remain the main methodological approach within the field. However, three additional points which emerge from this book are worth making. First, a comparative approach clearly pays dividends and that is a major contribution of this book. Second, Cole and John's analysis does indicate that utilizing a sociometric methodology can be useful. They use the technique to present a very clear picture of the networks in the two cities. However, it must be emphasized that this is a first step; to examine how these networks affect policy outcomes one still needs to adopt a more traditional methodology, relying to a large extent on interviews. Third, Hay's point that we need more dynamic studies, which look at the development of the network, and especially its formation and, perhaps, termination, needs particular emphasis.

A new mode of governance?

A review in English of the German literature on networks as a form of governance is overdue. However, it is clear that networks do play an important role in governance. Benington and Harvey develop this theme. They argue that governance cannot be seen exclusively in terms of the activities of public authorities and indicate how private interests interact with local authorities, national governments and the EU to produce a broad type of governance based upon resource exchanges within policy networks. Certainly, this argument fits well with the views of the Max Planck school.

More broadly, all the case studies here indicate how private interests and government interests operate within networks to make policy. Such relations are not new, but a number of processes have clearly accentuated their development. The increased emphasis on the market, and particularly on public–private partnership, has meant that the growth of networks linking public authorities and private interests has become inevitable. Similarly, a variety of processes, often, wrongly, lumped together as a single process of globalization, e.g. the internationalization of communications and culture, the growth of international trade and transnational companies and the growing importance of international organizations – both economic, like the IMF and the World Bank, and political, particularly the EU – often precipitate national and international responses which involve networking.

It is important to assess the extent to which policy networks are emerging as a response to such developments. However, the case studies here suggest that it would be unwise to overstress this process. Certainly, as we saw in the last section, the authors here place great emphasis upon the role of government or public authorities in the networks. As an example, even Benington and Harvey (and they pursue the issue most directly) argue that the European Commission plays a key role in the creation of the transnational networks. The Commission needs the networks to provide information and advice, given that the EU bureaucracy is small, and the process of consultation helps legitimize the decision. At the same time, the Commission is still the dominant partner. In addition, when the EU policy is administered the action of the national government often acts as a further constraint on the network members' achievement of the concessions thought to have been negotiated in Brussels. In this case, as in others examined here, it appears that there has been a shift towards networks as a new form of governance which must be tempered by the realization that hierarchy is still important.

The way forward

If it is accepted that the policy network concept can be useful as both a heuristic device and an explanatory tool when analysing policy making then there is still much to do. Here, I wish to highlight three issues which emerge from this book: the need to integrate the approach with associated approaches; the importance of focusing on the interrelationship between networks; and finally, but most importantly, the need to use, and the implications of using, a dialectical approach to the study of networks.

Policy networks and other approaches

To date the policy network literature has paid little attention to other bodies of literature which deal with the same or similar issues. Peters argues that the literature on advocacy coalitions and epistemic communities can be used to address some of the deficiencies in the policy network literature. In his view, the advocacy coalition approach can help explain policy change; different policy networks which advocate different policy options can negotiate to produce a change to the existing policy regimen. As far as the epistemic community approach is concerned, Peters suggests that the epistemic community can be viewed as a particular structural form of policy network whose membership is based upon knowledge.

Cole and John briefly examine the relationship between network theory and regime theory. Regime theory suggests that a particular pattern of governance has emerged in American cities, based upon a governing coalition between business and political elites; other interests are consistently excluded. Policy making is the result of an exchange of resources between, and a continual process of political learning involving, those two elites. There are thus obvious connections between regime theory and the policy network approach. However, Cole and John follow other authors in questioning the ethnocentrism of the regime theory model and question its transferability given the importance of public sector actors in Europe. As such, the policy networks model, which doesn't a priori focus on particular interests, may be more useful.

It is not my intention to examine the ways in which these different approaches can be integrated; rather I want to emphasize that while some attempt has been made in that direction more is essential (see also Cairney 1997, who deals with the relationship of network analysis and the advocacy coalition approach and Watt 1997, who deals with its relationship to the advocacy coalition and the actor network approaches).

The interrelationship between networks

Individual policy networks don't exist in isolation; although tight networks may succeed in isolating the interactions in their network from the attention of other networks. As such, other policy networks provide an important feature of the context within which particular networks operate. Marsh and Rhodes (1992) fail to examine this important exogenous constraint on networks. In a complex polity the relationship between networks is clearly crucial. In fact, there are at least two related problems here. First, the context within which networks operate is composed, in part, of other networks and this aspect of the context has a clear impact on the operation of the network, upon change in the network and upon policy outcomes. Here, Martin Smith's piece (1991) on the salmonella in eggs issue, where the agriculture and health network clashed, and Carsten Daugbjerg's analysis in this volume of how the shape of, and the outcomes from, the agricultural policy networks in Sweden and Denmark were affected by the rise of the environmental networks in the two countries, are particularly relevant and interesting. Second, the issue of the relationship between sectoral and sub-sectoral networks is particularly important. Authors like Jordan *et al.* (1995) argue that networks only exist at the sub-sectoral level. In contrast, I would argue that it is an empirical question whether there are networks at both levels and, if so, what are the relationships between the networks at these two levels?

It also may be worth paying some attention to the relationship between policy networks and implementation networks. In a given policy area they may not be synonymous. So, those actors involved in the policy network which discussed and shaped policy may not be the same actors as those involved in the implementation of those policies. In such circumstances, it is possible that those involved in the implementation network, but not in the policy network, will obstruct implementation; this may be a common cause of the implementation gap.

The need for a more dynamic, dialectical approach

As Hay pointed out, too much of the work in network analysis adopts a static analysis; it takes a snapshot of a network at a particular time. Hay emphasizes the necessity of adopting a dynamic approach. Most of the case studies here do take a longitudinal approach to the study of networks but, in my view, every analysis of networks and their putative effect on outcomes should emphasize the origins, development and, if appropriate, termination of the networks. More specifically, as I suggested in the Introduction, and as Hay argues in Chapter 3, we need a dialectical approach to the analysis of networks. While this is an easy statement to make, it is not always obvious what such an approach involves. Here, I want to develop such an approach which is outlined in Figure 11.1.

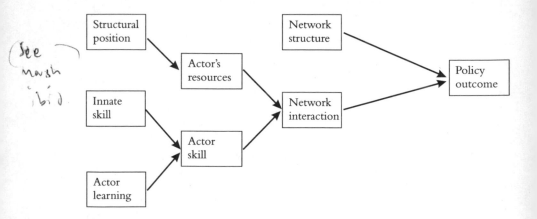

(*See* Marsh "ibid")

Figure 11.1   Policy networks and policy outcomes: an initial approach

A propositional analysis

The proposition that networks affect outcomes in fact involves three subsidiary propositions: (i) change in the policy network is associated with change in the policy outcome; (ii) any such correlation is not a spurious one, with change in both the network and the outcome caused by some other factor(s); (iii) the policy network is affecting the policy outcome, rather than vice versa. Here then are three questions which any study of policy networks needs to answer. Is change in the policy outcome related to change in the policy network? Is change in both the network and the outcome the result of change in a third (or fourth) variable? What is the causal direction; does change in the policy network lead to change in outcome?

However, as always, nothing is quite so simple; all these propositions need unpacking. Let us begin with the first proposition. The literature suggests that two separate, but related, aspects of the policy network affect the outcome: the structure of the network; and the interaction between the actors in the network. This again is more complicated than it sounds, because the interactions which shape outcomes are a product of the resources which the actors control and the skill with which they are used. Furthermore, the resources which individual actors control are not given; they are a reflection of the structural position occupied by the group which the actor represents. In addition, the actor's skills, while to an extent innate, are also the product of the actor learning from experience. These relationships are summarized in Figure 11.1. This means that any analysis of the effect of networks on outcomes needs to examine each of these relationships. What is more, this throws up a series of more sophisticated questions, upon which this volume has focused. What is the relative importance of the structure of the network and the interaction of the agents within the network to policy outcomes? What is the importance of the resources which the actor possesses as representative of a group relative to the personal skills of the actor? Why do some actors possess more resources than others? How important is the process by which actors learn from experience?

The second proposition is perhaps a little more straightforward. It is important to identify the other factors which might have affected any change in both the policy network and the policy outcome. It is particularly important here to look at the role of contextual factors. For example, changes in the broader political structures and climate may affect the structure of the network, the resources of the actors within it and the policy outcomes. In this way, many argued that the election of a Conservative Government in 1979 committed to 'New Right' ideology led to major changes in policy networks and policy outcomes; to them 'Thatcherism' was the key explanatory variable. Similarly, Marsh and Rhodes (1992: Conclusion) argue that, in the case studies on which they reflect, three contextual factors, political structure, economic structure and knowledge, shaped change in both the network and the outcome. Of course, this throws up another key question for network research. What are the relative importance of the structure of, and interactions within, the network

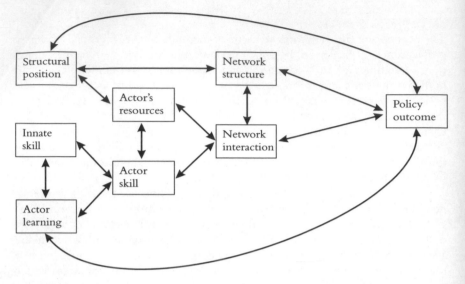

Figure 11.2   Policy networks and policy outcomes: a dialectical approach

and the context within which the network is located, in relation to change in the policy network and change in policy outcomes?

The third proposition is also relatively straightforward. To establish the causal direction we need to examine changes in the policy network and changes in policy outcomes over time in order to discover the temporal sequence. As we shall see later, this has significant methodological implications.

Towards a dialectical approach

In my view, the existing literature fails to acknowledge that when we try to unpack the proposition that networks affect outcomes this in fact involves three dialectical relationships; that is an interactive relationship between two variables in which each affects the other (see Hay 1995). The model is outlined in Figure 11.2.

Beyond network structure versus resource exchange among agents. My propositional analysis distinguishes between structure and agency, for example between network structure and network interaction, that is the pattern of resource exchange between agents within networks. As we saw in Chapter 1, Marsh and Rhodes privileged the former and Dowding the latter. However, in order to provide a grounded, but dynamic, account of how networks affect policy outcomes, it is essential to recognize that policy networks are structures within which agents operate. Agents are, in a sense, 'bearers' of those positions, but they interpret, deconstruct and reconstruct these structures; in this way the relationship between structures and agents is dialectical. At the same time, networks are not unchanging, they change in part because of the strategic decisions of the agents within the structure; and these strategic decisions represent a response to both exogenous and endogenous factors, a second dialectical relationship.

Adopting a dialectical approach emphasizes that policy networks are dynamic, not static; they are political structures, but not unchanging structures. They change because the behaviour of the strategically calculating subjects who make up the network changes and/or because the wider structural context within which they operate changes. In addition, outcomes cannot be explained solely by reference to the structure of the network; they are the result of the actions of strategically calculating agents. However, those agents are located within a structured context, which is provided by both the network and the broader political and social–structural context within which the network operates. Significantly, the agents do not control either aspect of this structured context. At the same time, they do interpret that context and it is as mediated through that interpretation that the structural context affects the strategic calculation of the actors.

As such, the key to any attempt to conceptualize how policy networks affect outcomes is the acknowledgement that the relationships involved in policy networks are both structural and interpersonal. They are based upon information and communication exchanges which create 'resource dependencies'; these resource dependencies are crucial to any understanding of the operation of the network. The relationships within the network are structural because they define the roles which actors play within networks; prescribe the issues that are discussed and how they are dealt with; have distinct sets of rules; and contain organizational imperatives, so that, at the very least, there is major pressure to maintain the network. At the same time, we need to acknowledge both that resource dependencies are not fixed and that the way in which they are discursively constructed by the participants affects their behaviour and the policy outcomes. So, it is agents who choose policy options, bargain and conflict and break up networks; although all of these are also affected by the broader context.

Beyond network versus context. In order to understand how networks may affect outcomes, we also need to recognize that there is a dialectical relationship between networks and the broader context within which they are located. There are two different, but related, points here. First, policy networks reflect exogenous structures; for example, class and gender structures. So, the structure of networks often reflects the broader pattern of structured inequality within society. Certainly, policy networks are structures which cannot be treated as given; we need to explain their origin, and a key part of this is showing how they embody other structural relations. At the same time, agents are located in various structural positions and, while membership of a policy network may give them structural privilege, other structural positions, for example based upon class, gender or ethnicity, may be both more important generally and reflected in policy network membership. Second, network structure, network change and policy outcome may be partly explained by reference to factors exogenous to the network but those contextual factors are dialectically related to the network structure and network interaction. Certainly, if we are to argue that networks affect policy outcomes and, thus, that changes in networks can result in change in policy, then we also have to address the question: what leads to network change?

Many empirical studies of networks have highlighted change within the networks they identified and attempted to explain those changes largely in relation to changes in the environment or the context within which the networks are located. As such, the change is usually explained in terms of factors exogenous to the network; as the external environment changes it may affect the resources and interests of actors within a network. However, the extent and speed of change is clearly influenced by the networks' capacity to mediate, and often minimize the effect of, such change.

Networks are often faced by very strong external uncertainties and that does affect network structure, network interactions and policy outcomes. As we saw earlier, Marsh and Rhodes emphasize three broad categories of network-environment changes, economic, political and knowledge-based, which may undermine the certainties and values within particular networks; but following on a previous discussion, I would also highlight the role of other networks. Political authority is perhaps the most important external constraint (see Judge 1993). If a minister, or particularly the Prime Minister, is prepared to bear the costs of breaking up a policy community, he or she has the resources and the authority, although the costs of doing so may be high. Certainly, it is often argued that the Thatcher Government successfully challenged existing policy networks, although at the cost of significant implementation problems (see Marsh and Rhodes 1992, Chapter 11); so, in both health (Wistow 1992) and education (Hu 1995) it is clear that political goals and ideology affected both the membership and policies of the network. The key point is that it is difficult, although far from impossible, for networks to ignore direct political pressure for change.

However, economic and knowledge-based change are also important. For example, in the case of nuclear power in Britain it is evident that technological advances were a crucial source of network change, while the shift to a more commercial ethos by key actors and organizations in the network owed much to the deepening economic recession in the early 1970s (Saward 1992). Similarly, new knowledge about the relationship between smoking and health (Read 1992) and concerning salmonella in eggs (Smith 1991) affected relationships within the respective networks.

Overall, it is evident that exogenous changes can affect the resources, interests and relationships of the actors within networks. Changes in these factors can produce tensions and conflicts which lead to either a breakdown in the network or the development of new policies. However, these changes don't have an effect independent of the structure of, and interactions within, the network. All such exogenous change is mediated through the under-

standing of agents and interpreted in the context of the structures, rules/
norms and interpersonal relationships within the network. So, any simple
distinction between endogenous and exogenous factors is misleading (see
Stones 1992).

Beyond networks versus outcomes. Although policy networks may affect policy
outcomes, these outcomes also affect the shape of the policy network directly,
as well as having an effect on the structural position of certain interests in civil
society and the strategic learning of actors in the network. Certainly, there is
not a unidirectional causal link between networks and outcomes.

Outcomes may affect networks in at least three ways. First, a particular
policy outcome may lead to a change in the membership of the network or to
the balance of resources within it. In this way, Conservative industrial relations
policy in the 1980s led in large part to the exclusion of trade union interests
from the youth employment policy network; in 1988 the Manpower Services
Commission, on which the trade unions had a third of the membership, was
abolished and replaced by a system of Training and Enterprise Councils (with
Local Enterprise Companies in Scotland) on which unions had very limited, if
any, representation (see Marsh 1992). Similarly, the changing government
policy on health, while it clearly didn't lead to the exclusion of the doctors
from any networks, nevertheless weakened their bargaining position within
those networks (Wistow 1992).

Second, policy outcomes may have an effect on the broader social structure which weakens the position of a particular interest in relation to a given
network. Thus, a whole series of economic policies, as well as industrial relations policy, weakened the position of trade unions in civil society, removed
them from a series of interest groups and virtually removed their role in the
policy-making process (Marsh 1992).

Third, policy outcomes can affect agents. Clearly, agents learn by experience. If certain actions within a network fail to produce an outcome beneficial
to an actor within the network and the organization he or she represents, or
more broadly to the network as a whole, then that actor is likely to pursue
other strategies and actions. As Hay emphasizes, strategic learning is obviously
an important feature of political activity (see Hay 1995).

In my view, it is crucial to refine Figure 11.1 in the light of the subsequent discussion (see Figure 11.2). Figure 11.2 differs from Figure 11.1 in four
key respects. First, all the arrows are two-way to emphasize that dialectical
relationships are involved. Second, the lines highlight the importance of the
interaction between certain variables, an interaction which was ignored in the
earlier formulation. Third, a new link is added, structural position → network
structure, to represent the direct effect which the broader patterns of privilege,
which are a key feature of the context within which networks operate, have on
the network structure. Finally, the links between policy outcome and structural
position and policy outcome and actor learning emphasize that outcomes have
an indirect as well as a direct effect on network outcomes.

Bibliography

Adler, E. and Haas, P.M. (1992) 'Epistemic communities, world order and the creation of a reflective research program', *International Organizations*, 46(3): 367–90.

Aldrich, H. and Whetton, D.A. (1981) 'Organization-sets, action-sets, and networks: making the most of simplicity', in P.C. Nystrom and W.H. Starbuck (eds) *Handbook of Organizational Design*. Oxford: Oxford University Press.

Almond, G. and Powell, G.B. (1965) *Comparative Politics: A Developmental Approach*. Boston: Little Brown.

Andersen, M.S. and Daugbjerg, C. (1994) 'Land-use policy in Denmark', in K. Eckerberg, P.K. Mydske, A. Niemi-Iilahti and K.H. Pedersen (eds) *Comparing Nordic and Baltic Countries – Environmental Problems and Policies in Agriculture and Forestry*. Copenhagen: Nordic Council of Ministers.

Andersen, M.S. and Hansen, M.W. (1991) *Vandmiljplanen. Fra forhandling til symbol*. Harlev J.: Niche.

Andersen, S.S. (1984) *Conflict over Labour Relations in the Norwegian Petroleum Sector*. Sandvika: Institute of Energy.

Andresen, R.G. (1992) *The Norwegian Authorities' Expectations and Activities Relevant to the Concept of Total Management in the Offshore Industry*. Stavanger: NPD.

Antonelli, C. (1988) *New Information Technology and Industrial Change*. Dordrecht: Klumer.

Arlacchi, P. (1986) *Mafia Business: The Mafia Ethic and the Spirit of Capitalism*. London: Verso.

Arp, Hennig (1991) 'Interest groups in EC legislation: the case of car emission standards', paper presented at the European Consortium for Political Research Joint Session of Workshops, University of Essex, Colchester, UK, 22–8 March.

Ashford, D. (1982) *British Dogmatism and French Pragmatism: Central–Local Policymaking in the Welfare State*. London: George Allen and Unwin.

Association of Chief Police Officers in Scotland (1994) *Constitution and Rules*. Edinburgh: Lothian and Borders Police Print Unit.

Atkinson, M.M. and Coleman, W.D. (1985) 'Corporatism and industrial policy', in A. Cawson (ed.) *Organized Interests and the State: Studies in Meso-Corporatism*. London: Sage.

Atkinson, M.M. and Coleman, W.D. (1989) 'Strong states and weak states: sectoral policy networks in advanced capitalist economies', *British Journal of Political Science*, 19(1): 47–67.

Atkinson, M.M. and Coleman, W.D. (1992) 'Policy networks, policy communities and the problems of governance', *Governance*, 5(2): 154–80.

ATV (Akademiet for de Tekniske Videnskaber) (1990) *Vandmiljøoplanens tilblivelse og iværksættelse*. Lyngby: ATV.

Bache, I. (1992) 'Bypassing the centre: assessing the value of UK local authority participation in E.C. transgovernmental coalitions'. Unpublished MA thesis, International Studies department, University of Sheffield.

Bache, I., George, S. and Rhodes, R.A.W. (1996) 'The EU, cohesion policy and subnational authority in the UK', in L. Hooghe (ed.) *Cohesion Policy and European Integration*. Oxford: Clarendon Press.

Baine, S., Benington, J. and Russell, J. (1992) *Changing Europe: Challenges Facing the Voluntary and Community Sectors in the 1990s*. London: NCVO, Bedford Square Press.

Baker, W. (1990) 'Market networks and corporate families', *American Journal of Sociology*, 96(3): 589–625.

Baldock, D. (1991) 'The Polluter Pays Principle and agriculture', in D. Baldock and G. Bennett (eds) *Agriculture and the Polluter Pays Principle. A Study of Six EC Countries*. Arnhem and London: Institute for European Environmental Policy.

Baldock, D. and Wenning, M. (1990) *The EC Structural Funds – Environmental Briefing 2*. London: World Wide Fund for Nature (WWF).

Baldock, D. et al. (1992) *The Integration of Environmental Protection into the Definition and Implementation of Other EC Policies*. London: IEEP.

Bales, R.F. (1950) *Interaction Process Analysis*. Cambridge, MA: Addison-Wesley.

Barlow, H. (1993) 'Police chief's cry for help', *The Dominion*, Wellington, 25 May.

Barrett et al. (1987) *Safety in Offshore Petroleum Industry*. London: Kogan Page.

Baumgartner, F.R. and Jones, B.D. (1993), *Agendas and Instability in American Politics*. London and Chicago: University of Chicago Press.

Baumgartner, F.R. and Talbert, J.C. (1995) 'From setting a national agenda on health care to making decisions in Congress', *Journal of Health Politics, Policy and Law*, 20(3): 437–45.

Bayley, D.H. (1979) 'Police function, structure, and control in Western Europe and North America: comparative and historical studies', *Crime and Justice*, Vol. 1. Chicago: University of Chicago Press.

Bayley, D.H. (1992) 'Comparative organisation of the police in English-speaking countries', in M. Tonry and M. Morris (eds) *Modern Policing: Crime and Justice*, Vol. 15. Chicago and London: University of Chicago Press.

Beckett, A. (1991) 'Structural Options for the New Zealand Police Service', unpublished research paper. Wellington, New Zealand: Victoria University of Wellington.

Benington, J. and Harvey, J. (1994) 'Spheres or tiers? The significance of trans-national local authority networks', in P. Dunleavy and J. Stanyer (eds) *Contemporary Political Studies 1994*. Belfast: Political Studies Association.

Benington, J. and Stoker, G. (1989) 'Local government in the firing line', in N. Buchan and T. Sumner (eds) *Glasnost in Britain*. London: Macmillan.

Benington, J. and Taylor, M. (1993) 'Changes and challenges facing the United Kingdom welfare state in Europe of the 1990s', *Policy and Politics*, 21(2): 121–34.

Benson, J.K. (1982) 'A framework for policy analysis', in D. Rogers, D. Whitten and associates, *Interorganisational Co-ordination*. Ames IL: University of Chicago.

Benyon, J. (1993) *Law and Order Review 1993: An Audit of Crime, Policing and Criminal Justice Issues*. Leicester: Centre for the Study of Public Order.

Benyon, J. *et al.* (1994) 'Understanding police cooperation in Europe: setting a framework for analysis', in M. Anderson and M. den Boer (eds) *Policing Across National Boundaries*. London: Pinter.

Benz, A. (1995) 'Politkenetzwerke in der Horizontalen Politkverflechtung', in D. Jansen and K. Schubert (eds) *Netzwerke und Politikproduktion, Konzepte, Methoden, Perspektiven*. Marburg: Schuren.

Berg-Schlosser, D. and De Meur, G. (1994) 'Conditions of democracy in inter-war Europe – reduction of complexity for a small-N analysis', paper for panel, 'The Methodology of Comparative Political Research: Recent Advances', World Congress of Sociology, July 18–23.

Birley, S. (1985) 'The role of networks in the entrepreneurial process', *Journal of Business Venturing*, 1(1): 107–17.

Birnbaum, J.S. and Murray, A.S. (1987) *Showdown at Gucci Gulch: Lawmakers, Lobbyists and the Unlikely Triumph of Tax Reform*. New York: Random House.

Blau, P.M. (1982) 'Structural sociology and network analysis: an overview', in P.V. Marsden and N. Lin (eds) *Social Structure and Network Analysis*. Beverley Hills, CA: Sage.

Bomberg, E. (1994) 'Policy networks on the periphery: EU environmental policy and Scotland', *Regional Policy and Politics*, 4(1): 45–61.

Bomberg, E. (1998) *Green Parties and Politics in the European Union*. London: Routledge.

Bomberg, E. and Peterson, J. (1993) 'Prevention from above? Preventive policies and the European Community', in M. Mills (ed.) *Health, Prevention and British Politics*. Aldershot: Avebury Press.

Bonacich, P. (1987) 'Power and centrality: a family of measures', *American Sociological Review*, 92(5): 1170–82.

Borgatti, S.P. and Everett, M.G. (1992) 'The notion of position in social network analysis', in P.V. Marsden (ed.) *Sociological Methodology 1992*. Oxford: Blackwell.

Borgatti, S.P., Everett, M.G. and Freeman, L.C. (1992) *UCINET IV*. Columbia: Analytic Technologies.

Borzel, T. (1997) 'What's so special about policy networks? An exploration of the concept and its usefulness in studying European governance', Mimeo, European University, Florence.

Boston, J., Levine, S., McLeay, E. and Roberts, N.S. (1996) *New Zealand Under MMP: A New Politics?* Auckland: Auckland University Press.

Boston, J., Martin, J., Pallot, J. and Walsh, P. (1996) *Public Management: The New Model*. Auckland: Oxford University Press.

Bovaird, T. (1994) 'Managing urban economic development: learning to change or the marketing of failure?', *Urban Studies*, 31(4/5): 573–603.

Braakman, G. (1993) Interview in *Europe Environmental Fortnightly*, No. 413, October 12, Section II, 2–5.

Brand, J. (1992) *British Parliamentary Parties: Policy and Power*. Oxford: Clarendon Press.

Brass, D.J. and Burkhardt, K. (1992) 'Centrality and power in organizations', in N. Nohria and R. Eccles (eds) *Networks and Organizations: Structure, Form and Action*. Harvard: Harvard Business School Press.

Buksti, J.A. (1980) 'Udviklingen i landbrugets organisationsforhold 1972–79', in J.A. Buksti (ed.) *Organisationer under forandring: Studier i organisationssystemet i Danmark*. Århus: Forlaget Politica.

Burt, R.S. (1976) 'Positions in networks', *Social Forces*, 55(1): 93–122.

Burt, R.S. (1982) *Toward a Structural Theory of Action*. New York: Academic Press.

Cabinet Office (1996) *Cabinet Office Manual*. Wellington: Cabinet Office, Department of Prime Minister and Cabinet.

Cairney, P. (1997) 'Advocacy coalitions and policy change', in J. Stanyer and G. Stoker (eds) *Contemporary Political Studies*. Oxford: Blackwell.

Callon, M. (1991) 'Techno-economic networks and irreversibility', in J. Law (ed.) *A Sociology of Monsters: Essays on Power, Technology and Domination*. London: Routledge.

Callon, M. and Law, J. (1989) 'On the construction of sociotechnical networks: context and content revisited', *Knowledge and Society*, 8(1): 57–83.

Cameron, G. *et al.* (1991) 'The economic outlook for the regions and countries of the United Kingdom in the 1990s', *Cambridge Economic Review*.

Cameron, N. (1986) 'Developments and issues in policing New Zealand', in N. Cameron and W. Young (eds) *Policing at the Crossroads*. Wellington: Allen and Unwin.

Campbell, D. (1994) 'Police chiefs agree new lobbying voice', *Guardian*, 28 October.

Carrell, S. (1994) 'More chance of conflict as accountability goes by the board', *The Scotsman*, 3 November.

Carson, W.G. (1982) *The Other Price of Britain's Oil*. London: Martin Robertson.

Cater, D. (1964) *Power in Washington*. New York: Random House.

Cavanagh, M., Marsh, D. and Smith, M. (1995) 'The relationship between policy networks and the sectoral and the sub-sectoral levels', *Public Administration*, 73(4): 627–33.

CEC (1992) *Towards Sustainability: A European Community Programme of Policy and Action in Relation to the Environment and Sustainable Development*, Com(92)23 Final, Brussels: EC.

Chisholm, D. (1989) *Coordination Without Hierarchy*. Berkeley: University of California Press.

Christiansen, P.M. (1996) 'Denmark', in P.M. Christiansen (ed.) *Governing the Environment*. Copenhagen: Nordic Council of Ministers.

Clark, C.E. (1991) 'The need for a national policy', *Policing*, 7(2): 117–31.

Cole, A. and John, P. (1995) 'Local policy networks in Britain and France: policy coordination in fragmented political sub-systems', *West European Politics*, 18(4): 89–109.

Coleman, W.D. and Skøgstad, G. (1990) 'Policy communities and policy networks: a structural approach', in W.D. Coleman and G. Skøgstad (eds) *Policy Communities and Public Policy in Canada*. Toronto: Copp Clark Pitman.

Collier, D. (1993) 'The comparative method', in A. Finifter (ed.) *Political Science: The State of the Discipline*. Washington DC: APSA.

Collins, K. and Earnshaw, D. (1992) 'The implementation and enforcement of European Community environmental legislation', *Environmental Politics*, 1(4): 213–49.

Cooke, P. and Morgan, K. (1993) 'The network paradigm: new departures in corporate and regional development', *Environmental and Planning D*, 11(5): 543–64.

Court of Auditors (1992) Special Report No. 3/92 with the Commission's Replies, *Official Journal* 92/c245/01, vol 35, 23 September.

Damgaard, E. (1982) 'The public sector in a democratic order. Problems and non-solutions in the Danish case', *Scandinavian Political Studies*, 5(4): 337–58.

Damgaard, E. (1986) 'Causes, forms, and consequences of sectoral policy-making: some Danish evidence', *European Journal of Political Research*, 14(3): 273–87.

Daniel, P. and Jamieson, J. (1992) *Coal Production Prospects in the EC*. London: Institute for Economic Affairs.

Danske Husmandsforeninger (1991) *Danske Husmandsforeningers politik på et bæredygtigt landbrug*. Copenhagen: Danske Husmandsforeninger.

Daugbjerg, C. (1994a) 'Dansk industri og det indre marked: Policy-netværk i Bruxelles og København', *Politica*, 26(4): 456–73.

Daugbjerg, C. (1994b) *Policy Networks and Changing Environments. Environmental Regulation and Agricultural Reform: Some Theoretical Considerations*. Aarhus: Department of Political Science, Aarhus University.

Daugbjerg, C. (1995) 'Er miljøpolitik teknik eller politik? En komparativ analyse af miljøpolitik i den svenske og danske landbrugssektor', *Nordisk Administrativt Tidsskrift*, 76(1): 33–47.

Daugbjerg, C. (1996) 'Policy networks and net agendas in agriculture'. PhD dissertation, Department of Political Science, Aarhus University, Denmark.

Den Boer, M. (1994) 'The quest for European policing: rhetoric and justification in a disorderly debate', in M. Anderson and M. den Boer (eds) *Policing Across National Boundaries*. London: Pinter.

Department of Employment (1972) *Safety and Health at Work*, vols 1 and 2, Cmnd 5034. London: HMSO.

Department of Energy (1967) *Report into the Inquiry into the Causes of the Accident to the Drilling Rig Gem*. Cmnd 3409. London: HMSO.

Department of Energy (1980) *Offshore Safety*, Cmnd 7866. London: HMSO.

Department of Energy (1990) *The Public Inquiry into the Piper Alpha Disaster*, Cm 1310. London: HMSO.

Department of Justice (1993) *Briefing Papers for the Minister of Justice, Vol. 1: Key Policy Issues*. Wellington: Department of Justice.

Department of Prime Minister and Cabinet (1995a) *Report of the Department of Prime Minister and Cabinet*. Wellington: Department of Prime Minister and Cabinet.

Department of Prime Minister and Cabinet (1995b) *Strategic Result Areas*. Wellington: Department of Prime Minister and Cabinet.

Döhler, M. (1991) 'Policy networks, opportunity structures and neo-Conservative reform strategies in health policy', in B. Marin and R. Mayntz (eds) *Policy Networks: Empirical Evidence and Theoretical Considerations*. Frankfurt am Main/ Boulder, Colorado: Campus Verlag/Westview Press.

Dowding, K. (1994a) Behaviouralism, Rational Choice Theory and the 'New Institutionalism': A Critique and Synthesis. Paper delivered at the ECPR workshops in Limerick.

Dowding, K. (1994b) 'Policy networks: don't stretch a good idea too far', in P. Dunleavy and J. Stanyer, *Contemporary Political Studies, 1994*. Belfast: Political Studies Association.

Dowding, K. (1995) 'Model or metaphor? A critical review of the policy network approach', *Political Studies*, 43(2): 136–58.

Dubgaard, A. (1991) *The Danish Nitrate Policy in the 1980s. Report No. 59*. Copenhagen: Statens Jordbrugsøkonomiske Institut.

Dunleavy, P. (1981) *The Politics of Mass Housing in Britain 1945–1975*. Oxford: Oxford University Press.

Dupuy, F. and Thoenig, J.–C. (1983) *Sociologie de l'Administration Française*. Paris: Armand Colin.

Dyson, K. (1980) *The State Tradition in Western Europe*. Oxford: Martin Robertson.

Eckerberg, Katarina (1994) 'Consensus, conflict or compromise: the Swedish case', in K. Eckerberg, P.K. Mydske, A. Niemi-Iilahti and K.H. Pedersen (eds) *Comparing Nordic and Baltic Countries – Environmental Problems and Policies in Agriculture and Forestry*. Copenhagen: Nordic Council of Ministers.

Eckhoff, D. (1995) 'Big changes in the administration of the justice system', Press Release, Justice Communications Unit, 5 April.

Edmund-Davies, Lord (1979) *Committee of Inquiry on the Police Reports on Negotiating Machinery and Pay*, Cmnd 7283. London: HMSO.

EU Committee of the American Chamber of Commerce in Belgium (1995) *EU Environment Guide 1995*. Brussels: EU Committee.

Evans, M. (1995) 'Elitist theories of the state', in D. Marsh and G. Stoker (eds) *Theories and Methods in Politics*. Basingstoke: Macmillan.

Fairburn, M. (1989) *The Ideal State and its Enemies. The Foundations of Modern New Zealand Society 1850–1990*. Auckland: Auckland University Press.

Foster, J. and Woolfson, C. (1992) *Trade Unionism and Health Safety Rights in Britain's Offshore Oil Industry*. London: International Centre for Trade Union Rights.

Fothergill, S. (1992) 'The new alliance of mining areas', in J. Benington and M. Geddes (eds) *Restructuring the Local Economy*. London: Longman.

Freeman, J.L. (1965) *The Policy Process*. New York: A.A. Knopf.

Freeman, L.C. (1955) *The Political Process*. New York: Random House.

Freeman, L.C. (1979) 'Centrality in social networks: conceptual clarification', *Social Networks*, 1(3): 215–39.

Friedmann, R.R. (1992) *Community Policing. Comparative Perspectives and Prospects*. Hemel Hempstead: Harvester Wheatsheaf.

Galaskiewicz, J. (1979) *Exchange Networks and Community Politics*. Beverley Hills: Sage.

Galaskiewicz, J. and Wasserman, S. (1993) 'Social network analysis: concepts, methodology and directions for the 1990s', *Sociological Methods and Research*, 22(1): 3–22.

Gambetta, D. (1991) 'In the beginning was the word: the symbols of the Mafia', *Archives Européenes de Sociologie*, 32(1): 53–67.

Gambetta, D. (1993) *The Sicilian Mafia: The Business of Protection*. Cambridge, MA: Harvard University Press.

Gambetta, D. (1994) 'Godfather's gossip', *Archives Européenes de Sociologie*, 32(2): 199–223.

Glover, F. (1989) 'Tabu search – Part I', *ORSA Journal of Computing*, 1(3): 190–206.

Glover, F. (1990) 'Tabu search – Part II', *ORSA Journal of Computing* 2(1): 4–32.

Goldsmith, A.J. (ed.) (1991) *Complaints Against the Police. The Trend to External Review*. Oxford: Clarendon.

Golub, J. (1996) 'State power and influence in European integration: lessons from the Packaging Waste Directive', *Journal of Common Market Studies*, 34(3): 313–40.

Goodman, L.A. (1961) 'Snowball sampling', *Annals of Mathematical Statistics*, 32(2): 148–70.

Government Offices for the Regions (1994) *Bidding Guidance: A Guide to Funding for the Single Regeneration Budget*. London: HMSO.

Gramsci, A. (1971) *Selections from Prison Notebooks*. London: Lawrence and Wishart.

Grant, W. (1978) 'Insider groups, outsider groups and interest group strategies in Britain', Working Paper No. 19. Warwick: University of Warwick.

Grant, W. (1993) *Business and Politics in Britain*. Basingstoke: Macmillan.

Grant, W., Paterson, W. and Whitson, C. (1988) *Government and the Chemical Industry: A Comparative Study of Britain and West Germany*. Oxford: Clarendon Press.

Green Group in the European Parliament (1994) Press Release, 5 May.

Greenwood, J. (1994) 'Representing interests in the EU: the contribution of case-study methods', paper presented at the XVIth World Congress of the International Political Science Association, 21–25 August.

Griffiths, G. (1995) 'Executive coordination mechanisms in comparative perspective', Unpublished Paper, Office of the Cabinet, State of Queensland, Brisbane, Queensland.

Haas, P.M. (1990) *When Knowledge is Power*. Berkeley, CA: University of California Press.

Hall, J.A. and Ikenberry, G.J. (1989) *The State*. Milton Keynes: Open University Press.

Hall, P.A. (1986) *Governing the Economy: The Politics of State Intervention in Britain and France*. Cambridge: Polity Press.

Hanf, K. and Scharpf, F.W. (eds) (1978) *Interorganizational Policy Making*. London: Sage.

Hanf, K. and Toonen, T.A.J. (1985) *Policy Implementation in Federal and Unitary Systems*. Dordrecht: Kluwer.

Harding, A. (1997) 'Development coalitions in European cities', *Frontières*, 6(1): 83–119.

Harris, S., Swinbank, A. and Wilkinson, G. (1983) *The European Food and Farm Policies of the European Community*. Chichester and New York: John Wiley and Sons.

Hay, C. (1994a) 'Structural and ideological contradictions in Britain's post-war reconstruction', *Capital and Class*, 54(1): 25–60.

Hay, C. (1994b) 'Werner in Wunderland, or notes on a Marxism beyond pessimism and false optimism', in F. Sebsi and C. Vercellone (eds) *École de la Régulation et Critique de la Raison Économique*. Paris: *Futur Anterieur*, Editions L'Hormatton.

Hay, C. (1995) 'Structure and agency: holding the whip hand', in D. Marsh and G. Stoker (eds) *Theories and Methods of Political Science*. London: Macmillan.

Hay, C. (1995/96) 'Rethinking crisis: narratives of the New Right and constructions of crisis', *Rethinking Marxism*, 8(2): 60–76.

Hay, C. (1996a) *Re-Stating Social and Political Change*. Buckingham: Open University Press.

Hay, C. (1996b) 'Narrating crisis: the discursive construction of the Winter of Discontent', *Sociology*, 30(2): 253–77.

Hay, C. (1997) 'Divided by a common language: political theory and the concept of power', *Politics*, 17(1): 45–52.

Hay, C. (forthcoming) 'Marxism and the state: flogging a dead horse?', in A. Gamble, D. Marsh and T. Tant (eds) *Marxism and the Social Sciences*. London: Macmillan.

Heclo, H. (1978) 'Issue networks and the executive establishment', in A. King (ed.) *The American Political System*. Washington, DC: AEI.

Heclo, H. and Wildavsky, A. (1974) *The Private Government of Public Money*. London: Macmillan.

Heinz, J.P. and Laumann, E.O. (1990) 'Inner circles or hollow cores? Elite networks in national policy systems', *Journal of Politics*, 52(3): 356–90.

Heinz, J., Laumann, E., Nelson, R. and Salisbury, R. (1993) *The Hollow Core: Private Interests in National Policy-Making*. Cambridge, MA: Harvard University Press.

Her Majesty's Inspectorate of Constabulary (1992) *Annual Report*. London: HMSO.

Hill, R. (1986) *Policing the Colonial Frontier: The Theory and Practice of Coercive Social and Racial Control in New Zealand 1767–1867*. Wellington: GP Books.

Hill, S. (1995) 'The social organisation of boards of directors', *British Journal of Sociology*, 46(2): 245–78.

Hilliard, B. (1994) 'Hopes fading as NCIS fails to flourish', *Police Review*, 10 June.

Hjern, B. and Porter, D.O. (1980) 'Implementation structures: a new unit of administrative analysis', *Organization Studies*, 2(2): 211–34.

Hoddinott, J.C. (1994) 'Justice for the next generation', paper presented at the Bar Council Conference, 1 October.

Hogwood, B. (1995) 'The Integrated Regional Offices and the Single Regeneration Budget', Commission for Local Democracy Report 13. London: Commission for Local Development.

Home Office (1993) *White Paper on the Government's Proposals for the Police Service in England and Wales*, Cmnd 2281. London: HMSO.

Home Office (1996) 'Fighting crime: head of Crime Prevention Agency announced', Press Release, 17 June.

House of Commons Committee of Public Accounts (1991) *Promoting Value for Money in Provincial Forces: Minutes of Evidence*. London: HMSO.

House of Commons Energy Committee (1992) *Seventh Report: Offshore Safety Management, HC 343*. London: HMSO.

Howe, S. (1994) 'Pay our £250-a-year ACPO subscriptions, Chiefs plead', *Police Review*, 21 January: 7.

HSE (1992) *A Guide to Offshore (Safety Case) Regulations*. London: HMSO.

HSE (1993) Documents supplied directly to the author, 6 November 1993.

Hu, K.–C. (1995) 'Policy networks in democratic and authoritarian regimes', unpublished PhD thesis, University of Sheffield.

Hughes, H.W.D. (1994) 'Developments within safety, health and environment standards and the regulator systems in north-west Europe', paper presented at the Offshore Northern Seas Conference, Stavanger.

Hunter, F. (1953) *Community Power Structure*. Chapel Hill, NC: University of North Carolina Press.

Imai, K. and Baba, Y. (1989) *Systemic Innovation and Cross-Border Networks*. Paris: OECD.

Ingham, B. (1991) *Kill the Messenger*. London: Fontana.

Jarillo, J.C. (1988) 'On strategic networks', *Strategic Management Journal*, 9(1): 31–41.

Jenkins-Smith, H.C. and Sabatier, P.A. (1993) 'The dynamics of policy-oriented learning', in P.A. Sabatier and H.C. Jenkins-Smith (eds) *Policy Change and Learning. An Advocacy Coalition Framework*. Boulder, CO, San Francisco, CA, Oxford: Westview Press.

Jessop, B. (1990) *State Theory: Putting the Capitalist State in Its Place*. Cambridge: Polity.

John, P. (forthcoming) 'Urban economic policy networks in Britain and France: a sociometric approach', *Government and Policy*.

John, P. and Cole, A. (1995) 'Models of local decision-making networks in Britain and France', *Policy and Politics*, 23(4): 303–12.

John, P. and Cole, A. (1998) 'Urban regimes and local governance in Britain and France: policy adaption and coordination in Leeds and Lille', *Urban Affairs Review*, 33(3): 382–404.

Johnson, S. and Corcelle, G. (1989) *The Environmental Policy of the European Communities*. London: Graham and Trotman.

Johnston, L. (1992) 'The politics of private policing', *Political Quarterly*, 63(3): 341–9.

Jones, C.O. (1979) 'American politics and the organization of energy policy-making', *Annual Review of Energy*, 4: 99–121.

Jones, C.O. (1982) *An Introduction to the Study of Public Policy* (3rd ed.). Monterey, CA: Brooks/Cole.

Jones, T., Newburn, T. and Smith, D.J. (1994) *Democracy and Policing*. London: Policy Studies Institute.

Jordan, A.G. (1990a) 'Policy community realism versus "new" institutionalist ambiguity', *Political Studies*, 38(3): 470–82.

Jordan, A.G. (1990b) 'Sub-government, policy communities and networks: refilling the old bottles', *Journal of Theoretical Politics*, 2(2): 319–38.

Jordan, A.G. (1990c) 'The pluralism of pluralism: an anti-theory?', *Political Studies*, 38(2): 286–301.

Jordan, A.G. and Richardson, J.J. (1987) *British Politics and the Policy Process*. London: Unwin Hyman.

Jordan, A.G. and Schubert, K. (1992) 'A preliminary ordering of policy network labels', *European Journal of Political Research*, 21(1/2): 7–27.

Jordan, G., Maloney, W. and McLaughlin, A. (1994). 'Characterizing agricultural policy networks', *Public Administration*, 72(4): 505–26.

Jordbruksdepartementet (1987) *Intensiteten i jordbruksproduktionen. Miljöpåverkan och spannmålsöverskott. Betänkande av arbetsgruppen med uppgift att utreda vissa frågor rörande en lägre intensitet i jordbruksproduktionen.* Stockholm: Ds Jo.

Jordbruksutskottets (1989/90) 'Jordbruksutskottets betänkande 1989/90: JoU25', in *Riksdagstrycket 1989/90*. Stockholm: Livsmedelspolitiken.

Judge, D. (1993) *The Parliamentary State*. London: Sage.

Just, F. (1992) *Landbruget, staten og eksporten 1930–1950*. Esbjerg: Sydjysk Universitetsforlag.

Just, F. (1994) Agriculture and corporatism in Scandinavia', in P. Lowe, T. Marsden and S. Whatmore (eds) *Agricultural Regulations*. London: David Fulton.

Kamminga, M. (1994) 'Environment requirements in EC policies', *European Environmental Law Review*, 12: 23–5.

Katzenstein, P.J. (1978) 'Conclusion: domestic structures and strategies of foreign economic policy', in P.J. Katzenstein (ed.) *Between Power and Plenty. Foreign Economic Policies of Advanced Industrial States*. Madison: University of Wisconsin Press.

Kay, S. (1996) 'Organisational discretionary decision-making in the police with particular reference to the prosecution of serious matters'. PhD dissertation, Victoria University of Wellington.

Kenis, P. and Schneider, V. (1991) 'Policy networks and policy analysis: scrutinizing a new analytical toolbox', in Martin and Mayntz (eds) *Policy Network: Empirical Evidence and Theoretical Considerations*. Frankfurt am Main: Campus Verlag.

Keohane, R. and Nye, J. (1974) 'Transgovernmental relations and international organisations', *World Politics*, 27: 39–62.

Kickert, W.J., Klijn, E. and Koppenjan, J. (1997) *Managing Complex Networks*. London: Sage.

Kilsworth, P. and Bernard, H.R. (1974) 'A new sociometric and its application to a prison living unit', *Human Organisation*, 33(4): 335–50.

King, D. (1996) 'Justice network scheme winning overseas attention', *The Dominion*, Wellington, 2 September.

Kingdon, J. (1994) *Agendas, Alternatives and Public Policy* (2nd ed.). Boston: Little Brown.

Kirby, T. (1989) 'Police chiefs retreat over identity cards', *Independent*, 28 January.

Kitchen, J. (1977) *Labour Law and Offshore Oil*. London: Croom Helm.

Kjeldsen-Kragh, S. (1995) 'Svensk og dansk jordbrug – En sammenligning', *Tidsskrift for Landøkonomi*, 182(2): 113–31.

Klijn, E. (1997) 'Policy networks: an overview', in W.J. Kickert *et al. Managing Complex Networks*. London: Sage.

Knoke, D. (1990) *Political Networks: The Structural Perspective*. Cambridge: Cambridge University Press.

Knoke, D. and Kuklinski, J.H. (1982) *Network Analysis*. Beverley Hills, CA: Sage.

Knoke, D. and Laumann, E.O. (1987) *The Organizational State: Social Change in National Policy Domains*. Madison: University of Wisconsin Press.

Knoke, D. *et al.* (1996) *Comparing Policy Networks: Labour Politics in the US, Germany and Japan*. Cambridge: Cambridge University Press.

König, T. (1997) 'Macro stability and micro change. German policy networks before and after unification', paper presented to Annual Meeting of the American Political Science Association, Washington, 28–31 August.

Laclau, E. and Mouffe, C. (1985) *Hegemony and Socialist Strategy*. London: Verso.

Lagrove, J. and Wright, V. (eds) (1979) *Local Government in Britain and France*. London: Allen and Unwin.

Landboforeninger(ne), De danske (1986) *Beretning 1986*. Copenhagen: Landboforeninger(ne).

Landboforeninger(ne), De danske (1991) *En bæredygtig udvikling i landbruget*. Copenhagen: Landboforeninger(ne).

Landbrugsministeriet (1991) *Bæredygtigt landbrug: En teknisk redegørelse*. Copenhagen: Landbrugsministeriet.

Lane, J.–E. and Ersson, S.O. (1991) *Politics and Society in Western Europe* (2nd ed.). London: Sage.

Latour, B. (1986) 'The powers of association', in J. Law (ed.) *Power, Action and Belief: A New Sociology of Knowledge?* London: Routledge.

Latour, B. (1987) *Science in Action: How to Follow Scientists and Engineers Through Society*. Cambridge, MA: Harvard University Press.

Laumann, E. and Knoke, D. (1987) *The Organizational State: A Perspective on National Energy and Health Domains*. Madison: University of Wisconsin Press.

Laumann, E. and Pappi, F. (1973) 'New directions in the study of community elites', *American Sociological Review*, 38(2): 212–30.

Laumann, E. and Pappi, F. (1976) *Networks of Collective Action: A Perspective on Community Influence Systems*. New York: Academic Press.

Laumann, E., Marsden, P. and Prensky, D. (1992) 'The boundary specification problem in network analysis', in L. Freeman, D. White and A. Romney, *Research Methods in Network Analysis*. New Brunswick: Transaction.

Law, J. (1994) *Organizing Modernity*. Oxford: Blackwell.

Lazer, D. (1995) 'Social comparison processes in political networks'. PhD dissertation, University of Michigan.

Lembruch, G. (1991) 'The organization of society, administrative strategies, and policy networks', in R. Czada and A. Windhoff–Héritier (eds) *Political Choice: Institutions, Rules, and the Limits of Rationality*. Frankfurt am Main/Boulder, CO: Campus Verlag/Westview Press.

Liberatore, A. (1991) 'Problems of transnational policymaking: environmental policy in the European Community', *European Journal of Political Research*, 19(3): 281–305.

Linder, S.H. and Peters, B.G. (1989) 'Instruments of government: perceptions and contexts', *Journal of Public Policy*, 9(1): 35–58.

Long, T. (1995) 'Shaping public policy in the European Union: a case study of structural funds', *Journal of European Public Policy*, 2: 672–9.

Loughlin, M. (1986) *Local Government in the Modern State*. London: Sweet and Maxwell.

Lov no. 16 (1987) 'Lov om støtte til miljøforbedrende investeringer i mindre landbrug m.v.'. Copenhagen: *Loutidende A*.

Lov no. 1172 (1992) 'Beckendgørelse af lov om støtte til miljøforbedrende investeringer i mindre landbrug m.v.'. Copenhagen: *Loutidende A*.

Lowi, T. (1969) *The End of Liberalism*. New York: Norton.

Lowi, T. (1972) 'Four systems of policy, politics and choice', *Public Administration Review*, 32 (July/August): 298–310.

Lundvall, B.-A. (1988) 'Innovation as an interactive process', in G. Dosi *et al.* (eds) *Technical Change and Economic Theory*. London: Frances Pinter.

Lustgarten, L. (1986) *The Governance of Police*. London: Sweet and Maxwell.

Mabileau, A. (1991) *Le Système Local en France*. Paris: Montchrestien.

McConnell, G. (1966) *Private Power and American Democracy*. New York: Knopf.

McFarland, A. (1984) *Common Cause: Lobbying in the Public Interest*. Chatham, NJ: Chatham House.

McFarland, A. (1987) 'Interest groups and theories of power in America', *British Journal of Political Science*, 17(1): 129–47.

McGill, D. (1992) *No Right to Strike. The History of the New Zealand Police Service Organisations*. Wellington: Silver Owl Press.

McKelvey, D. (1982) *Organizational Systematics*. Berkeley: University of California Press.

Mackie, T. and Marsh, D. (1995) 'The comparative method', in D. Marsh and G. Stoker (eds) *Theories and Methods in Political Science*. Basingstoke: Macmillan.

McLaughlin, E. (1992) 'The democratic deficit. European Union and the accountability of the British police', *British Journal of Criminology*, 32(4): 473–87.

McLeay, E. (1990) 'Defining policing policies and the political agenda', *Political Studies*, 38(4): 620–37.

McLeay, E. (1992) 'The state in New Zealand', in H. Gold (ed.) *New Zealand Politics in Perspective*. Auckland: Longman Paul.

McLeay, E. (1995) *The Cabinet and Political Power in New Zealand*. Auckland: Oxford University Press.

McPherson, A. and Raab, C. (1988) *Governing Education*. Edinburgh: Edinburgh University Press.

March, J.G. and Olsen, J.P. (1989) *Rediscovering Institutions: The Organizational Basis of Politics*. New York: Free Press.

Marin, B. (1990) 'Generalized political exchange, governance and generalized exchange', in B. Marin (ed.) *Governance and Generalized Exchange*. Frankfurt am Main: Campus.

Mariolis, P. (1983) 'Interlocking directorates and financial groups: a peak analysis', *Sociological Spectrum*, 3: 237–52.

Markowsky, B. *et al.* (1988) 'Power relations in exchange networks', *American Sociological Review*, 53(1): 220–36.

Marsh, D. (1992) 'Youth employment policy 1970–1990: towards the exclusion of Trade Unions', in D. Marsh and R. Rhodes, *Policy Networks in British Government*. Oxford: Clarendon.

Marsh, D. (1994) 'Coming of age but not learning from the experience: one cheer for rational choice theory', paper presented at the European Consortium for Political Research, Madrid, May. Published in the *Caledonian Papers in Social Science Series*, Department of Social Sciences, Glasgow Caledonian University.

Marsh, D. (1995a) 'The convergence between state theories', in D. Marsh and G. Stoker (eds) *Theories and Methods in Political Science*. London: Macmillan.

Marsh, D. (1995b) 'State theory and the policy network model', Strathclyde Paper in Politics and Government. Glasgow: University of Strathclyde.

Marsh, D. and Rhodes, R.A.W. (eds) (1992) *Policy Networks in British Government*. Oxford: Clarendon.

Marsh, D. and Smith, M.J. (1995) 'The role of networks in an understanding of Whitehall: towards a dialectical approach', paper presented at the ESRC Local Governance Programme's Conference on Networks, University College Wales, Cardiff, May.

Martin, B. and Mayntz, R. (eds) (1991a) *Policy Network: Empirical Evidence and Theoretical Considerations*. Frankfurt am Main: Campus Verlag.

Mawson, J. *et al.* (1995) *The Single Regeneration Budget: The Stocktake*. Birmingham: Centre for Urban and Regional Studies, Birmingham University.

Mayntz, R. (1994) 'Modernization and the Logic of Interorganizational Networks', MIPGF Working Paper No. 4, Koln: Max-Planck-Institut Fur Gesellschaftsforschung.

Mazey, S. and Richardson, J. (1992) 'Environmental groups and the EC: challenges and opportunities', *Environmental Politics*, 1(4): 109–28.

Mazey, S. and Richardson, J. (1993) *Lobbying in the European Community*. Oxford: Oxford University Press.

Micheletti, M. (1990) *The Swedish Farmers' Movement and Government Agricultural Policy*. New York: Praeger.

Miles, R.E. and Snow, C.C. (1992) 'Causes of failure in network organizations', *California Management Review*, 34(4): 53–72.

Miljøstyrelsen (1984) *NPO-redegørelse*. Copenhagen: Miljøstyrelsen.

Mills, M. and Saward, M. (1994) 'All very well in practice, but what about the theory? A critique of the British idea of policy networks', in P. Dunleavy and J. Stanyer (eds) *Contemporary Political Studies*. Belfast: Political Studies Association.

Ministry of Local Government and Labour (1992) *Safety and Working Environment in the Offshore Petroleum Industry*. Oslo: NPD.

Mintz, B. and Schwartz, M. (1985) *Power Structure of American Business*. Chicago, IL: University of Chicago Press.

Mizruchi, M.S. (1994) 'Social network analysis: recent achievements and current controversies', *Acta Sociologica*, 37(4): 329–43.

Morgan, R. (1989) 'Police accountability: current developments and future prospects', in M. Weatheritt (ed.) *Police Research: Some Future Prospects*. Aldershot: Gower.

Murdoch, J. (1995a) 'Actor-networks and evolution of economic forms: combining description and explanation in theories of regulation, flexible specialisation and networks', *Environment and Planning A*, 27(11): 731–57.

Murdoch, J. (1995b) 'Government in action: some (sociological) thought on policy networks as actor-networks', paper presented at the ESRC Local Governance Programme's Conference Networks, University College Wales, Cardiff, May.

Myhre, L. (1989) Nopef Presentation to the Piper Alpha Inquiry. Mimeo supplied to author.

National Audit Office (1992) *Report by the Comptroller and Auditor-General: Control of Police Manpower in Scotland*. London: HMSO.

Neuberger, H. (1989) 'The economics of 1992', *Local Government Policy Making*, 16(3): 3–10.

Newton, K. (1976) *Second City Politics*. Oxford: Oxford University Press.

New Zealand Police (1987) *Annual Report of the New Zealand Police*. Wellington: New Zealand Police.

New Zealand Police (1989) *Briefing Papers for the Information of the Minister of Police*. Wellington: New Zealand Police.

New Zealand Police (1996) *Animal Report of the New Zealand Police, 1995/6*. Wellington: New Zealand Police.

Nordlinger, E. (1981) *On the Autonomy of the Democratic State*. Cambridge, MA: Harvard University Press.

Noreng, O. (1980) *The Oil Industry and Government Strategy in the North Sea*. London: Croom Helm.

Norton, P. (1991) 'The changing face of Parliament: lobbying and its consequences', in P. Norton (ed.) *New Directions in British Politics? Essays on the Evolving Constitution*. Aldershot, Brookfield: Edward Elgar.

OECD (1989) *Economic Instruments for Environmental Protection*. Paris: OECD.

OECD (1994) *Agricultural Policies, Markets and Trade: Monitoring and Outlook 1994*. Paris: OECD.

Ognedal, M. (undated) *Offshore Safety – The Response to Cullen*. NPD Paper.

Ohmae, K. (1989) 'The global logic of strategic alliance', *Harvard Business Review*, 67(2): 143–54.

OILC (1991) *Striking Out: New Directions for Offshore Workers and their Unions*. Aberdeen: Offshore Information Centre.

OILC (1992) *Submission on the Draft Offshore Installations (Safety Case) Regulations*. Aberdeen: OILC.

OILC (1993) *Presentation to the Human Factors in Emergency Response Conference*. Aberdeen: OILC.

Olsen, J.P. (1983) *Organized Democracy: Political Institutions in a Welfare State – The Case of Norway*. Bergen: Universitetsforlaget.

Olsen, J.P., Roness, P. and Sætren, H. (1982) 'Norway: still peaceful coexistence and revolution in slow motion?' in J. Richardson (ed.) *Policy Styles in Western Europe*. London: George Allen and Unwin.

Opp, K.D. (1986) 'Soft incentives and collective action: participation in the antinuclear movement', *British Journal of Political Science*, 16: 87–112.

Orr, G. (1986) 'Policy accountability to the executive and Parliament', in N. Cameron and W. Young (eds) *Policing at the Crossroads*. Wellington: Allen and Unwin.

Ouchi, W.G. (1980) 'Markets, bureaucracies and clans', *Administrative Science Quarterly*, 25(2): 129–42.

Padgett, J.F. and Ansell, C.K. (1993) 'Robust action and the rise of the Medici 1400–1434', *American Journal of Sociology*, 98(6): 1259–319.

Page, E. (1991) *Localism and Centralism in Europe*. Oxford: OUP.

Page, E. and Goldsmith, M. (1987) *Central and Local Government Relations*. London: Sage.

Panebianco, A. (1988) *Political Parties: Organisation and Power*. Cambridge: Cambridge University Press.

Papi (1990) *Piper Alpha Public Inquiry, Day 169*. Croydon: Palantype Reporting Services.

Peck, J. (1995) 'Moving and shaking: business elites, state localism and urban privatism', *Progress in Human Georgraphy*, 19(1): 16–46.

Peck, J. and Tickell, A. (1995) 'Business goes local: dissecting the "business agenda" in Manchester', *International Journal of Urban and Regional Research*, 19(1): 55–78.

Perchard, D. (1993) 'Packaging and the environment: the draft EC directive', *European Environment*, 3: 2–6.

Peters, B.G. (1992) 'Bureaucratic politics and the institutions of the European Community', in A. Sbragia (ed.) *Euro-Politics: Institutions and Policymaking in the 'New European Community'*. Washington, DC: Brookings Institute.

Peters, B.G. (1994) 'Overload in American Government', in R. Maidment (ed.) *Democracy*. London: Hodder and Stoughton.

Peters, B.G. (1996) *Managing Horizontal Government: The Politics of Policy Coordination*. Ottawa: Canadian Centre for Management Development.

Peterson, J. (1989) 'Hormones, heifers and high politics: biotechnology and the Common Agricultural Policy', *Public Administration*, 67(4): 451–71.

Peterson, J. (1991) 'Technology policy in Europe: explaining the framework programme and Eureka in theory and practice', *Journal of Common Market Studies*, 22(1): 269–90.

Peterson, J. (1995) 'Decision-making in the European Union: towards a framework for analysis', *Journal of European Public Policy*, 2(1): 69–93.

Peterson, J. and Bomberg, E. (1996) Decision-making in the European Union: Reflections on EU governance, Working Document No 98. Centre for European Policy Studies.

Pollack, M. (1995) 'Regional actors in an intergovernmental play: the making and implementation of EC structural policy', in C. Rhodes and S. Mazey (eds) *The State of the European Union Building a European Policy?* Essex: Longman.

Porter, M. and Fuller, M.B. (1986) 'Coalition and global strategy', in M. Porter (ed.) *Competition in Global Industries*. Harvard, MA: Harvard University Press.

Porter, M. and Philip, A.B. (1993) 'The role of interest groups in EU environmental policy formulation: a case study of the draft packaging directive', *European Environment*, 3: 16–20.

Powell, P. (1990) 'Neither markets nor hierarchy: network forms of organisation', *Research in Organisational Behaviour*, 12(1): 74–96.

Przeworski, A. and Teune, H. (1970) *The Logic of Comparative Social Inquiry*. New York: John Wiley.

Proposition 1983/84: 76 'Regeringens proposition 1983/84: 76 om vissa livsmedelpolitiska frågor', in *Riksdagstrycket 1983/84*, Stockholm.

Proposition 1987/88: 85 'Regeringens proposition 1987/88: 85 om miljöpolitikken inför 1990-talet', in *Riksdagstrycket 1987/88*, Stockholm.

Pryce, R. (1973) *The Politics of the European Community*. London: Butterworth.

Rajan, A. (1990) *1992, A Zero Sum Game: Business Know-How, and Training Challenges in an Integrated Europe*. London: Industrial Society Press.

Rauch, J. (1992) 'Demosclerosis', *National Journal*, 5 September.

Read, M. (1992) 'Policy networks and issue networks: the politics of smoking', in D. Marsh and R. Rhodes *Policy Networks in British Government*. Oxford: Clarendon Press.

Reiner, R. (1991) *Chief Constables: Bobbies, Bosses or Bureaucrats?* Oxford: Oxford University Press.

Reiner, R. (1993) 'Accountable policing', in R. Reiner and S. Spencer (eds) *Accountable Policing: Effectiveness, Empowerment and Equity*. London: Institute for Public Policy Research.

Rhodes, R.A.W. (1981) *Control and Power in Central-Local Relations*. Aldershot: Gower.

Rhodes, R.A.W. (1986) *The National World of Local Government*. London: Allen and Unwin.

Rhodes, R.A.W. (1988) *Beyond Westminster and Whitehall: The Sub-Central Governments of Britain*. London: Unwin Hyman.

Rhodes, R.A.W. (1990) 'Policy networks: a British perspective', *Journal of Theoretical Politics*, 2(3): 293–317.

Rhodes, R.A.W. (1992) *Beyond Westminster and Whitehall* (2nd ed.). London: Routledge.

Rhodes, R.A.W. and Marsh, D. (1992) 'New directions in the study of policy networks', *European Journal of Political Research*, 21(1/2): 181–205.

Rhodes, R.A.W. and Marsh, D. (1994) 'Policy networks: "defensive" comments, modest claims, and plausible research strategies', paper presented at the PSA Annual Conference, University of Swansea, 29–31 March.

Richardson, J. and Jordan, G. (1979) *Governing Under Pressure*. Oxford: Martin Robertson.

Richardson, J.J., Maloney, W.A. and Rudig, W. (1992) 'The dynamics of policy change: lobbying and water privatization', *Public Administration*, 70(1): 157–75.

Ripley, R. and Franklin, G. (1980) *Congress, the Bureaucracy and Public Policy*. Homewood, IL: Dorsey.

Ripley, R. and Franklin, G. (1984) *Congress, the Bureaucracy and Public Policy* (2nd ed.). Homewood, IL: Dorsey.

Ritchie, E. (1992) 'Law and order', in M. Harrop (ed.) *Power and Policy in Liberal Democracies*. Cambridge: Cambridge University Press.

Robinson, J., Young, W. and Cameron, N. (1989) 'Measuring police effectiveness. A literature review', in W. Young and N. Cameron (eds) *Effectiveness and Change in Policing*. Study Series 3, Wellington: Institute of Criminology, Victoria University of Wellington.

Rokkan, S. (1966) 'Norway', in R.A. Dahl (ed.) *Political Oppositions in Western Democracies*. New Haven: Yale University Press.

Rose, R. (1980) 'Government against sub-government: a European perspective on Washington', in R. Rose and E.N. Suleiman (eds) *Presidents and Prime Ministers*. Washington: American Enterprise Institute.

Rothenberg, L.S. (1992) *Linking Citizens to Government*. Cambridge: Cambridge University Press.

Sabatier, P.A. (1988) 'An advocacy coalition model of policy change and the role of policy oriented learning therein', *Policy Sciences*, 21(2): 129–68.

Sabatier, P.A. (1991) 'Toward better theories of the policy process', *PS: Political Science and Politics*, 24(1): 144–56.

Sabatier, P.A. and Jenkins-Smith, H. (eds) (1993) *Policy Change and Learning: An Advocacy-Coalition Approach*. Boulder, CO, San Francisco, CA, Oxford: Westview.

Sanderson, J. (1995) *Current Issues in Local Government Finance*, research report. London: Commission for Local Democracy.

Sartori, G. (1991) 'Comparing and mis-comparing', *Journal of Theoretical Politics*, 3(3): 243–57.

Saunders, P. (1980) *Urban Politics: A Sociological Interpretation.* Harmondsworth: Penguin.
Saward, M. (1992) 'The civil nuclear network in Britain', in D. Marsh and R. Rhodes, *Policy Networks in British Government.* Oxford: Clarendon.
Schattschneider, E.E. (1960) *The Semisovereign People: A Realist's View of Democracy in America.* Hinsdale, IL: Dryden Press.
Schneider, A. and Ingram, H. (1993) 'Social construction of target populations: implications for policy and politics', *American Political Science Review,* 87(2): 334–47.
Schön, D.A. and Rein, M. (1994) *Frame Reflection: Resolving Intractable Policy Issues.* New York: Basic Books.
Scott, J. (1986) *Capitalist Property and Financial Power.* Brighton: Wheatsheaf.
Scott, A. (1990) *Ideology and the New Social Movements.* London: Unwin and Hyman.
Scott, J. (1991) *Social Network Analysis.* London: Sage.
Scottish Police Federation (1993) *Joint Central Committee: Annual Report.* Edinburgh: Scottish Policy Federation.
Seelye, K.Q. (1994) 'Lobbyists are the loudest in the health care debate', *New York Times,* 16 August.
SFS 1989: 12, 'Förordning om statsbidrag till miljöförbättrande åtgärder i jordbruket', in *Svensk författningssamling 1989* Stockholm.
SFS 1991: 238, 'Förordning om ändring i förordning (1989: 12) om statsbidrag till miljöförbättrande åtgärder i jordbruket', in *Svensk författningssamling* Stockholm.
Sheehy, P. (1993) *Inquiry into Policy Responsibilities and Rewards I and II (Sheehy Report),* Cmnd 2280. London: HMSO.
Simon, H. (1982) *Models of Bounded Rationality,* Vol. 2. Cambridge, MI: MIT Press.
Skocpol, Theda (1985) 'Bringing the state back in: strategies of analysis in current research', in P. Evans, D. Rueschemeyer and T. Skocpol (eds) *Bringing the State Back In.* Cambridge: Cambridge University Press.
Skocpol, T. and Finegold, K. (1982) 'State capacity and economic intervention in the early New Deal', *Political Science Quarterly,* 97(2): 255–78.
Smith, M.J. (1989) *The Politics of Agricultural Support in Britain: The Development of the Agricultural Policy Community.* Aldershot: Dartmouth Publishing Company.
Smith, M. (1991) 'From policy community to issue network: salmonella in eggs and the new politics of food', *Public Administration,* 69: 235–55.
Smith, M.J. (1992) 'The agricultural policy community: the rise and fall of a closed relationship', in D. Marsh and R. Rhodes (eds) *Policy Networks in British Government.* Oxford: Clarendon.
Smith, M.J. (1993) *Pressure, Power and Policy. State Autonomy and Policy Networks in Britain and the United States.* London: Harvester Wheatsheaf.
Smith, M.J. (1995) 'Pluralism', in D. Marsh and G. Stoker (eds) *Theories and Methods in Politics.* Basingstoke: Macmillan.
SOU 1977: 17, *Översyn av jordbrukspolitiken. Betänkande av 1972 års jordbruksutredning,* Stockholm: Liber/Allmänna Förlaget.
SOU 1983: 10, *Använding av växtnäring. Betänkande av udredningen om använding av kemiska medel i jord- och skogsbruket,* Stockholm: Liber/Allmänna Förlaget.
SOU 1984: 86, *Jordbruks och livsmedelspolitik. Huvudbetänkande av 1983 års livsmedelkommitté,* Stockholm: Liber/Allmänna Förlaget.
Southworth, B. (1993) 'Packaging and the environment. The challenge', *European Environment,* 3: 7–9.
Steen, A. (1985) 'The farmers, the state and the Social Democrats', *Scandinavian Political Studies,* 8(1/2): 45–63.

Steen, A. (1988) *Landbruket, staten og sosialdemokratene. En komparativ studie av inter-essekonflikterne i landbrukspolitikken i Norge, Sverige og England 1945–1985*. Oslo: Universitetsforlaget.

Stoker, G. and Wilson, D. (1986) 'Intra-organisational politics in local authorities', *Public Administration*, 70(2): 241–67.

Stones, R. (1992) 'Labour and international finance, 1964–1967', in D. Marsh and R.A.W. Rhodes (eds) *Policy Networks in British Government*. Oxford: Clarendon.

Strategos Consulting Ltd (1989) *New Zealand Policy: Resource Management Review*. Wellington: Strategos Consulting Ltd.

Sunde, G. (1996) 'Breaking the international tradition: the merger of oil service companies into a Norwegian industrial strategy', *International Journal of Maritime History*.

Taylor, G. (1995) 'Marxist theories of the state', in D. Marsh and G. Stoker (eds) *Theories and Methods in Political Science*. Basingstoke: Macmillan.

Thompson, G. *et al.* (1991) *Markets, Hierarchies and Networks*. London: Sage.

Thomsen, J.P.F. (1996) *British Politics and Trade Union Pressures in the 1980s: Governing Against Pressure*. Aldershot: Dartmouth.

Thorelli, H.B. (1986) 'Networks: between markets and hierarchies', *Strategic Management Journal*, 7(1): 37–51.

Tracy, M. (1993) *Food and Agriculture in a Market Economy: An Introduction to Theory, Practice and Policy*. La Hutte: Agricultural Policy Studies.

Truman, D. (1971) *The Governmental Process* (2nd ed.). New York: Knopf.

Udvalget vedr. en Bæredygtig Landbrugsudvikling (1991) 'Beretning om en bæredygtig landbrugsudvikling (miljøinitiativer)', *Folketingstidende 1991–92*. tillæg B, Copenhagen.

van Waarden, F. (1992) 'Dimensions and types of policy network', *European Journal of Political Research*, 21(1): 29–52.

Visher, M.G. and Remoe, S.O. (1984) 'A case study of the cuckoo nestling: the role of the state in the Norwegian oil sector', *Politics and Society*, 13(3): 321–41.

Vogel, D. (1989) *Fluctuating Fortunes*. New York: Basic Books.

Waddington, P.A.J. (1994) 'A shoulder to cry on', *Police Review*, 15 July.

Wahlen, M. and Rydning, G. (1993) The Development of the Norwegian Offshore Safety Environment', in *Workforce Involvement and Health and Safety Offshore: Power, Language and Information*. Glasgow: Scottish TUC.

Ward, H. (1995) 'Rational choice theory', in D. Marsh and G. Stoker (eds) *Theories and Methods in Political Science*. London: Macmillan.

Wasserman, S. and Faust, K. (1994) *Social Network Analysis: Methods and Applications*. New York: Cambridge University Press.

Watt, R. (1997) 'An historical relationship between agency and structure; synthesising actor network, policy network and advocacy coalition interpretations of policy making', in J. Stanyer and G. Stoker (eds) *Contemporary Political Studies*. Oxford: Blackwell.

Weale, A. and Williams, A. (1992) 'Between economy and ecology? The single market and the integration of environmental policy', *Environmental Politics*, 1: 45–64.

Wellman, B. (1979) 'The community question: intimate networks of East Yorkers', *American Journal of Sociology*, 84(5): 1201–31.

Wellman, B. (1988) 'Structural analysis', in B. Wellman and S.D. Berkowitz (eds) *Social Structures*. Cambridge: Cambridge University Press.

Weston, J. (1988) *The Mafia and Clientalism: Roads to Rome in Post-War Calabria*. London: Routledge.

Wilkes, S. and Wright, M. (1987) 'Conclusion: comparing government–industry relations: states, sectors and networks', in S. Wilkes and M. Wright (eds) *Comparing Government–Industry Relations: Western Europe, the United States, and Japan*. Oxford: Clarendon Press.

Wilson, E. (1993) 'Strategic environmental assessment: evaluating the impacts of European policies, plans and programmes', *European Environment*, 3: 2–6.

Wilson, G.K. (1985) *The Politics of Safety and Health*. Oxford: Clarendon Press.

Wilson, G.K. (1990) *Interest Groups*. Oxford: Blackwell.

Wilson, J.Q. (1980) 'The politics of regulation', in J.Q. Wilson (ed.) *The Politics of Regulation*. New York: Basic Books.

Wistow, G. (1992) 'The health service policy community: professionals pre-eminent or under challenge?', in D. Marsh and R. Rhodes, *Policy Networks in British Government*. Oxford: Clarendon Press.

Woolfson, C. and Beck, M. (1995) *Seven Years After Piper Alpha: Safety Claims and the new Safety Case Regime*. Glasgow: University of Glasgow.

Yin, R.K. (1989) *Case Study Research: Design and Methods*. London: Sage Publications.

Index

UNDERSTANDING GOVERNANCE
POLICY NETWORKS, GOVERNANCE, REFLEXIVITY AND ACCOUNTABILITY

R.A.W. Rhodes

Understanding Governance asks:
- What has changed in British government over the past two decades, how and why?
- Why do so many government policies fail?
- What does the shift from government to governance mean for the practice and study of British government?

This book provides a challenging reinterpretation which interweaves an account of recent institutional changes in central, local and European Union government with methodological innovations and theoretical analysis. It emphasizes: the inability of the 'Westminster model', with its accent on parliamentary sovereignty and strong executive leadership, to account for persistent policy failure; the 'hollowing out' of British government from above (the European Union), below (special purpose bodies) and sideways (to agencies); and the need to respond to the postmodern challenge, rethinking the methodological and theoretical assumptions in the study of British government. Professor Rhodes makes a significant and timely contribution to our understanding of government and governance.

Contents
Part 1: Introduction – Governing without Government: order and change in British politics – Part 2: Theory – Policy networks in British political science – The new governance: governing without Government – Part 3: Methodology – The institutional approach – Part 4: Applications – Reinventing Whitehall, 1979–95: hollowing out the state? – Now nobody understands the system: the changing face of British local government, 1979–95 – The European Union, cohesion policy and sub-national authorities in the United Kingdom – Part 5: Developments – From institutions to dogma: tradition, eclecticism and ideology in the study of British Public Administration – Towards a post-modern Public Administration: epoch, epistemology or narrative? – References – Name index – Subject index.

256pp   0 335 19727 2 (Paperback)   0 335 19728 0 (Hardback)

THE STATE UNDER STRESS
CAN THE HOLLOW STATE BE GOOD GOVERNMENT?

Christopher D. Foster and Francis J. Plowden

This is a comprehensive account of the changes that have taken place in British government in recent years – since 1979 but, more especially, since 1988. It argues that (and explains why) there has been a general decline in competence and ability to deliver good government. Ministers are increasingly overloaded, their long-standing relationships with civil servants have altered and the power of Parliament has declined. And the machinery of government has been transformed, at one level, by changes in the use of Cabinet and at another by privatization, contractorization and the creation of executive agencies. Any new government will find government transformed to a point where most memories of how it used to work in the 1970s are irrelevant. *The State Under Stress* argues that, while the clock cannot be turned back, urgent reforms are needed if democracy is not to be further undermined.

Contents
The causes of fiscal crisis – The politics of fiscal crisis – New public management examined – Separating provision from production – Complete separation: social objectives and regulation of privatization – Impermanent separation: contractorization – Decentralization: empowering local communities – The agency: incomplete separation – Ministers and agencies: separation as metaphor? – The role of minister – What future for politics? – Conclusion – References – Index.

288pp   0 335 19713 2 (Paperback)   0 335 19714 0 (Hardback)

QUALITY IN PUBLIC SERVICES
MANAGERS' CHOICES

Lucy Gaster

This book closes the gap between politicians' rhetoric, public expectations and the day-to-day dilemmas facing managers wanting to improve the quality of public services. It offers a mixture of conceptual clarification and practical awareness of the environment in which public service managers have to work. This is no 'missionary' or 'how to' book that peddles instant solutions. Instead, a variety of approaches to quality definition, implementation and measurement are critically examined. Lessons and experience from practice and research in the public and private sectors give a solid background for readers to develop their own views.

Lucy Gaster disentangles the important aspects of quality, challenges assumptions, and shows that there are no simple solutions. At the same time she provides a framework to enable public service managers to develop and integrate ideas about quality in ways which are relevant to their own day-to-day practice. This framework shows that real choices *are* available to managers. Values and participation, combined with a real commitment to the ideal of 'public service', are at the heart of the approach adopted in this book. It will appeal to all those wanting a more objective and informed approach to providing quality services.

Contents
Introduction − Whose quality? − What quality? − Principles of implementation − The practice of implementation − Quality standards − Measuring, monitoring, evaluating − Choices of quality − Bibliography − Index.

160pp   0 335 19160 6 (Paperback)   0 335 19349 8 (Hardback)